The Beginnings of Writing

Second Edition

Charles Temple
Hobart and William Smith Colleges

Ruth Nathan
Oakland University

Nancy Burris
University of Houston

Frances Temple
Children's Hours School

ALLYN AND BACON, INC.
Boston • London • Sydney • Toronto

Series Editor: Susanne F. Canavan
Senior Editorial Assistant: Elizabeth Brooks
Production Administrator: Annette Joseph
Production Coordinator: Susan Freese
Editorial-Production Service: Kailyard Associates
Cover Administrator: Linda K. Dickinson
Cover Designer: Susan Slovinsky

Library of Congress Cataloging-in-Publication Data

The beginnings of writing.

   Rev. ed. of: The beginnings of writing / Charles A.
Temple, Ruth G. Nathan, Nancy A. Burris. c1982.
   Bibliography: p.
   Includes index.
   1. English language—Composition and exercises.
2. Children—Writing. I. Temple, Charles A., 1947–
II. Temple, Charles A., 1947–   . The beginnings of
writing.
LB156.T44   1987   372.6   87-19305
ISBN 0-205-11107-6
ISBN 0-205-11392-3 (International Edition)

Acknowledgments:
Figure 1–1 on p. 2 is reprinted by permission from *Word,* Vol. 27 (1971).
Figure 3–13 on p. 34 is from *Typed Lettering* (4th ed.) by William Longyear. Copyright © 1966 by Watson-Guptill Publications. Reprinted by permission.
Figures 7–1 and 7–2 on p. 99 are reprinted by permission of J. Richard Gentry, Ph.D.
Figure 11–22 on p. 241 is reprinted by permission of Donald M. Murray, Professor of English Emeritus, University of New Hampshire.
Quotation on p. 249 is from POP CORN & MA GOODNESS by Edna Mitchell Preston. Copyright © 1969 by Edna Mitchell Preston. Reprinted by permission of Viking Penguin Inc.
Quotation on p. 250 is a text excerpt from pages 30–31 of WILLIAM'S DOLL by Charlotte Zolotow. Text Copyright © 1972 by Charlotte Zolotow. By permission of Harper & Row, Publishers Inc.
Quotation on p. 251 is a text excerpt from HOLD MY HAND by Charlotte Zolotow. Text Copyright © 1972 by Charlotte Zolotow. By permission of Harper & Row, Publishers Inc.
Quotation on p. 251 is from Sheb Wooley, "The Purple People Eater." By permission of Channel Music Company.

Printed in the United States of America

10 9 8 7 6 5 4 3 2 1   92 91 90 89 88 87

Overview

Preface **xi**

1/   *A Child Discovers How to Write*   **1**

Part One   **The Beginnings of Writing**   **17**

2/   *The Precursors of Writing*   **18**
3/   *Features of Children's Early Writing*   **26**
4/   *What Children Do with Early Graphics*   **41**

Part Two   **The Beginnings of Spelling**   **53**

5/   *Invented Spelling*   **55**
6/   *Learning Standard Spelling*   **79**
7/   *Making Progress in Spelling*   **99**

Part Three   **The Beginnings of Composition**   **117**

8/   *The Functions and Forms in Children's Composition*   **118**
9/   *Writing in the Poetic Mode*   **144**
10/   *Approaching the Transactional Mode*   **187**
11/   *Writing: The Child, the Teacher, and the Class*   **211**

Epilogue   *Playing with Literature and Language: Amy's Story*   **249**

Appendix   **259**
Selected Further Reading   **263**
Index   **265**

Contents

Preface **xi**

1/ ***A Child Discovers How to Write*** **1**
How Children Learn to Talk **3**
How Writing Systems Are Organized **11**
References **15**

Part One **The Beginnings of Writing** **17**

2/ ***The Precursors of Writing*** **18**
Early Writing and a Theory of Perception **19**
How Children Perceive Writing **21**
Conclusion **25**
References **25**

3/ ***Features of Children's Early Writing*** **26**
The Recurring Principle **27**
The Generative Principle **28**
The Sign Concept **29**
The Flexibility Principle **31**
Linear Principles and Principles of Page Arrangement **33**
Spaces between Words **38**
Conclusion **39**
References **40**

4/ ***What Children Do with Early Graphics*** **41**
Children Write on Their Own **41**
Strategies for Early Writing **45**
Conclusion **52**
References **52**

Part Two   The Beginnings of Spelling   53

    5/   Invented Spelling   55
        The Disappointments of English Spelling   55
        Letter-Name Spelling   56
        How We Make Speech Sounds: A Long but Necessary Digression   61
        How Vowels Are Produced   68
        The Developmental Dimension of Invented Spelling   73
        Letters to Represent Sounds   76
        Conclusion   77
        References   77

    6/   Learning Standard Spelling   79
        How English Got Its Strange Spelling   80
        Some Learnable Patterns of Modern English Spelling   82
        Conclusion   96
        References   98

    7/   Making Progress in Spelling   99
        The Stages of Spelling Development   100
        Assessing Children's Spelling Development   105
        Helping Children Make Progress in Spelling   107
        Conclusion   115
        References   116

Part Three   The Beginnings of Composition   117

    8/   The Functions and Forms in Children's Composition   118
        Self, Audience, Topic, and Purpose: A Menu of Writing Forms   127
        The Expressive Mode   131
        Transitional Writing: Expressive Traces in the Other Two Modes   134
        The Transactional Mode   136
        The Poetic Mode   140
        Conclusion   142
        References   143

    9/   Writing in the Poetic Mode   144
        The Shape of Otherness: Children's Stories   144
        Joey's Works: A First Grader Learns to Write Stories   148
        Sarah's Works: Literature Influences Story Development   165
        Developing the Poetic Mode in School   170
        Conclusion   185
        References   186

    10/   Approaching the Transactional Mode   187
        Assignments for Expository Writing   188
        An Assignment for Argumentative Writing   200

Encouraging Writing in a Variety of Modes **205**
Conclusion **210**

11/ ***Writing: The Child, the Teacher, and the Class* 211**
Writing as a Social Activity **211**
A Description of the Writing Process **212**
Atmosphere, Assignment, and Response: The Teacher's Role in the Writing Process **215**
The Kindergarten Year **216**
The Primary Years **219**
Conclusion **247**
References **247**

Epilogue ***Playing with Literature and Language: Amy's Story* 249**

Appendix **259**
Magazines That Publish Children's Work **259**
Publishing Possibilities for Children **260**
Selected Further Reading **263**
Index **265**

Preface

Nearly ten years have passed since we began writing the first edition of *The Beginnings of Writing,* and this second edition goes out to a language teaching profession that has dramatically changed. The process approach to teaching writing is by now, if not universally practiced, at least familiar to teachers throughout the English-speaking world. Language-experience, the whole-language approach, and the study of children's emergent literacy—these allied movements have generated a climate of deeper appreciation of children's discovery processes in the tasks of learning to read and write and a greater understanding of the constructive role teachers play in children's literacy development.

More and more teachers are persuaded by the wisdom of teaching reading and writing together. Research shows unequivocally that early writing helps children develop concepts about written language they need in order to read, and reading makes children familiar with language structures they need in order to write.

As these movements have matured, teachers have recognized that the techniques of managing whole-language or process-writing classrooms cannot be successful without a deep commitment to letting children express themselves in their own voices and an informed appreciation of children's development as literate people. It is here that the first edition of *The Beginnings of Writing* has most valuably served the profession. The book is a clear and richly illustrated description of children's writing development from preschool through about fourth grade. Readers of the first edition have told us that it has helped them to learn much more from their children's writing.

The second edition of *The Beginnings of Writing* adds exciting new material to the original work. Frances Temple, who provided much of the inspiration and all of the artwork for the first edition, has signed on as an author of this second one. She has opened up her classroom at the Children's Hours School, where she has taught the same children for two consecutive years. She has been in a unique position to observe the factors that influence children's writing and reading over the long term, and has made connections that visiting researchers inevitably would have missed. She brings to this volume a careful study of the influence of literature on children's writing development. Also included is an observation of first, second, and third graders who used writing in a social studies unit, and we see how her assignment allows them to translate content that they have heard, read, and acted out into texts that they write.

Another big addition in this volume is the detailed guide to setting up and managing a process approach to teaching writing. Ruth Nathan has distilled the best instruction from her successful work as a writing consultant in the Detroit area and written up a set of procedures that has helped scores of teachers carry out the process approach in their own classrooms. With this new material, readers of this newest edition can develop an understanding of children's writing processes and also find explicit guidance for setting up a classroom environment in which children can learn to write.

ACKNOWLEDGMENTS

We are grateful to the children, teachers, and parents who have shared their work and their insights with us. They are too numerous to name here, but we appreciate each one.

The administration of Hobart and William Smith Colleges extended valuable support for this work. Evelyn Sperry and Anita Barton provided timely typing, and in the case of the former, irreverent commentary.

Margaret Quinlan first made the decision to publish this book, and Sue Canavan, also at Allyn and Bacon, shepherded this work from its inception to its second edition in her own delightful way. Susan Mesner of Kailyard Associates edited the final manuscript with admirable skill and a supportive spirit, for which the authors are very grateful.

We also wish to thank Allyn and Bacon's reviewers, who evaluated the book at various stages: David Bloome of the University of Michigan; Martha King of Ohio State University; and Eileen Tway of Miami University (Oxford, Ohio).

1/   A Child Discovers How to Write

At a preschool in Cambridge, Massachusetts, a four-year-old girl had just completed a drawing of a person fishing. At her side was a language researcher who was studying the beginnings of writing in young children. The researcher wondered what would happen if she asked the girl to write about her picture. The girl looked at her quizzically for a moment and then began to write these letters:

YUTS A LADE YET FEHEG AD HE KOT FLEPR

She whispered laboriously to herself as she wrote the letters one at a time. The researcher was elated, and she read the words immediately: "Once a lady went fishing and she caught Flipper."[1] (See Figure 1–1.)

There are at least two mysteries in that story: How was the girl able to write those words? She was too young to have been taught to write, and anyway, nobody would have taught her to write like that. And how was the researcher able to read her words? This second question we can answer quickly. The researcher could read what the girl wrote because the made-up system of spelling she used to write her words was exactly like the invented spelling of many other children that the researcher had observed, and therefore the researcher knew what to expect. The first question, how the girl was able to write those words, will take us much of the rest of this book to answer.

Children can discover how to write if adults surround them with print and encourage them to produce print of their own. Writing, the act of expressing thoughts by means of written symbols, is a mysterious process. No one understands exactly how we learn to do it, but it appears that we learn to write at least as much by discovering how as by being taught. Learning to write is largely an act of discovery. This book is about that act. It is also about another act of discovery, as parents and teachers see revealed in children's early productions outlines of the nature of the writing process, the nature of our written language, and the nature of the process by means of which children learn to write.

If every child went about discovering how to write in his or her own unique way, this book could not have been written, for there would have to be as many books on young children's writing as there were young children. But research and the experience of teaching and parenting have shown us a remarkable thing: Even when they are not taught about writing, most children make essentially the same discoveries about it, in essentially the same order.

This is truly mysterious, for our writing system and how to use it is a vast and complex matter. That most children should follow the same path in coming to understand it is remarkable, and it is not the result of mere coincidence. Children, it seems, have a unique biological endowment that disposes them to learn to talk.[2] Given the proper circumstances, it is likely that this language-learning facility extends to the learning of written language as well. Children learn to talk by following a very narrow path. Moreover, they learn to talk by exerting an intellectual effort that appears natural, yet has tremendous force.

Learning to talk has been more thoroughly scrutinized and is better understood than learning to write, and the dynamics involved are clearer and closer to general recognition. Therefore, a brief sketch of how children learn to talk is in order. In many ways, this discussion will continue to inform us through the rest of the book.

HOW CHILDREN LEARN TO TALK

Have you ever wondered how children learn to talk? Many people, when asked that question, respond that they do it by imitating. This is at least partially true. Without imitation, we couldn't account for the fact that children in Texas usually learn Texan English, children in Paris usually learn Parisian French, and not vice versa. But imitation as an answer doesn't take us very far. For one thing, children routinely say things they've never heard: "Mommy, come quick—Waldo swallowed a frog!" That is a novel statement for a novel situation. When you think about it, it is inconceivable that children could learn in advance by imitation all of the sentences they will ever have to say.

At this point some would amend their position to say that children don't imitate others sentence by sentence. Instead, they imitate the nouns and verbs and sentence structures of others around them; they can fit their own words into these imitated structures to create novel sentences. But the facts of children's speech do not fit this explanation either. Children produce many sorts of grammatical constructions that they have not heard before. A two year old says, "Allgone milk" and "Daddy bye-bye" and for a time, rarely utters sentences of more than two words. A three year old says, "I seed two gooses" and "I have small foots"—two particular plural forms that nobody else in the family uses.

At any given point in development, a child's speech more closely resembles the speech of other children at the same stage of development than it does the speech of adults in the child's environment—even if there are not other children around. Any explanation of children's speech that depends on strict imitation cannot stand up to these facts.

What *do* children do as they learn to talk? Children seek from their early days to make sense of the communication around them. As their minds and muscles mature, they attempt—through a sort of gradual trial-and-error process—to construct a system of *rules* that will allow them to produce sentences like those they hear others use. "Rules" is used here in a loose sense. They are not consciously saying to themselves: "Hmm . . . whenever I mean more than one, I must put an S on the end of the noun." Yet some sort of unspoken assumption close to this must have been made or else why would the three year old say "gooses" and "foots"?

There is much evidence that children's early sentences result from the use of some sort of rules—and not simply from the haphazard imitation of adult sentences.

Imagine that you are in a kitchen with a two year old and his mother. The child is seated in his highchair eating. Suddenly he bangs his cup on the highchair tray and says, "Mommy milk, Mommy milk." We assume from the context—his gesture with the cup and so forth—that he means something like, "Mommy, get me some more milk." If we have spent much time around this child, this may seem like one of his typical sentences: typical for one thing in that, for the past few weeks, at least, we have rarely heard him utter sentences with more than two words in them.

On reflection, we may be struck by what a good sentence it is for having only two words! If we had to pick two words to convey the idea in "Mommy, get me some more milk," we could not improve on "Mommy milk." A lot of young children's sentences are like this; that is, they are of a uniform shortness, starting out as one-word sentences. Later, as children mature a bit, they begin to use two-word sentences and then move up to three-word sentences and so on.

Most early sentences are like this sample sentence, too, in that children show a knack for picking the most important words to convey their meanings. "Mommy milk" packs a lot of information; "get more" conveys less. Early sentences use informative words and leave out in-between words such as "and," "to," "with," "should," "have," "will," "the," "very," and the like. We assume that the limits to the number of words children can put in their early sentences have to do with biology and maturity. But the nature of their choice of words and the order they put them in reveals some deliberation, some rules.

Another piece of evidence for the operation of rules in early speech is seen when a child is asked to imitate adult sentences. Normally, young children cannot correctly imitate a sentence that is more complicated than one they could produce on their own. The following exchange between a psychologist and his young daughter illustrates this point:

Child: Want other one spoon, Daddy.
Father: You mean, you want the other spoon.
Child: Yes, I want other one spoon, please Daddy.
Father: Can you say, "The other spoon"?
Child: Other . . . one . . . spoon.
Father: Say, "other."
Child: Other.
Father: "Spoon."
Child: Spoon.
Father: "Other spoon."
Child: Other . . . spoon. Now give me other one spoon?[3]

Similar difficulty was encountered by a researcher who attempted to lead another child away from an incorrect use of a past tense of the verb "hold":

Child: My teacher holded the baby rabbits and we patted them.
Adult: Did you say your teacher held the baby rabbits?
Child: Yes.
Adult: What did you say?
Child: She holded the baby rabbits and we patted them.
Adult: Did you say she held them tightly?
Child: No, she holded them loosely.[4]

This child apparently is not going to say "held" until she changes the rule in her head that produces that form. And language rules, like rules in other aspects of human life, take some time to change!

Children do not trade in their immature speech for mature speech all at once. They always go through a sequence of stages of language use, moving from simple to complex. Thus, we hear a child at two years of age ask, "Why you singing?" and we note that all of her questions are of the same form. At two years, four months, we hear her ask, "Why you are singing?" and other questions of this more complex form. Just before the age of three, she arrives at the standard form for the English question, "Why are you singing?"[5]

It is obvious that this child is not learning to talk simply by memorizing sentences or sentence types. Rather, she is formulating her own rules to help her understand sentences she hears around her to produce sentences like them. Once she formulates a rule, she uses it confidently until she begins to notice differences between her sentences and the sentences adults use. Then she will gradually add to and amend her rules so that she is able to produce sentences more like adults'. She doesn't junk her old rules altogether; this would be too disruptive. Feature by feature, she makes her rules more and more like those adults must be using to produce mature sentences.[6]

Remarkably, children usually go through the same *sequence* of rule learning as they mature in speech production. A study by Brown[7] showed that three separate children started using major grammatical features in roughly the same order:

present progressive	I rid*ing*
plural nouns	two skate*s*
linking verbs	I *am* big
articles before nouns	*the* birds
past tense markers	we skat*ed*

Child language researchers are not sure why children tend to acquire language rules in the same order, although one theorist has suggested that it may be because children are born "prewired" to learn language in a certain way.[2]

The uniformity of order surely has nothing to do with what we teach. The language children hear around them cannot be much different from age one to age two, or from age two to age three—though their own language changes dramatically during that time. Whatever the explanation turns out to be, it is bound to be related to language-learning processes going on inside the child.

Not all of children's early speech is different from adult speech. Sometimes we do hear two and three year olds repeating phrases—learned by imitation—that seem more advanced than normal speech for that age. We sometimes hear "Why *dincha* tell me" at two and a half, but later, oddly enough, the child reverts to a less mature form: "Why *you didn't* tell me?" Eventually he will come to use the correct form: "Why *didn't you* tell me?"

The implication is that some imitated but unassimilated forms may be used for a time as *formulas*—that is, as whole structures that the child hasn't analyzed and for which rules have not been found that will generate them. But as language development advances, the rules invade the formulas; the utterances produced by formula disappear, and they may not be heard again until the rules have been developed to produce them.

If children construct their own rules to use and understand language, how is it that everyone winds up speaking English instead of her or his own private language?

We sometimes do hear of sets of twins who—being raised in isolation from others or in other unusual circumstances—make up a private idiomatic language that makes no sense to anyone but themselves.[8] But that doesn't happen very often. Every year, millions and millions of children learn to speak English (and, in their respective settings, hundreds of other languages) through their own efforts, without being taught. That is the normal pattern of things.

Clearly, when children construct language rules, they are attempting to find rules or patterns that account for the language used by others in their presence. It is as if they were carefully feeling and probing the language to find its joints and seams, its outer shape and its inner workings.

Children's early hunches about the way spoken language works can be wrong, of course. An area of language where this is sometimes seen is in naming things. We have an example in our young friend, Will, who produced voluminous speech throughout his second and third year. Except for a few words, most of Will's speech was unintelligible to his parents or other adults. One of Will's recognizable words was "bupmum," used to refer to his favorite vehicle, the family's Land-Rover (a British-made jeep). According to Will's father, "bupmum" was a pretty fair rendering of the sound made by the exhaust popping out of the Rover's rusted tailpipe. When the family sold it and bought a Volkswagon, Will reflected the change in his name for the new car: "mummum" (a smoother-sounding name for a better-running engine!). Later, he used "mummum" to refer to all cars and trucks. Still later, an element of the name showed up in his name for motorboat: "boatmum." At four, Will was speaking standard English. But in those early years, it seemed to those who knew him that he was seeking names for things in the sounds that emanated from them—a perfectly sensible strategy, really, but not one around which English is organized.

Thus far we have observed some basic notions of how children come to string words together grammatically and name things correctly. But there is more to the language than this, as the reader may have already discerned. A different but equally fruitful way to look at language learning is to examine what children use it for; that is, we can examine the different functions to which children learn to put language.

Michael Halliday, an English linguist, has noted that children can direct their utterances to serve different functions before they use any recognizably grammatical utterances.[9] A certain kind of baby's cry or coo, for instance, can clearly be meant as a request (or demand) for some thing or some service from a parent. It may mean "Pick me up" or "Put me down" or "Feed me, I'm hungry" or "Change me, I'm wet." This cry or coo will be altogether different from another coo that is done apparently for the sheer pleasure of hearing the sound in the air and feeling the vibrations in the mouth. The baby intends the utterances differently and the parent understands them differently.

In all, Halliday has identified seven different functions for which children use language. They are summarized here, and a characteristic utterance appears beside each one for easy reference.

Gimme!   *The instrumental function:* Language is used to get something for the speaker. Language is used as an extension of the hand; hence, this is called instrumental language use.

Stop that!   *The regulatory function:* Language is used to get somebody else to do something, to regulate somebody else's behavior, though not necessarily for the direct benefit of the speaker.

You know?   *The interactional function:* Language is used to build a "we-ness," a sense of closeness or group membership between the speaker and his listener or listeners. "How do you do?" and other such utterances that lack literal meaning have this interactional function and are important for the bond they create between the speaker and others.

I love you.   *The personal function:* Language is used to share inner material. The speaker's feelings and attitudes toward things and other people, and the speaker's understanding of himself are shared by means of such utterances.

What's that?   *The heuristic function:* Language is used to ask questions and find things out. "Heuristic" means "related to discovering things" ("eureka" is a cousin word). Children and others use the heuristic function when they use language to learn things or to satisfy their curiosity.

Baa Baa Black Sheep.   *The imaginative function:* Language is used in this mode for the pure fun of it, to amuse the speaker and perhaps also the listener. Speakers using the imaginative function play with sounds, rhythms, and associations in language.

It's snowing!   *The representative function:* Language is used here to communicate facts about the real world, to convey information. Such language represents reality with words.

After the age of about two, children rely more and more on words and syntax and less and less on coos and grunts to communicate their meanings. But even after that, Halliday believes, their language learning proceeds differentially across a repertoire of language functions. They must use language to get things done, to get along with other people, to explore their feelings, to entertain, to investigate the world, and to share the truth as they see it. How successful they are in developing each of these functions depends upon the opportunities they have to use language and hear language used in each of these ways.

In a long-term observational study in which he recorded hundreds of hours of children's speech both at home and at school, Gordon Wells concluded that even his least verbal subjects learned to use a full range of expression at home. The real bottleneck occurred at school: Children had far fewer opportunities to talk at school; their language was drawn out by an adult far less often; and the less confident children, in particular, reverted to a very truncated form of expression—often using only one or two words per sentence at school, whereas they would use far lengthier and more expressive sentences at home.[10]

So far in this discussion of children's language learning, we have emphasized the child's own efforts to make sense of and construct rules for the language she hears around her. But what do the adults contribute? Have they only to keep up a patter of talk, from which the child can abstract rules of grammar? Such may have been the drift of earlier descriptions of language acquisition, but now it is widely recognized that adults—parents or "primary caregivers"—are much more actively involved in children's language learning.

First of all, adults do provide the raw material of language from which children construct their own ideas of the way language works. In those fortunately rare cases in which children have been kept isolated from human contact, the children have been found not to have developed language—to no one's surprise. But secondly, it seems clear that when adults are speaking to children, they modify their speech considerably, into a form of speech that is sometimes called "motherese": they use fewer words per utterance and simpler syntax; they speak more slowly and in a higher range (babies have been shown to prefer high-pitched voices to low-pitched ones); and they exaggerate the stress and intonation of their speech. One researcher has compared all this exaggeration to the way an instructor demonstrates a golf swing: it is as if the mother were saying, "Here, pay attention to upness and downness and stress and words—these are the important things."[11]

But there's more. Most parents in English-speaking countries read to their children. The practice of reading to children has long been believed to help those children learn to read. However, recent assessments of its benefits are more specific. Some argue that reading to children leads them to associate pleasure with written language and enables them to formulate schemata for stories and other forms of written discourse. Other researchers go further and suggest that children who are read to *learn a written form of language from the very beginning:* they learn that language can be elaborated to explain things that are not in the context of the speech. This *decontextualized language* is just the sort of language that is used in reading and writing.[12]

So the picture that emerges from more recent studies of language learning shows that (1) parents are actively involved in their children's language learning, that they tend to direct a form of language toward their children that is easier to learn from than the speech they use with older people, and (2) written language—complete with the word choices and structures of stories, and the use of language to create a world of understanding on its own, a world removed from the context in which it is read—is often part of children's language experience from the very beginning.

Space does not permit a more extensive discussion of children's oral language development here. We can summarize the points we have made in our brief discussion this way:

1. When children learn to talk, they appear to be constructing for themselves a set of rules that enable them to produce and understand sentences.
2. The rules children use gradually change—are added to and amended—as children gain experience and maturity.
3. There are biological controls on the timetable of oral language learning, but experience in hearing and using language is involved in making progress through the stages of language acquisition.
4. Though children may make some complicated utterances at an early point in their development, this usually turns out to be the result of verbatim memorization; at a later stage such utterances will regress to a more primitive outer form as they become subject to the use of rules. Still later they will emerge stably in the correct form.
5. In the process of constructing rules for English, children sometimes try approaches that are not English at all before finding rules that do produce English.
6. Learning to use language is to grow in not one ability but in a cluster of abilities. Language has at least seven demonstrably different functions for which it is regularly used, and a speaker must learn to use each one by having experience in that function.
7. Exposure to language is not enough for children to learn it. Parents use a particular kind of slowed down and simplified speech when they address young children. Similarly, by reading to children, parents present them with language in very familiar and predictable settings, and this

comforting activity seems to help children learn to talk. It also acquaints them with the words, the structures, and the decontextualized nature of written language.

To some extent learning to talk and learning to write follow similar dynamics. For the present, we don't understand if they are both enabled by some master capacity in the human brain. The similarities between the two processes suggest that they might be. In any case, the learning of spoken language and written language have at least the following points in common:

1. Children normally take a great deal of the initiative both in learning to talk and in learning to write.
2. Children must be surrounded by language used in meaningful ways if they are to learn to talk; the same is true of written language if they are to learn to write (and read).
3. Children learn to talk by formulating tentative rules about the way language works, trying them out, and gradually revising them. At first, they make many mistakes in speech, but they gradually correct them. In writing we see errors of letter formation, spelling, and composition occurring as children make hypotheses about the rules that govern the writing system; errors give way to other errors before children arrive at correct forms.
4. Children generally do not start using correct forms of speech as a result of direct teaching; speech forms change only gradually. In writing, too, spelling forms and composition strategies may not be immediately improved by corrective teaching but through gradual conceptual learning that is controlled by the child as much as by the teacher.
5. Children learn to talk to meet a range of personal needs, and they learn to vary their use of language as their needs and purposes change and as they have opportunities to use language functionally. Writing serves different purposes, too, and there are unique forms of writing for each function. Children must have opportunities to use writing meaningfully, serving different purposes in order to develop complete literacy.
6. Any spoken language is an immensely complicated thing; no one yet has succeeded in writing down all of the rules that explain how any natural language works. Thus, it is absurd to suppose that we could teach our children to talk by explaining the language to them—we don't understand the language well enough ourselves to do that. People somehow learn spoken language on a working level, but this does not enable them to explain their knowledge of it to others. Written language has never been fully and satisfactorily described, either. None of us understands writing well enough to explain to someone else how to write, unless that other person exerts her powers to learn for herself.

This last point needs some discussion. No one can describe the knowledge inside someone's head that enables that person to read and write. But we know enough about writing to understand what an amazingly complex thing it is. It is important to try to visualize some of the workings of our writing system in order to appreciate the range of choices open to a child who undertakes to gain control over written English.

HOW WRITING SYSTEMS ARE ORGANIZED

When you and I write, we employ letters of the alphabet to represent words. The letters represent parts of words—the individual sounds that make them up. But this is not the only way we *could* write if we chose to use letters in a different way. There are other approaches to writing—to the representing of words with symbols—that have been used by different peoples. There is no reason to believe English-speaking children are genetically programmed to use symbols for the sound components of words. So we should consider some different ways to write in order to clarify the alternatives that are open to a child when she decides to represent a spoken message with written symbols.

Symbols for Ideas: Ideographic Writing

One approach to writing is to let each symbol stand for an idea, in the manner that a road sign ⟨⚡⟩ conveys the idea to motorists that a winding road lies ahead.

Chinese writing is a modern system based on the principle of using a single symbol to represent an idea. In ancient times the symbols were pictures of the things they represented. Through constant usage, the symbols came to look less like pictures, and the meanings became abstracted from the original concrete things that the symbols stood for.

The ancient drawing 山 used to stand for "fire," by representing its jumping, dancing quality. The modern character for fire has changed to 火 . By abstraction, two fires, 炎 means "brilliant."[13] The ancient drawing for "sunrise" depicted the sun between the branches and the roots of a tree 東 . Gradually the symbol was changed to 東 , and the meaning was extended to include the direction "east," since that is where the sun is seen to rise.[13]

As a result of the abstraction of both symbol and meaning, modern Chinese writing has evolved as an elaborate and versatile system capable of representing approximately the same range of ideas that English writing can. The pictorial basis of Chinese writing gives it one advantage that alphabetic writing systems do not have: Chinese writing can be read and understood by people who speak dialectical versions of Chinese that are so different that speakers of some different dialects cannot understand each other.

Both a Peking man and a Cantonese will understand 日 means day, and 月 means moon. But a Peking man will pronounce the words r and ywe, while the

Cantonese will pronounce yat and ut. . . . If the Peking man reads to the Canton man, the Canton man will not understand one word. If each man reads a text for himself, he can understand it, completely.[13]

This is so because the Chinese symbol is independent of the *sound* of the word and represents directly the *idea* that is conveyed by the spoken word. Because the symbols represent ideas and not spoken words, they have come to be called *ideographs,* which means, simply, "idea writing." We use a few of them in our own writing system: $, c, $; the number symbols 1, 2, 3, 4, etc.; and the mathematical operation signs ×, −, and +. Note that these symbols are found in languages other than English and are paired with different words: 1, 2, 3 can stand for one, two, three in English; *uno, dos, tres* in Spanish; *eins, zwei, drei* in German; and *moja, mbili, tatu* in Swahili.

Writing words with a single symbol, then, is a perfectly workable approach to writing.

Children and Ideographic Writing.   Children who are first working on the *sign principle* (see Chapter 4) are producing something that could be called ideographic writing. Note the use of the Valentine shape in five-year-old Jessie's sample (Figure 1–2).

At age four, Annabrook used her mother's initial (F) and her father's (C) to symbolize her parents standing beside her as she appeared as a bride, or is that a dazzling princess? (See Figure 1–3.)

FIGURE 1–2
Jessie (left)
Age 5
A somewhat
ideographic
message

FIGURE 1–3
Annabrook (right)
Age 4
A more clearly
ideographic
message

Symbols for Syllables: Syllabic Writing

A few thousand years ago, an Egyptian scribe thought up a joke that eventually revolutionized writing His language had a hieroglyph ➤—→ that stood for the Egyptian word for "arrow," called *ti*. There was another Egyptian word, also called *ti*, that meant "life," an idea not easily represented by a picture. The scribe's joke was to represent *ti*, meaning "life," with the hieroglyph ➤—→ which stood for "arrow."[14] With that pun he invented the phonetic principle—the principle that relates symbols with words on the basis of *sound*.

For an illustration of the sort of writing that resulted, consider *rebus*—the picture writing found in many young children's prereading books. We write 🐝 4 for "before" and intend that the reader ignore the honey-gathering insect and the numerical quantity of "four" and think only of the sounds of their respective names. This is a phonetic use of hieroglyphics.

With this first use of the phonetic principle, the scribe may have been using symbols to spell whole words, but it is more likely that he was using them to spell syllables. After the invention of the phonetic principle, Egyptian hieroglyphics spelled syllables of words. That writing system has been obsolete for centuries; but the system of syllabic writing lives on in modern Japanese.

The spoken language of Japanese makes use of forty-six different syllables. Combinations of syllables from those forty-six make up every word in the language. A Japanese writing system, called *kana*, provides a symbol for each of the forty-six syllables. The syllable *ro* is written ⃞ ; the syllable *ku* is written ⟩ . The word for "green," *roku*, may thus be written ⃞⟩ . If we know that ⟩ represents the syllables *tsu*, then we can write the word *kutsu*, "to bend" ⟩⟩ . Note that the syllable symbols ⟩ , ⃞ , and ⟩ mean nothing in themselves. They gain significance only by representing the sounds of the syllables of Japanese words.[15]

There are few syllabic writing systems besides Japanese in active use nowadays. But in ancient times these systems were widespread.[14] Just as ideographic writing systems mostly gave way to syllabic systems, the latter mostly evolved into alphabetic writing systems or disappeared altogether.

Children and Syllabic Writing. Do our young spellers in English attempt to produce syllabic writing? Sometimes we see writings that have words represented at the level of the syllable. In one kindergartner's sentence (Figure 1–4), the number 2 and the letter T in DELTKO represent syllables.

The next sample is another kindergartner's response to the question: "If you could go anywhere in town for lunch, where would you go?" (See Figure 1–5.) The B and Z in Bonanza also serve as syllables.

Both of these samples differ from true syllabic writing because they have

FIGURE 1–4
*Melanie
Kindergarten
Syllabic use of
"2" and "T"*

FIGURE 1–5
*Annabrook
Kindergarten
Syllabic use of
"B" and "Z"*

LSNT WE   WNT S DELTKO

I WEᑕ.
GO TO.
BNA S.

other symbols in them that represent units smaller than syllables. Few children seem to spell consistently at the level of the syllable—though, as we shall see in Chapter 5, they occasionally do represent syllables with single consonants, a practice that standard English spelling does not allow.

Symbols for Small Units of Sound: Alphabetic Writing
The use of the alphabet as we know it was a Greek invention. Five thousand years ago, the Greeks discovered that the syllabaries in circulation at the time did not fit their language. For example, the word *anthropos,* meaning "man," was rendered a-to-ro-po-se by an early syllabary. "The crown," *ton choron,* was written to-ne-ko-ro-ne. It wouldn't do. What was plainly needed was a writing system that would let the scribes choose what combinations of consonants and vowels they wanted.

So they made some changes in the syllabaries. Instead of representing a whole syllable (a vowel plus a consonant), the new Greek symbols would represent either a consonant or a vowel but not both. Thus the alphabet and the alphabetic principle were born.[14]

It may be that some children who seek to understand how English writing works reject the syllabic approach for the same reasons the Greeks did.

English *could* be spelled syllabically, if the names of the letters of the alphabet could be associated with syllables in words—but it wouldn't work very well.

English is better suited to the alphabet than it is either to ideographs or to syllables. It has too many words for an ideographic system. A large dictionary has more than 130,000 entries; if we used ideographs, we would have to learn to look up that many! English is not suited to any syllabary either, because—unlike Japanese—the syllable patterns in English are many and varied and would require a large number of characters to represent them. The twenty-six letters of the alphabet can, in some combination, represent all of the sounds contained in all 130,000 plus words in a large English dictionary. No other writing system offers such economy.

The match between our alphabet and the sounds of our words is far from perfect, however. English has forty-four sounds but only twenty-six letters. A few of the letters, moreover, are redundant: the letters K and C can represent the same sounds, as can S and C, and Y and I. Some letters represent many different sounds, and some sounds may be spelled with many different letters. All of these features have consequences for learning to write in English.

That is enough about writing systems. To review, we have briefly described three major types: (1) the ideographic system (which uses symbols to represent whole words or ideas), (2) the syllabic system (which uses symbols to represent syllables), and (3) the alphabetic system (which uses symbols to represent individual speech sounds, or *phonemes,* as linguists call them). All three systems are in use today.

There is no inherent reason why children who speak English should expect writing to work by the alphabet principle. It is reasonable to suppose that children's early suppositions about the way writing works might for a time light on ideographic and syllabic writing, as well as on alphabetic writing. In fact, alphabetic writing requires that writers be able to break a word into its individual speech sounds before they can write it (assuming they are inventing the spelling). This breaking out of speech sounds is a sophisticated language act, far more sophisticated than breaking sentences into words (as ideographic writing requires) or words into syllables (as syllabic writing requires). These matters will be given a more thorough discussion in the ensuing chapters.

From our discussion of writing systems, one point should be clear: Discovering how to write in English involves making choices from a very large range of alternatives. Children may very well be more aware of the alternatives than adults are because our long experience with alphabetic writing tends to blind us to the possibility that there may be ways of representing words with symbols that are different from the way we do it.

REFERENCES

1. Carol Chomsky. "Invented Spelling in the Open Classroom." *Word* 27(1971): 499–518.
2. Noam Chomsky. *Language and Mind.* (Enlarged ed.) New York: Harcourt Brace Jovanovich, 1972.

3.   Martin Braine. "The Acquisition of Language in Infant and Child." In C. E. Reed (ed.), *The Learning of Language*. New York: Appleton-Century-Crofts, 1971. (Quoted in Aitchison, *The Articulate Mammal*. London: Hutchinson, 1973, p. 74.)

4.   Courtney Cazden. *Child Language and Education*. New York: Holt, Rinehart and Winston, 1972. (Quoted in Aitchison, *The Articulate Mammal*, p. 72.)

5.   Jean Aitchison. *The Articulate Mammal*. London: Hutchinson, 1973.

6.   Jill DeVilliers and Peter DeVilliers. *Language Acquisition*. Cambridge: Harvard University Press, 1979.

7.   Roger Brown. *A First Language*. Cambridge: M.I.T. Press, 1973.

8.   Catherine Gorney. " 'Gibberish' Language of Identical Twins Still Baffles the Experts." *The Houston Chronicle*, 29 July 1979, sec. 10, p. 4.

9.   Michael Halliday. *Explorations in the Functions of Language*. London: Edward Arnold, 1973.

10.   Gordon Wells. *The Meaning Makers*. Portsmouth, N.H.: Heinemann Educational Books, 1986.

11.   Daniel Stern. *The First Relationship: Infant and Mother*. Cambridge: Harvard University Press, 1977.

12.   David Olson. " 'See! Jumping!' Some Oral Antecedents of Literacy." In Hillel Goelman, Antoinette Oberg, and Frank Smith (eds.), *Awakening to Literacy*. Portsmouth, NH: Heinemann Educational Books, 1984.

13.   Diane Wolff. *An Easy Guide to Everyday Chinese*. New York: Harper Colophon Books, 1974.

14.   Ignace Gelb. *A Study of Writing*. Chicago: University of Chicago Press, 1963.

Part One
The Beginnings of Writing

When does writing begin? Is it when the child composes a readable message to serve some communicative purpose? Is it when the child uses letters to spell words with some approximate degree of accuracy? Or is it when the child makes some wiggly lines on paper and pretends that she is writing?

It is clear that much writing development unfolds in children well before they spell or compose.

The earliest tasks in learning to write concern making marks that look like writing—whether they be long wiggles that fill a page the way writing does or smaller shapes that resemble letters. Thanks to the work of Eleanor Gibson, Linda Lavine, Emilia Ferreiro, and Marie Clay, we can list and describe the concepts and principles children must master in order to make marks that look like writing. We turn to these matters in the next three chapters.

2/   The Precursors of Writing

A four year old was bent over a piece of paper, deeply engrossed in the act of making the marks shown in Figure 2–1, when her older sister, a first grader, entered the room.

"Jessie, what are you doing?" asked the sister.

"I'm writing," she replied.

"No, you're not."

"Yes, I am."

"You can't be. I don't see any letters!"

Jessie's sister is certainly a realist, a clear-sighted spotter of naked emperors. But we rather agree with Jessie. Her marks do contain many of the rudiments of writing. Our purpose in this chapter and in the two succeeding ones will be to demonstrate the growth of writing—starting with youngsters who "write" as Jessie does and continuing until we see children begin to spell.

Consider the samples in Figures 2–2 and 2–3. How is it possible to examine samples like these and find elements of writing in them? Real writing is composed of combinations of discrete symbols that stand in some socially agreed upon relation to language.[1] These scribbles do not meet this definition by any stretch of the imagination. Indeed, as Jessie's sister pointed out, they don't even have letters in them.

FIGURE 2–1
Jessie
Age 4
Early writing

FIGURE 2–2
No Name
Kindergarten
The child called
this writing

FIGURE 2–3
No Name
Kindergarten
This, too, was
called writing

EARLY WRITING AND A THEORY OF PERCEPTION

People who know how to read and write, even newcomers to this endeavor like Jessie's sister, think of writing as something composed of letters and words. Learning to write, it would seem, is nothing other than learning to make letters and to combine them into words. But studies of writing development carried out against a theory of perceptual learning have suggested that young children learn to write through a process that is really quite the opposite. Rather than learning to write by mastering first the parts (letters) and then building up to the whole (written lines), it appears that children attend first to the whole and only much later to the parts. But what is there is to be attended to in the whole of written language if not words and letters?

Let us now explore the process of perceptual learning for a bit to establish a background for an answer to this question. (Our discussion will draw mostly from Eleanor Gibson.)[2] Imagine a newborn baby just home from the hospital, lying in a crib in his nursery. What does he see? At first his eyes are closed in sleep much of the time, and for several months he cannot focus on objects more than a foot or two away from his face. But from the time he opens his eyes he is bombarded by sensations: light, shadow, and dark; objects that loom into view and withdraw; and objects that do not move.

What does he hear? There is the constant sound of his own breathing, the sound of voices—some loud and distinct (voices of people close by) and some less loud and echoing (voices of people further away). He may hear sounds of traffic outside, sounds of lawnmowers, sounds of birds chirping and dogs barking. The child is surrounded by a "blooming, buzzing, bustling confusion" of sights, sounds, and feelings.

At first we may imagine that the sensations are all undifferentiated—that is, the baby has no way to distinguish one sight, sound, or feeling from another. But soon he must begin to do some basic sorting. Things that move can be distinguished from things that are static. Human voices can be separated from other non-human noises, such as passing motorcycles, ringing telephones, and barking dogs.

These first gross distinctions can be taken further. Things that move can be sorted into parts of the baby himself, and other things that move. Or they can be sorted into things that move on their own accord, and other things that move (people and animals versus balls and mobiles). Sounds can be carried to further distinctions as voices that are close by are distinguished from voices that are far away, a woman's voice from a child's, and so on.

This process of sorting and classifying is the child's way of finding out about the world and getting some control over it. The process continues throughout childhood and adult life, though it never again reaches the intensity of the child's first four years.

When the child begins to use words to stand for things, we begin to get a clearer idea of how this sorting process works. Take the case of Annabrook, for example. The first word uttered by this little girl was "dog." During that phase of language development when all of her sentences consisted of a single word, she delighted in pointing to the family beagle and sagely pronouncing him, "dog." But the beagle was not the only animal to qualify for that label. Goats, sheep, cats, and even an occasional cow (she lived on a farm) were all pronounced "dog." During this period it happened that Annabrook was taken to a circus. She and her family had taken their seats and were arranging themselves when a large elephant appeared at the back of the circus tent and swayed into the center ring. "Dog!" cried Annabrook, and in fear and amazement she clapped her hand over her eyes.

It seems that what Annabrook had been doing was lumping together several objects in the world into the category that she labeled "dog." She did the lumping on the basis of features these objects had in common. "Dogs" apparently were four-legged, self-propelled living things. Chickens, having two legs, were never called "dog." Annabrook must have been aware that there are differences in the appearance of dogs, sheep, goats, cats, and certainly cows. For the time being, she chose to ignore the differences and group them together because of the features they did have in common. When she saw the elephant, however, she seemed to realize at once that her category for "dog" must be amended to take size into account. In other words, she found it necessary to add another *distinctive feature,* size, to the set of features that defined "dog."

Distinctive features are central to an understanding of perceptual learning. They are the necessary set of features or attributes that we use to define a category of things. For Annabrook, "four-legged," "living," and "self-propelled" appeared to be the distinctive features that made up her category "dog." Distinctive features are acquired with experience. In general, the more experience we have in the world, the more distinctive features we add to our categories. Then two things happen: Membership in a particular category becomes reserved to fewer varieties of objects, while at the same time we set up new categories to include those items that were not adequately described by our earlier categories.[3]

To summarize our points about perceptual learning, we can say

1. Our environment presents us with an abundant potential of sense data all of the time. The task of perceptual learning is to carve out classes of objects and events from the undifferentiated confusion around us— classes of things that somehow act or can be acted upon in the same way.
2. The differentiation of things in the environment usually starts with gross categories defined by gross distinctions and then proceeds to finer categories defined by finer distinctive features.
3. We assign things to categories on the basis of distinctive features that the things share. In doing this, we initially ignore some differences. However, if the differences become important enough, we will create a new category and assign some things to the new category that will not fit the old.

HOW CHILDREN PERCEIVE WRITING

If the perception of things in the environment starts with gross distinctions and moves progressively to finer ones, it stands to reason that letters—being the fine elements of writing—would be the last elements to be differentiated. The theory of perceptual learning would lead us to believe that children should first discover gross differences between writing and other similar things. When children first become aware of writing as a separate thing, they must have some rough set of distinctive features to help them decide when something is writing and when it is not. As they gain experience, they should become aware of finer and finer distinctive features that separate writing from other kinds of graphic displays, and the smaller components of writing, such as letters, from each other.

In recent years, there have been several productive inquiries into the question of what children think writing is—that is, into the distinctive features of writing to which children attend to at different points in childhood. These inquiries have been carried out in two ways. First, there have been experiments in which children are asked to make distinctions between several different sorts of graphic displays. Second, children's own productions, which they themselves call writing, have been examined for the features that they have in common. The findings of the first kind of experiment will concern us through the remainder of this chapter. The second kind of experiment will be discussed in Chapter 3.

Several years ago, Eleanor Gibson, a psychologist at Cornell University, put forth the idea that children might come to know about writing through its features—not through its letters.[4] She stated that we might expect children's progress in learning about writing to proceed from the discrimination of gross shapes to the discrimination of letters themselves. Gibson then proceeded to conduct a long program of experiments, using young children as subjects, to test her ideas of how they might think about writing. One of the most elaborate of these experiments was carried out by her doctoral student, Linda Lavine.[1,5]

Lavine sought to find out what sorts of graphic forms children of different ages call writing and which sorts they don't. She designed a set of cards, each featuring a graphic display of some sort (see Figure 2–4). Then she made up a game, which she played with her three-, four-, and five-year-old subjects. Showing them the cards, she told the children to decide which cards had writing on them. They were to place the ones that did in a toy mailbox. The ones that did not have writing on them were placed in a garbage can.

On the cards Lavine had printed four kinds of graphic displays (see Figure 2–4). The first were pictures of familiar and unfamiliar objects and of geometric designs. The other three kinds she designated as follows:

- Class I dealt with real English writing and included both cursive and printed letters and words.
- Class II was made up of writings that looked very much like Roman letters (that is, the writing shared many distinctive features with Roman letters), but were written in the Hebrew alphabet.
- Class III consisted of designs that did not look like Roman letters. These were Chinese letters and a Mayan design motif.

FIGURE 2–4
Cards from Lavine's experiment

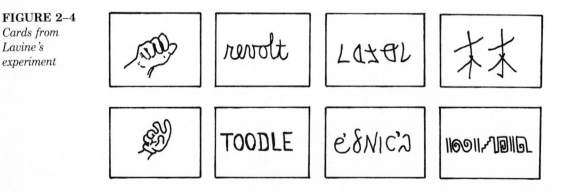

All the types of figures were presented in several formats to contrast the different features that children might respond to. The normal presentation was horizontal, linear, six units to a line (see Figure 2–5). But variations were single unit presentations (see Figure 2–6), same unit six times (see Figure 2–7), and nonlinear arrays of varied units (see Figure 2–8).

When the responses of the three age groups—three, four, and five year olds—were tallied and compared, they showed some very interesting patterns. No one said the pictures were writing—not even the three year olds. Only the youngest subjects called the Class III figures writing (these were the Chinese and Mayan figures). But all the age groups called both Class I (writing) and Class II (Hebrew characters) writing. Class II figures shared features with Roman letters, but they were not Roman letters and they were not likely to have been seen in the children's environment. On this finding, Gibson's hypothesis was supported: Children did seem to be using *features* of the writing system and not just an inventory of known letters as the basis for making judgments as to whether or not a display could be called writing.

The younger children appeared to use both linearity (whether the figures were presented in a straight horizontal line) and variety (whether there was a composition of different sorts of figures rather than one figure repeated) as distinguishing features of writing. That is, unlinear and unvaried displays were usually rejected by the younger subjects. But the older subjects tended to ignore such features as linearity and variety and focus instead on the appearance of the individual figures. Thus, they tended to class unlinear or unvaried arrays as writing, so long as the figures that composed them were Roman letters or Roman-like letters (see Figure 2–9). This finding, too, was in accordance with Gibson's hypothesis: Gross features such as linearity and variety were distinctive in the judgments of the younger subjects; but finer features such as the details of the letters themselves were distinctive for the older subjects.

FIGURE 2–5
(left)
*Horizontal, linear,
six units per line*

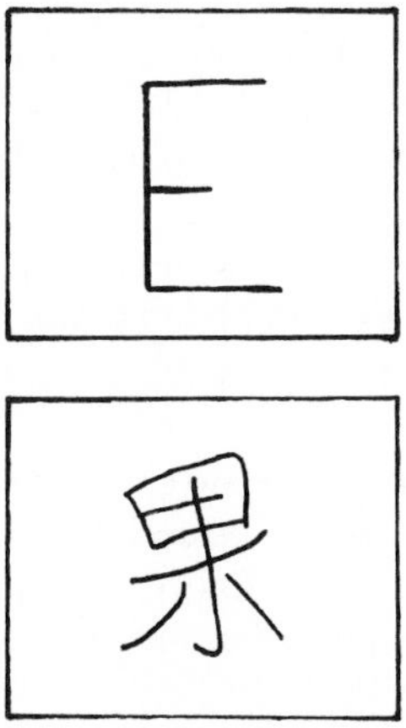

FIGURE 2–6
(right)
*Single-unit
variations*

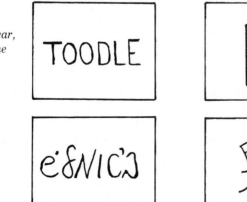

FIGURE 2–7
(left)
*Variations with
the same symbol
repeated*

FIGURE 2–8
(right)
*Nonlinear
variations*

FIGURE 2–9
*Linearity and
variety were
distinctive to
younger children*
(left) *and Roman
letters were
distinctive to older
children* (right)

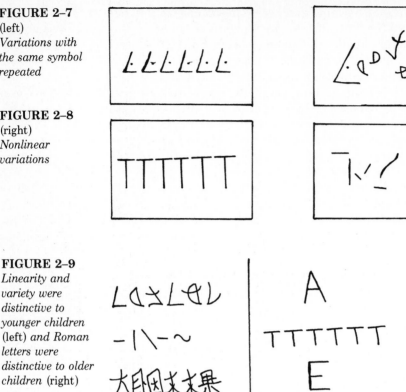

Lavine's study supported the supposition that children come to know about writing through the process of perceptual learning. Children appear to identify distinctive features in separating writing from other graphic displays. Moreover, they progressively refine the sets of distinctive features they use to define writing.

Lavine reasoned from her experiment that several distinctive features must be included in children's categories of "writing." The features apparently considered distinctive by even the youngest subjects were

- *nonpictoriality*—whatever is considered writing may not be a picture;
- *linearity*—the figures must be arrayed horizontally in a straight line;
- *variety*—figures in a display should vary from one another;
- *multiplicity*—writing consists of more than one figure.

The features used by the older subjects appeared to be:

- *Roman-like*—the individual units of writing should share the distinctive features of letters in the Roman alphabet (what these features are was not detailed in this experiment); and
- *being Roman letters themselves*—writing is composed of letters we can recognize from our knowledge of individual letters.

CONCLUSION

"What looks like writing to you?" That, essentially, was the question Lavine asked her subjects. In their answers, the children revealed the distinctive features that they considered to define writing at their respective ages. And since these features differed from the younger children to the older ones, these findings were interesting indeed.

We may still want to ask what all this has to do with children's writing. Judging designs to be writing or nonwriting is one thing; producing designs that look like writing may be quite another. That objection is reasonable, but Lavine's study nevertheless tells us much that is important. For one thing, it is likely that the features to which the children in her study responded parallel the features children notice in the writing they find in their environment. With repeated exposure to print—in books, on billboards, in buses and subways— these features may become more and more important to children and more stable in their minds.

When children make their own early attempts to produce designs that look like writing, we might expect features similar to those identified by Lavine to emerge in their designs. In the next chapter, in which we look closely at the first writings children produce themselves, we will see whether or not this prediction is borne out.

REFERENCES

1. Linda Lavine. "The Development of Perception of Writing in Prereading Children: A Cross-Cultural Study." Unpublished Ph.D. dissertation, Cornell University, 1972. Xerox University Microfilms, 73–6657.
2. Eleanor Gibson and Harry Levin. *Psychology of Reading.* Cambridge: M.I.T. Press, 1975.
3. Jerome Bruner. "On Perceptual Readiness." In Jeremy Anglin (ed.), *Beyond the Information Given.* New York: Norton, 1976.
4. Eleanor Gibson. *Principles of Perceptual Learning and Development.* New York: Appleton-Century-Crofts, 1969.
5. Linda Lavine. "Differentiation of Letterlike Forms in Prereading Children." *Developmental Psychology,* 13(2) (1977): 89–94.

3/ Features of Children's Early Writing

Jessie crept up beside one of the authors as he ate his breakfast and put down the strange message shown in Figure 3–1. "Read it!" she said. He knew from previous occasions that it wouldn't do to protest that she hadn't written anything readable.

"Rrbuhdow!" he said. This was just what she wanted. She disappeared into her bedroom and returned almost at once with four more sheets of the same.

"Read it!" she demanded.

In this chapter we are going to look closely at writings by children like Jessie. These are children whose written productions have stopped being pictures but have not yet become writing (if by "writing" we really mean spelling—using letters to represent words *by their sounds*). We will study the features that emerge in children's productions—the features that make their productions more and more like writing.

Following the example of Marie Clay,[1] a New Zealander whose research forms the backbone of this chapter, we will cease to use the term *features* and now speak of *principles*. The reason for the shift is this: When children sort writing from nonwriting (as we observed in the previous chapter), they do it on the basis of the visual features of the graphic displays—horizontal nature of the figures, variety of figures, nonpictoriality, and so on.[2] But when children produce early pseudowriting, they appear to be trying to discover and manipulate principles that can make their productions look like writing. Hence, *principles* and *features* are active and passive versions of the same thing. When we produce writing, we employ principles; when we discriminate writing, we use features.

FIGURE 3–1
Jessie
Age 4
Early writing

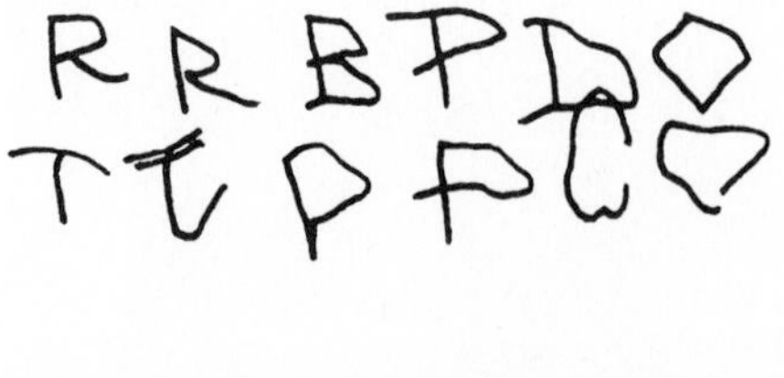

In the following pages we will describe the *recurring principle,* the discovery that writing uses the same shapes again and again; the *generative principle,* the discovery that writing consists of a limited number of signs in varied combinations; the *sign concept,* the idea that print stands for something besides itself; and the *flexibility principle,* the idea that there is a limited number of written signs, and a limit to the number of ways we can make them. Finally, we will describe a number of principles related to the way print is arranged on a page, *page-arrangement principles.* All of these principles must be learned by children before it can be said they write. And many of them may be seen emerging in children's scribbles before anyone notices that they are trying to produce writing.

THE RECURRING PRINCIPLE

Study the picture and the handwriting sample in Figure 2–2. On a very general level, what makes the writing look different from the picture? You may notice several differences. The writing is arranged in rows across the page, while the picture makes more use of two-dimensional space. If you squint your eyes and look at the writing and the picture, the individual letters lose their identity. Now you may notice that the writing seems to be composed of loops and tall sticks repeated over and over again. Children's early attempts to imitate writing often have this characteristic repetition of loops or sticks or circles.

Clay applied the label *recurring principle* to the idea that writing consists of the same moves repeated over and over again. She noted that children derive a great deal of satisfaction from filling whole lines or pages by repeating the same moves over and over.

FIGURE 3–2
Picture and words for the same idea

There was a house. It had a chimney with smoke coming out, and two flowers in the yard. There was a bird and a cloud in the sky.

FIGURE 3–3
Carlene
Age 4
Recurring principle

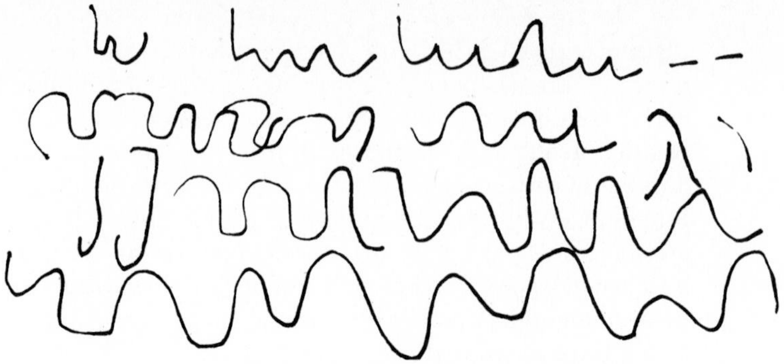

FIGURE 3–4
Matt
Kindergarten
Recurring principle

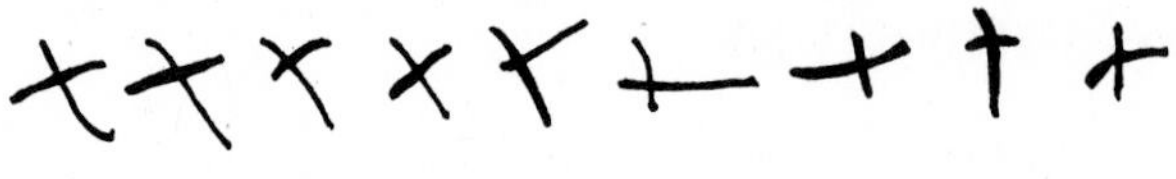

The displays in Figures 3–3 and 3–4 were produced by children who said they were writing. Note how each gives evidence of the recurring principle.

THE GENERATIVE PRINCIPLE

It is possible to fill an entire page with repetitions of the same basic mark. That is what the child in Figure 3–5 has done. But as we saw in the previous chapter, children learn early on that the same character repeated over and over again is not writing. To be called writing, there must be variety in the arrangement of marks.

It *is* possible to create writing with just a few characters, *but they must be repeated in different combinations.* Every book written in English simply combines and recombines fifty-two letter symbols. The writer in Figure 3–6 uses considerably fewer, but it is clear that she has discovered the same principle around which English writing is organized: A limitless amount of writing can be generated by using a small set of letters, provided they are combined in different ways. This is what Clay calls the *generative principle* (see Figure 3–7).

The generative principle may be employed with words, too. In Figure 3–8, note how Wes has recombined a small repertoire of words to make a list of sentences covering a whole page.

FIGURE 3–5
No Name
Age 3
Filling a line with
the same form

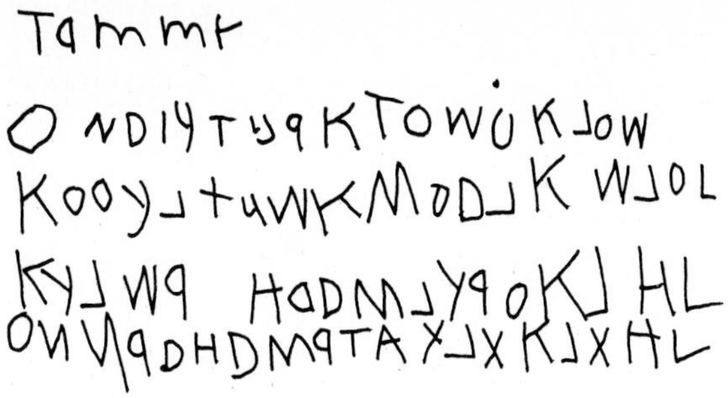

FIGURE 3–6
Tammy
Kindergarten
Generative
principle

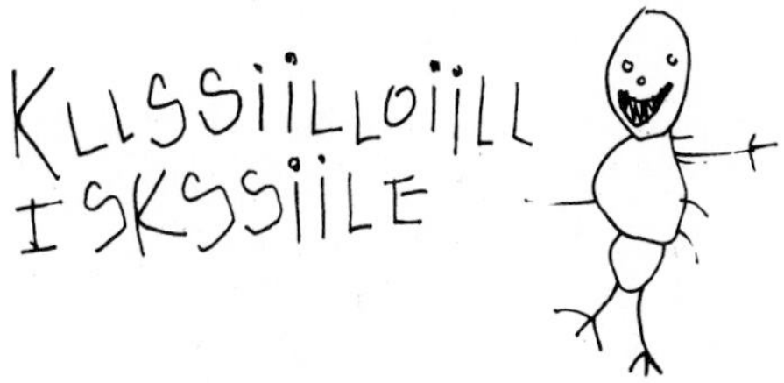

Tammy

O NDIYTY9KTOWUKJow
KOOyJtUWKMODJK WJOL
KYJW9 HODMJY9OKJ HL
OWNqDHDMqTAXJXKJXHL

FIGURE 3–7
No Name
Age 4
Generative
principle

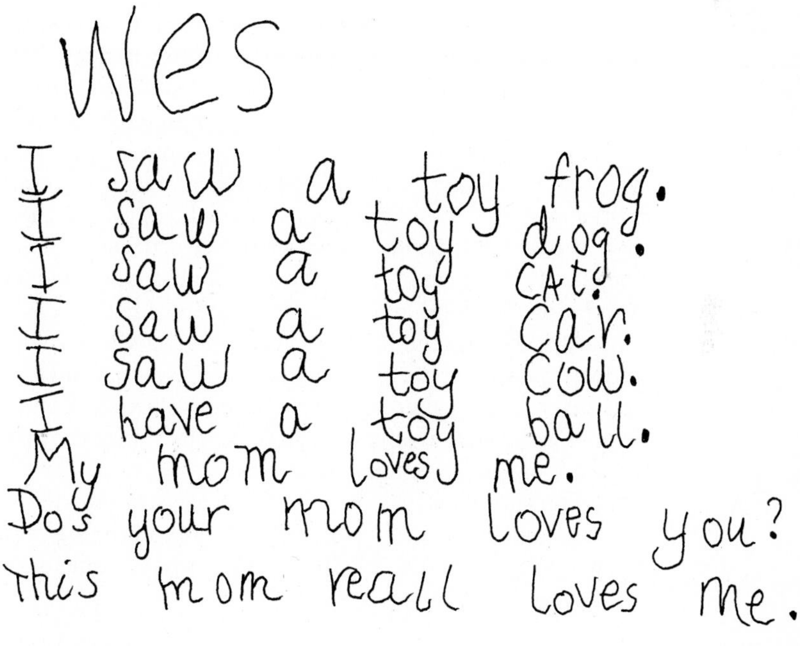

KLLSSiiLLOïiLL
I SKSSiiLE

FIGURE 3–8
Wes
Grade 1
Generative
principle applied
to sentences

Wes

I saw a toy frog.
I saw a toy dog.
I saw a toy cat.
I saw a toy car.
I saw a toy cow.
I have a toy ball.
My mom loves me.
Do's your mom loves you?
This mom reall loves me.

THE SIGN CONCEPT

All of the items in Figure 3–9 could be called *graphic displays,* but only some of them could be called *signs.* Figure 1) is a picture, not a sign. Figure 2) is a design, such as might decorate the hem of a skirt; it is not a sign either. Figure 3) *might* be a sign to someone who reads Chinese (the author made it up!).

FIGURE 3–9
*Varieties of
graphic displays*

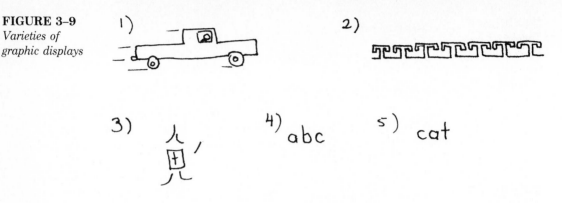

Figure 4) contains three signs—the graphic configurations for the letters a, b, and c, respectively. Figure 5) contains the three signs c, a, and t; collectively these make up the sign "cat," the English word for a small feline animal.

What is a sign? A sign is a display that stands for something else. In writing, signs are arbitrary—that is, there is no reason why a particular graphic display *has* to stand for what it does. There is no particular reason why a sideways hook should stand for the letter C. Generations of readers and writers of English have simply agreed that it does. This is what separates *writing* from *pictures*: writing represents something arbitrarily, while drawing does not.[2] The relation between the graphic display in Figure 3–10 and the idea "truck" is *not* arbitrary. The graphic display shares many features (wheels, back and front, steering wheel, window, etc.) with the object it represents. But the written word *truck* has none of these things in common with the object "truck." The written word can represent the object only because the community of literate English speakers agrees that the word stands for the thing, and the letters stand for the word.

At some point in their development as writers, all children must come to understand that writing uses graphic displays to stand for something else. This understanding is called the *sign concept*. Children understand the sign concept when they intend, even in play, to have the things they put on paper stand for words, ideas, or messages.

The sign concept seems to be present when children make marks that begin to look like writing. Note the evidence of the sign concept in the piece by Shawn, a four year old (Figure 3–11). We need some background information

FIGURE 3–10
"Truck"

truck

FIGURE 3–11
Shawn
Age 4
About his father

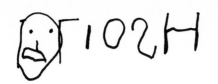

to interpret Shawn's markings. His father is a football coach at Stroman High School. Stroman High School students often wear sweatshirts emblazoned with a Teutonic letter S. The H in this passage probably stands not for the letter but for a goalpost. The face at the left-hand end of the figure has a mustache, just like Shawn's father. Thus, we can interpret this display to say something about the fact that Shawn's father is connected with football at Stroman High School.

Shawn's signs are not arbitrary. Perhaps he is showing us that it is natural for a beginning writer to think of concrete relations between signs and the things they stand for. Emilia Ferreiro has argued that this is the case.[3] (Her ideas will be discussed in Chapter 4.)

Most beginning writers are willing to *pretend* that the marks they wrote stand for something—leaving the relation between the marks and the things they stand for up to the reader's imagination. Note the grocery list written up by Susan, at her mother's suggestion (see Figure 3–12). After she had written down her marks for each item, her mother went back and asked her what each one was. To the left of each mark is written her answer.

Where does the sign concept come from? Children who grow up in homes where literacy is practiced have many indications that writing stands for things. Children whose parents read to them hear a certain story come from a certain book with certain pictures and print. And, although for a time they may believe that the story is somehow contained in the picture, it eventually dawns on them that the print is the source of the story.[4] Perhaps they notice that a variety of spoken comments may be induced by a picture, whereas an exact story line is stimulated by print. Recognition of the sign potential of the print is certainly made easier when parents occasionally run their finger along with the print as they read.

Even if children are not read to, there are other indications available to them of the sign potential of print. Logos on popular restaurants, such as McDonald's, Burger King, and the like, are quickly picked up by children. A three year old at home who is shown a McDonald's hamburger wrapper may easily say, "McDonald's!" No wonder businesses so jealously protect their logos from use by competitors!

THE FLEXIBILITY PRINCIPLE

In our discussion of the sign concept we noted that signs stand for things on the basis of social agreement. Hence, the figure D stands for the letter D, and the figure P stands for the letter P. We know this because it is taught in school and

FIGURE 3–12
Susan
Age 3
Grocery list

milk

eggs

bread
butter
ice cream

apples

noodles

soap

used consistently in any society where English is read and written. It follows that signs must be used *carefully*. In writing there is a limited set of agreed-upon signs. To write English, we *have to* use the agreed-upon signs and no others. On the present author's typewriter there are fifty-two of these: abcdefghijklmnopqrstuvwxyz, ABCDEFGHIJKLMNOPQRSTUVWXYZ. Some scripts add *a* and *g* to total fifty-four. If we use any other figures than these as signs for letters, we must not assume that others will know what we mean by them.

On the other hand, we know that letters are made up of combinations of a limited number of features. All of the letters we use are made up of lines that are horizontal, vertical, and diagonal; of loops that face left or right, up or down; or loops that are closed; and dots. These ten shapes account for all fifty-four of the letter forms in English. We can say that writing English letters is a matter of writing correct or allowable combinations of those ten basic shapes.

Once children begin to experiment with writing, a period of months or years may go by before they know all of the letter forms. During that time, they may be constantly surprised that letters they know can be varied to produce new letters. For example, the letter d may be turned upside down to make a letter p, or flipped around to make a letter b. If we add two horizontal bars to the letter L, we get E; if we take the lower bar off E, we get F. Children can discover ways to make letters they didn't previously know how to make. But in the process, they are likely to invent letters that do not exist.

Clay has referred to this whole problem as the *flexibility principle*. The flexibility principle might be stated as follows: By varying letter forms that we know, we can produce letters that we didn't know how to make. But we must be careful, because not all of the letter forms we produce in this way are acceptable as signs. There is one more aspect of the flexibility principle that is of great importance to beginning writers. That is the fact that the same letter form may be written many different ways. Depending on the reading matter a child picks up, he may see quite a variety of printed forms for the same letters (see Figure 3–13).

Observe in Figure 3–14 how Carlene, a four year old, came upon the flexibility principle. Which of her figures are allowable letters? Which are unallowable variations? Which ones are allowable forms that she might have invented? That is, has she produced some allowable letters by accident?

Jessie's figures all appear to be allowable letter forms (see Figure 3–15). But what might have influenced her to put the loops on her letters? The embellishments Jessie puts on her letters may be her attempt to imitate the serifs on standard type that she sees in books.

When young children explore the flexibility principle, this should be considered a positive sign.[1] In this way children gain active control over the features or principles of print. It is only speculation, but it seems likely that children who explore the flexibility principle will be better able to respond appropriately to varieties of print type encountered in their reading than children who memorize letter configurations one at a time. This is because practice with the flexibility principle helps children attend to the defining features of letters, to consider what features constitute a letter and what features make it something else.

LINEAR PRINCIPLES AND PRINCIPLES OF PAGE ARRANGEMENT

Perhaps one of the hardest things for young children to grasp in approaching early writing is the fact that the direction in which written characters face is so important. Psychologists of perception have taught us to marvel that a child can look at a chair from the top, from the bottom, and from any side and know that what she is looking at is still a chair.[5] The information available to the child's eyes changes markedly as she moves from one perspective to another vis-à-vis the chair. Still, the child learns to ignore the difference imposed by changes in perspective and attend to the features of the chair that do not change from one perspective to the next—the fact that it has four legs, a horizontal platform, and a vertical back (see Figure 3–16).

FIGURE 3–13
*Some variations
of print style*

FIGURE 3–14
Carlene (left)
Age 4
Flexibility
principle

FIGURE 3–15
Jessie (right)
Age 4
Flexibility
principle

FIGURE 3–16
A chair is still a
chair, regardless
of perspective

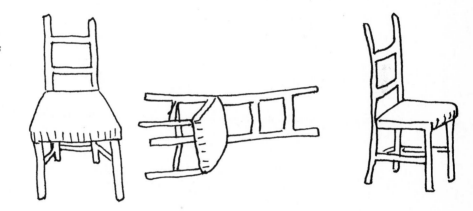

When the child begins to write, the rules change. Now the visual differences brought on by shifts in perspective change the very identity of the object! The same combination of circle and stick can be the letter b, p, d, or q, depending on its arrangement in space. Writing is one of very few areas of our experience where identity changes with direction. The orientation of letters gives children problems for months and even years after they begin to write (see Figures 3–17 and 3–18).

Directionality is also an important issue with regard to the arrangement of print on a page. When we write in English, we start on the left-hand side of the page at the top, proceed straight across to the right side, return to the left, drop down one line, and proceed to the right again. This fairly complicated directional pattern is arbitrary, and it does not extend to all writing systems. Hebrew readers read across from right to left. Chinese readers read top to bottom and right to left. Ancient Greeks used to read from left to right on the first line, then right to left on the second line, then left to right on the third line. Our English pattern of left to right and top to bottom is one set of choices selected arbitrarily from many possibilities.

FIGURE 3–17
Jessie (left)
Age 5
Letter direction
problems

FIGURE 3–18
Will (right)
Age 4
Started with "W"
and went both
ways

JESUS
JEZUS

Clay found in a study that directional problems were common in the five and six year olds she studied in New Zealand. Most of her five year olds and many of her six year olds had not yet settled on the left-right-top-bottom pattern. Her subjects read from right to left, from bottom to top, or from the middle of the line out to either end.[1] She also noted that children continue to have directional difficulty in writing well after this issue is settled in reading.

If children draw a picture first and then write, the direction in which they arrange their print is often a matter of the best use of the space available on the page. The child in Figure 3–19, for instance, glued a picture onto her page first, and then wrote the text in the vertically extended space that was left over.

Young children's habits of directionality are remarkably fluid. Adults cannot easily write their names backwards, but many beginning writers appear able to do this with little trouble (see Figure 3–20).

During the time when their notions of directionality have not yet been cast solidly in favor of left to right, top to bottom, we should avoid exercises with writing that violate this principle. Note, for example, what happened to the kindergartner in Figure 3–21 when she was given a commercially printed worksheet to complete. The worksheet asked that she fill in the letters of the alphabet in their proper order in the cells of the snake (or is it a tapeworm?).

FIGURE 3–19
No Name (left)
Kindergarten
Page arrangement
variations

FIGURE 3–20
Annabrook (right)
Age 5
Writing backwards
was easy for her

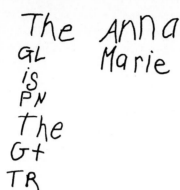

FIGURE 3–21
Shelley
Kindergarten
The "A" and "Z"
were already
printed

But since the snake meandered from left to right, then from right to left, then from left to right again, the girl took her cue from the snake's orientation and wrote those letters backwards that were to fill the blanks running from right to left. Then she straightened out and pointed them correctly when the snake ran from left to right again. This was a thoughtful response to a confusing exercise. Children deserve materials that are more sensitive to the real problems of learning to write than this sheet was.

When children violate directional principles in writing, part of the reason must be their tendency to focus on one letter or word at a time—they do not appear to give much forethought to the question of how the whole page is to be arranged (see Figure 3–22). It is therefore a good idea for the teacher to give them some guidance here. In an exercise where they are drawing a picture first and then writing about it, the teacher might first

- Fold the papers from side to side so as to leave a crease separating the top of the page from the bottom. Then instruct the child to draw their picture on the top (or the bottom) and do their writing on the bottom (or the top).
- Put a green arrow on the left-hand side of the page, pointing to the right, to remind the children where to begin and which way to arrange their writing.

SPACES BETWEEN WORDS

In Chapter 7 of this book, in which we discuss early spelling behavior, we raise the question of whether or not beginning readers and writers know what a word is. One reason that the question comes up is that so many beginning writers give no indication of what their word units are. Or when they do, they sometimes do so incorrectly (see Figure 3–23). Our writing system routinely indicates word boundaries by leaving spaces between the word units in print. Beginning writers quite often fail to leave these spaces.

Nevertheless, a child's failure to leave spaces between words should not be taken too quickly to indicate that she doesn't know that the words exist as separate units. It happens that leaving spaces is a highly abstract procedure for children to manage. The present writer remembers his difficulty some years ago when reading an introductory book on architecture. The book called attention to the use of positive and negative space in building design. Positive space is what you put in; negative space is what you leave out. At the time, negative space seemed a very difficult concept to work with. The space left between words is negative space, and the concept probably causes difficulty for children, also. Many children appear to prefer inserting periods between words rather than leaving spaces. It seems that they prefer to manipulate positive rather than negative space (see Figure 3–24).

FIGURE 3–22
Karan
Grade 2
Page arrangement
problems

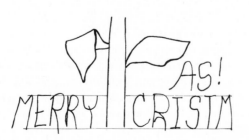

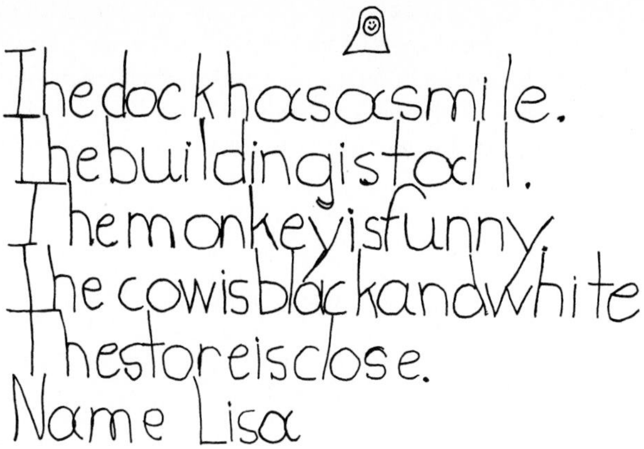

FIGURE 3–23
Lisa
Grade 1
Word spacing
problems

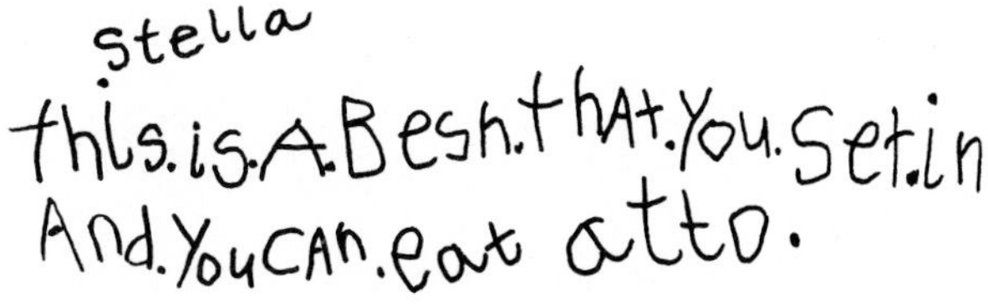

Thedockhasasmile.
Thebuildingistall.
Themonkeyisfunny.
The cowisblackandwhite
Thestoreisclose.
Name Lisa

FIGURE 3–24
Stella
Grade 1
Indicating word
spacing with
periods

stella
this.is.A.Besh.that.You.Set.in
And.YouCAn.eat atto.

CONCLUSION

The features of early writing that children use to distinguish writing from nonwriting (see Chapter 1) parallel very closely the principles and concepts that are displayed in the early writing children produce themselves.

Lavine's feature of *nonpictoriality*—that pictures are not writing—shows up as Clay's *sign concept*—that signs represent objects or ideas, but not directly the way pictures do. Lavine's *variety* feature—that writing consists of strings of different letters, not the same one repeated over and over—is much like Clay's *generative principle*—that a few letters can be made to look like writing if they are written over and over in varied order. Lavine's *multiplicity* feature—that writing must consist of many characters—reminds us of Clay's *recurring principle*—that a simple move may be repeated over and over and strung across a page to look like writing.

There are more parallels as well as some differences—these especially being related to the greater difficulty involved in producing forms that look like letters compared to the task of discriminating writing from nonwriting.

A more important difference between Lavine's work and Clay's is that Lavine associated certain features with greater levels of maturity in writing development. Clay made no such distinction but rather suggested that as more of her early graphic principles showed up in a child's writing, the more mature he was likely to be as a writer.

Future research may allow us to draw firmer conclusions about children's writing development from the examination of the emerging principles in their productions. At present, all we can say is that these principles do turn up in all the young children's writing we've seen. They seem to be signs that the child is actively exploring the writing system. This exploration normally leads to progress in writing.

REFERENCES

1. Marie Clay. *What Did I Write?* Portsmouth, N.H.: Heinemann Educational Books, 1975.
2. Linda Lavine. *The Development of Perception of Writing in Prereading Children: A Cross-Cultural Study.* Ph.D. dissertation, Cornell University, 1972. Xerox University Microfilms, 73–6657.
3. Emilia Ferreiro and Ana Teberosky. *Literacy before Schooling.* Portsmouth, N.H.: Heinemann Educational Books, 1983.
4. Marie Clay. *Reading: The Patterning of Complex Behavior.* 2d ed. Portsmouth, N.H.: Heinemann Educational Books, 1980.
5. Jerome Bruner. "On Perceptual Readiness." In Jeremy Anglin (ed.), *Beyond the Information Given.* New York: Norton, 1976.

4/ What Children Do with Early Graphics

In the previous two chapters we observed that children learn about writing not by acquiring letters one after another but by first becoming sensitive to the features of written language. Before children use a selection of letters with any stability, we see first a slow revelation of certain graphic principles in the children's scribbles—principles such as *directionality, flexibility, generativity,* and *recurrence.* With repeated writing practice children produce marks that more and more closely resemble the writing they see in the print around them. This learning proceeds not letter by letter but feature by feature. But *why* do children go through this learning process in the first place? What are children trying to do when they make scribble after scribble, only gradually producing letter forms that look like those of adults?

It will be our task in this chapter to consider children's purposes for their earliest writing. We will first try to understand what children are trying to get done when they commit marks to paper, considering both the reasons behind the marks they select and the overall communicative purposes. Then in a later section we will discuss ways that parents and teachers of young children can aid children in making a beginning in writing, by providing appropriate help but not pressure.

CHILDREN WRITE ON THEIR OWN

The Sign Concept, Revisited

In Chapter 3 we noted a basic difference between pictures and writing. We observed that writing uses signs to stand for things in an arbitrary way; we must refer to some previously agreed upon social meanings of written signs in order to interpret them correctly.

Children are capable of making signs on paper before they develop a concept of the way the signs represent things. It is interesting to examine children's early writing to determine how they think writing might represent things. Some of the most interesting research into this question has been performed by Emilia Ferreiro,[1] an Argentine psychologist. In order to understand Ferreiro's ideas, let us begin with an illustration. In the English that we adults read and write, we may say that written figures represent letters that combine into representations of words, which stand for real or imaginary things. We may illustrate this series of relationships by means of the diagram in Figure 4–1.

Some children who are new to writing hypothesize relations between writing and language that are different from the relations we described in Figure 4–1. Emilia Ferreiro worked with some four- and five-year-old children in Argentina who had some exotic notions about how writing represents language.

One little boy named Javier said "cat" could be written $O\,i\,A$, while "kittens" could be written $O A i\, O A i\, O A i$. Ferreiro concluded that he had the following hypotheses about the relation between writing and the things represented by writing:

1. Written words for similar things should *look* similar, even though the spoken words for those objects may not *sound* the same.
2. When characters refer to more than one object, the child uses *more* characters to represent them.

Ferreiro found many children who thought there might be a concrete relation between written marks and the things they stood for. She suggested that there may be a developmental continuum that would have children looking first for concrete relations between graphic characters and the things they stood for *without reference to sound.*

FIGURE 4–1
The way writing represents language for fluent readers

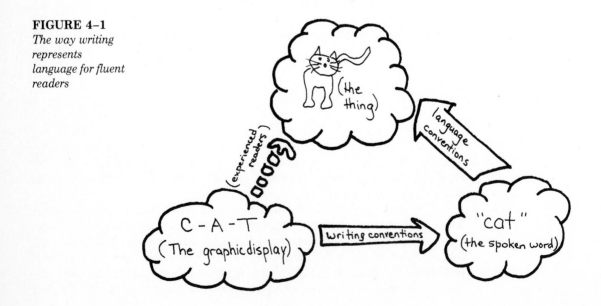

At a later stage, the relation between graphics and language became based on sound. Specifically, the children put the same number of letters in a graphic display as the number of syllables in the spoken word for which the graphic display stood. Thus, "chicken" was written ⌠ ∕ and "fencepost" ⌡ ℓ . There is no relation between the graphic characters and the individual speech sounds in either word. Letters are used as syllable counters only in this sort of writing.

In terms of the diagram in Figure 4–1, Ferreiro's finding was that children first

- look for a concrete relation between *A* and *C* (see Figure 4–2).
- and only later for a *sound* relation between *A* and *B* (see Figure 4–3).

Ferreiro gathered her findings from work with children who came from both uneducated and upper-class families in Argentina and Mexico. As a group, the subjects from uneducated families probably had less exposure to print than children in the United States. Perhaps that explains why we, the authors, have seen so little evidence of Ferreiro's findings in four year olds we have worked with. This whole issue needs further study with children in other cultures, including the United States.

FIGURE 4–2
Concrete relation of letters to language

FIGURE 4–3
*Sound relationship
of letters to
language*

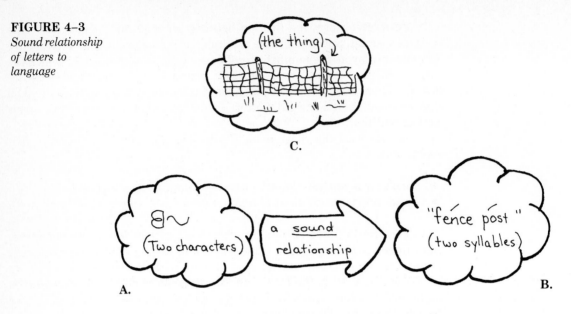

The *sign concept* in U.S. children's early graphics is still not fully understood in any depth. Among four and five year olds, many children think it natural that graphic characters stand for something—that they convey some sort of message. Exactly *how* they think sticks and circles could convey a message, if there is any consensus among young children, is still something of a mystery.

Writing Your Own Name

The first pieces of writing most children produce are their own names. In kindergarten the child's coat bin is marked with his own name. In first grade his name is printed neatly on tagboard and taped to his desk. When he draws a picture, his kindergarten or preschool teacher prints his name on the paper. In writing the child's name so often, the teacher may be motivated as much by management concerns as instructional ones. For the child, though, the result is that his own name is the meaningful printed array that he sees most often in his surroundings. It is certainly the message most children first attempt to write.

Writing their own names may teach children several lessons at once. Ferreiro notes that the child's own name provides the first real challenge to his early hypotheses about the relation of writing to language.[1] The child who thinks the *size* of the graphic display should be related to the size of the referent must wonder as he looks at name labels why Ted is the biggest boy in the class, while he, Anthony, is among the smallest. In a similar vein, the child who relates the number of characters in a graphic display to the number of syllables in the word for which it stands will wonder why "Ma-ry" has four letters while "Keith" has five.

The children's early hypotheses cannot explain the spelling of their own and their classmates' names. So they look for new hypotheses. As we shall see in Part Two of this book, children's thinking about spelling will go through many interesting changes before the children learn to spell correctly.

Learning to write one's own name carries with it another advantage for the learner. The name becomes a repertory of known letters. That is, letters that one gains in the course of learning to write one's own name can be recombined to form other words. Note in Figure 4–4 how Annabrook, age six, used many of the letters in her name to write two additional words. The child's own name as a repertory of known letters also pays off in a more abstract sense. As we noted in our discussion of Clay's *flexibility principle,* a beginning writer can start with a standard letter and embellish it until it becomes another letter. Thus, the letter L with a few more horizontal lines becomes ⌐, E, ⌐, and F, two of which are standard letters. Knowing how to write his own name may give a child a fairly good variety of letter forms, a point of departure for coming up with still other letter forms by means of the flexibility principle.

Learning their own names is a trailblazing event in children's writing for another reason. The process by which children learn to write their own names may be repeated to enable the children to write other words.

STRATEGIES FOR EARLY WRITING

Clay points to three common processes children use to begin writing words and longer messages—*tracing, copying,* and *generating.*[2] It is not claimed that children will always employ each of these processes in the order used here. However, tracing does seem to be the easiest of the three, with copying being the next most difficult, and generating being the most difficult process. Some children trace, then generate. Others copy, then generate.

Many children trace spontaneously, without being instructed to. Carlene, age 4:4, traced first, then copied. Her sample gives an indication of the relative difficulty of the two tasks (Figure 4–5).

Note in Figure 4–6, however, that she was generating letterlike graphics at the same time she produced Figure 4–5. Her generated products are more abundant than those she either traced or copied, but they are not limited to standard letters. This conforms to a finding of Clay's, namely, that copying may be a shortcut to accuracy, but most children prefer to generate letter forms on their own over copying. Her subjects stayed at the task much longer when they were generating, rather than copying.

FIGURE 4–4
Annabrook
Grade 1

ANNABROOK
SHOOK
A BOOK

FIGURE 4–5
Carlene
Age 4

FIGURE 4–6
Carlene
Age 4

Which strategy is best? Ultimately, we want children to be able to write letters on their own without having to rely on a model of correctly formed letters to copy. On the other hand, they must eventually learn to produce standard letter forms, not just invented ones. Generating letters is the process children should aim for, but they should pay attention to the details of standard letters. In our schools, many children need to be encouraged to take risks—to rely on their own devices and generate writing even if it's "wrong."

Nevertheless, there are a few children who are less mindful than they should be of the ultimately conservative nature of the writing system; that is, that there *is* a right way to make each letter. Teachers can safely encourage children to generate, knowing that they will copy anyway. With an occasional child it may be necessary to encourage copying. In our opinion, copying is probably encouraged far more often than need be.

Children's own names are usually the first objects of print to be traced, copied, and eventually generated. But after performing these feats with their names, children do not hesitate to carry them out with other words, known or unknown.

The Inventory Principle

Clay noted that "until I observed five year olds closely I had no idea that they took stock of their own learning systematically."[2] She was referring to what she called the *inventory principle*—the widespread tendency of beginning writers to make ordered lists of letters or words they can write. Next to writing their own names, then, are *listed inventories* as objects of children's first writing efforts.

Jessica's first compositions consisted of inventories of letters she could write. These were the sole content of her writing for some months. Another first-grade child offered inventories when her teacher asked the whole class to write something about a picture. She did not feel free to compose on that topic, apparently, so she listed her known words instead (see Figure 4–7).

Encouraging Children to Make Print

As we said at the beginning of this book, a child who knows that language can be written down has made a discovery that must come before she can make any other advances in writing and reading. Such a child can think about the medium of her thoughts and messages and not just their contents; she knows

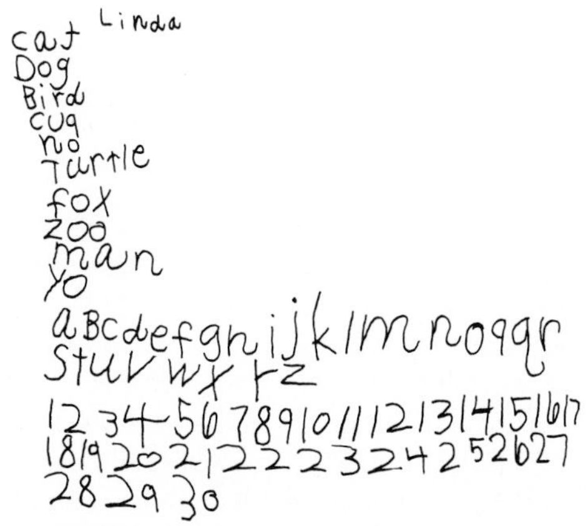

FIGURE 4–7
Linda
Grade 1

that language is a thing. David Olson believes that this discovery comes early to children whose parents read to them from infancy.[3] Indeed, such children's initial learning about language may include a budding consciousness that the medium can be reflected on, recorded, and read. For these children, opportunities to explore and produce print in preschool and kindergarten will be a natural extension of what they already know.

But what about the other children? Although we may associate very early writing experiences with preschools and kindergartens that serve the upper middle class, such activities can provide experiences in literacy that are at least as essential to children on the opposite end of the spectrum—the children from families that are poor and overworked, or unstable or neglectful or dominated by television or lacking in books and people to read them. Maria Montessori was the first to advocate giving children early experiences with writing before they began to read. Although her program is now fashionable with the well-heeled in North America, she developed it for the deprived children of Rome. And Marie Clay's study of five year olds' conceptions of written language, the subject of the previous chapter, was motivated by a need to learn about and help children who came from the diverse ethnic populations—some without traditions of literacy—that are served by the schools in New Zealand.

No, early writing is for the have-nots as much as for the haves. If we do not already, we should begin to conceive of preschools and kindergartens as places where all children—especially high-risk children—can gain rich exposure to the medium of print, by being read to and by having opportunities to produce print themselves. High-risk children can then be spared the often impossible task of learning what print is all about at the same time the first-grade program is trying to teach them to read.

The kind of encouragement children can profit by is of three types:

1. Having plenty of models of print at children's height around the classroom;
2. Having materials that the children can write upon, and utensils with which to write; and
3. Asking an occasional question, or setting up an occasional challenge, that will lead the child to emulate print.

Providing Models of Writing. Probably the best way to encourage children to explore writing—both the act of writing and the writing that is produced—is to have plenty of models around for children to imitate. The obvious starting point for showing children models of print is to read to them. Reading to children on at least a daily basis is a necessary nutrient for their growing literacy. This is true for many reasons, one of which is that the children gain, by being read to, a notion that print is somehow a means to a desirable end—a good story. When reading to children, it is a good idea occasionally to point to the words as you read.

Marie Clay has found that many children entering school do not realize that in a story book it is the print and not the pictures that provides the words that mother or father reads. Given a book that has both a picture and an array of print on a page, she tests this understanding by instructing the child, "Put your finger where I should read." She observes to see whether he puts his finger on the print or on the picture.[4]

There are static models of print, too. Obviously we label the child's desk and coathook; but labels on other things around the classroom are good sources of print: "clock," "coats," "flag," "paper," "crayons," and so forth. If the child draws a picture that the teacher wants to tape to the wall, it is useful to put the child's name on the picture. (For older children, the teacher can ask the child to "name" and describe the picture, writing the caption on the picture for him, too.) Things that belong to the child can be labeled, also. A crayon box with masking tape can be labeled, "Jimmy's Crayons."

Print makes messages. Print is arranged in horizontal displays. Print is made up of discrete graphic units, some of which are repeated, but never more than two right next to each other. All of these concepts can be brought home to children from meaningful print that is displayed in their surroundings.

Another sort of modeling that is valuable to children who may wish to explore writing is to have someone else write in their presence. Is writing a worthwhile activity? If it is, then adults should be seen doing it. Is writing a regular and important part of human communication? If it is, then adults should be seen doing it. For many adults, writing is a source of pleasure, an opportunity to reflect and think clearly. It is sometimes an occasion of frustration and hard work. Do children get a chance to see teachers and other adults approaching writing seriously? The ones who do are likely to be eager to get started becoming writers, too.

One of the authors was writing a children's book one year, at a time when her daughters were four and six years old. Every day the author would go into her bedroom and sit down before the big drafting table. There, for one or two hours, she would write and draw, throw away, and rewrite and redraw. Occasionally, the rest of the family got a glimpse of what she had produced. The children were captivated by the mystery of the quiet room where mother would go and create, and enthralled by the fragments of story and flashes of colorful pictures mother would share with them when she came out.

Soon the four year old had taken to stealing quietly away to her bedroom, too. She would stay sometimes for twenty or thirty minutes at a stretch, after which she would bring out writings for the rest of the family to read (see Figure 4–8). Nearly ten years have passed, and the girl's writing has picked up rules of spelling and composition, style, and originality; she has never really stopped writing since the day she decided to imitate her mother.

Teachers should take every opportunity to write important messages to others in the school and explain to the children what they are doing: "Look, I'm writing a note to the lunchroom to let them know our class will be going on a field trip during lunchtime tomorrow. See? I'm starting it out, 'Dear Mrs.

FIGURE 4–8
Jessie
Age 4

Washington . . .' See the letter 'D'? Now who will deliver the letter for me when I'm through?"

The central message teachers put across to children when they write in front of them is that writing is important; it is a worthy use of time. But there must be other messages as well. All of the *dynamic* principles of writing must be observed in process to be understood. If writing proceeds from left to right, then children must see someone doing it to comprehend this point. If writing can record a message and convey it to a distant receiver, then children must participate in the drama of remembering absent friends, thinking of messages for them, writing the messages down, sealing them up, and mailing them out.

To whom can young "prewriters" write? Certainly to a classmate who is home with an illness, to a visitor who is coming to the class, to a person in the school who has done the children a special favor or who needs cheering up.

Writing Materials in the Early Childhood Classroom. What materials are best for children to use when they are first writing? Almost anything will do, the only guiding considerations being (1) the safety of the child, (2) the well-being of your classroom walls and furniture, and (3) cheapness and convenience.

Safety concerns would militate against giving a sharp pencil to a very young child. But very young children do not sustain an interest in writing anyway. By the time children do become interested in writing—say, in their fourth and fifth years—a standard-size pencil is a fine thing for them to write with. We normally hear that children should use the big, fat "primary pencils" first. But children seem to find them unwieldy, and they are disappointed by the faint and indistinct silver trails they leave on paper. Our children prefer a *pencil* pencil, though they like colored marking pens even better.

For safety's sake, it is a good idea to make a rule against children moving around the classroom with pencils in hand, or generally crowding up on each other when they are writing. Writing is inherently a quiet and solitary activity, and writers know it. These rules are more necessary to enforce for the nonwriters in your classroom than the writers; that is, you sometimes have to point out to other children not to leap on the back of a child who is writing.

Practically any sort of paper is good for children to use to explore writing. It is probably best if it is not lined. Dealing with the proper height and staying on a horizontal line are unnecessarily difficult concerns to a child who is simply fooling around with the letter forms. The lines do not seem to help at first and may even be a hindrance. Therefore, there is no reason why parents or preschool teachers should buy paper for children to write on. The back side of practically any paper will do. Old memos from the office are perfect. Even better, perhaps, is computer paper, since the big format seems to invite big ideas. Any university computer center and most businesses have used computer paper around.

Suggestions That Get Children Writing. In addition to modeling writing and providing writing materials, a teacher can lead children to find challenge and delight in writing by well-considered and timely suggestions. The best of these suggestions seem to be situational. That is, a person who spends time with a child or a group of children will know the things that interest them and can often extend this interest into writing with a good suggestion.

A friend of ours invites her child to write each time she writes herself. When the mother is writing out a grocery list, she hands her daughter a piece of paper and asks her to make out a list of things she wants to buy, too.

Another parent works writing into the children's play. If a child comes to her and complains that her brother is not picking up his shoes from the living room floor, the mother says: "I'll tell you what. You be the policeman and write him a ticket. You can leave the ticket in his shoes."

Of course these writings will be unreadable by a stranger, but in the context of the situation they were written in, they have meaning. And they are fun ways for children to begin to explore writing. This sort of idea works in the classroom as well as at home.

Children like to be invited to slip a note into a letter that their parents are writing to a friend or relative. Contributing a note—whether it is on a separate piece of paper or is written on the bottom of someone else's page—is less responsibility than writing the whole letter, even if it is understood that the child doesn't really know how to write. The child knows that the parent can explain what the child meant to say; but it is an added pleasure to the recipient of the letter to hear directly from the child.

Another suggestion that works in some classrooms is for the teacher to hand the child some paper and some markers and invite her to write something. For many children, that is all they need to get started. But occasionally a child will not write. Perhaps it is reluctance to do something he knows he does not do correctly. After all, a child who has seen models of print around him in books recognizes immediately that what he himself writes on paper looks almost nothing like what he sees in books. (That is another reason why the teacher's own writing is a very important model for children who are beginning writers.) How do we get such children started? The first advice is for the teacher to write in the child's presence—and then invite the child to try it. But if that doesn't work, the teacher might show the child a page from this book. Show the child another child's bold efforts to make things that look like writing. We've known children to say: "Oh, I can do better than *that*!" and then write up a storm.

CONCLUSION

The earliest stage of writing is a sort of make-believe—children make designs that look like writing, but are still a long way from the real thing. Like other kinds of children's play, this make-believe writing is serious business—it is experience from which children learn.

As Ferreiro has shown us, children may be speculating on the ways in which written marks can represent ideas. They also seem to be experimenting to see where writing comes from, whether it is most efficiently produced by tracing, copying, or by generating marks of their own.

Finally, as in many other areas of endeavor, early writers are forming attitudes and behavior patterns. Some approach the task of writing with curiosity, energy, and confidence; others do not approach it at all. Some seek to make their own sense of how the writing system works; others wait to be shown. Some children experiment boldly and make mistakes; others do not experiment for fear of making mistakes. Some of the differences between children is attributable, no doubt, to deep-seated differences in personality. But to a degree, children's daring, initiative, and enthusiasm can be encouraged by parents and teachers. In the case of writing, it is certainly in their interests to give them this encouragement.

REFERENCES

1. Emilia Ferreiro and Ana Teberosky. *Writing Before Schooling.* Portsmouth, N.H.: Heinemann Educational Books, 1983.
2. Marie Clay. *What Did I Write?* Portsmouth, N.H.: Heinemann Educational Books, 1975.
3. David Olson. " 'See? Jumping!' Some Oral Antecedents of Literacy." In Hillel Goelman, Antoinette Goldberg, and Frank Smith (eds.), *Awakening to Literacy.* Portsmouth, N.H.: Heinemann Educational Books, 1984.
4. Marie Clay. *Concepts about Print Test.* Portsmouth, N.H.: Heinemann Educational Books, 1975.

Part Two
The Beginnings of Spelling

A four year old produces a string of letterlike forms that looks like writing (see Figure 1). A five year old deliberates carefully, inscribes a sparse collection of letters on the page, and claims it says: "Our car broke down" (see Figure 2).

These two presentations differ in more than appearance. The four year old is trying to make forms that look like writing, but the five year old is trying to make her letters do what writing does.

Writing uses marks to represent words. The marks represent words according to a socially agreed upon set of relationships. In some writing systems like Chinese, the relationship holds between symbols and whole words. In others like Japanese, it holds between symbols and syllables. In alphabetic systems like English, it holds between symbols and individual speech sounds, or *phonemes* as they are called. Anyone who wants to write must know what unit of language written symbols represent.

The would-be writer must also know how the symbols do the representing. In our English language, particularly, weathered old tongue that it is, the relations between symbols and phonemes have become somewhat peculiar—knowable, but peculiar. Beginning writers of English seem to proceed like this:

FIGURE 1
Jessie (left)
Age 4
These letters
represent no sounds

FIGURE 2
No Name (right)
Age 5
This says, "Our
car broke down."

53

They first discover the unit of language the symbols are to represent (word, syllable, or phoneme); they invent a plausible way for the symbols to represent language units; then they revise their invented spelling in favor of the standard spelling used around them.

5/ *Invented Spelling*

THE DISAPPOINTMENTS OF ENGLISH SPELLING

Some years ago George Bernard Shaw told of an acquaintance of his named Fish, who did not like the conventional way of writing his name and came up with the spelling GHOTIUGH. This spelling, he argued, found precedent in the spelling of common English words. The letters GH for the sound of *f* in his name was established in the spelling of the word "tou*gh*"; the O for the short sound of *i* is found in "w*o*men"; the TI for *sh* is heard in words like "ini*ti*al," "ter*ti*ary," and "spa*ti*al"; finally, the letters UGH are silent, as in "tho*ugh.*"

This story points out some of the more bizarre relations that seem to obtain between sounds in English words and the letters that represent them. And if each letter in a word is to have a clearly identifiable sound, some disappointment is inevitable. Just look at the spellings of some of the following words: What is the sound of the *i* in "complaint"? Of the *e* in "failure"? Of the second *l* in "spellings"? Of the *a* in "each"? And of the *h* in "paragraph"?

A large portion of the words in English contain letters that do not themselves directly represent sounds. Look, however, at the words in the sentences in Figures 5–1 and 5–2, written by the beginning speller, Annabrook.

FIGURE 5–1
Annabrook
Grade 1
Invented spelling

(I got bit by mosquitoes and it hurt.)

55

FIGURE 5–2
Annabrook
Grade 1
Invented spelling

(I am going to Virginia and I have a headache.)

Every one of Annabrook's letters represents a sound. There are no "silent" letters, no extra letters at all.

The early spellings that children produce on their own—we call them invented spellings—observe the same dictum: letters talk. Any letter that a child puts in a word is intended to represent some sound.

Why children select the letters they do to represent sounds presents a problem. Why is Virginia spelled FRJEYE? Why does it begin with the letter F? Why are the last two vowels E's? Why is "bit" spelled BET and not BIT? Why does "it," ET, follow the same pattern? As we shall see in this chapter, there are usually very good reasons why young spellers choose the letters they do to represent sounds. Seen together, these reasons constitute what has been called a system of spelling "logic."[1] Our purpose in this chapter will be to make this logic explicit, so that the reader can understand invented spelling the same way a child does.

LETTER-NAME SPELLING

Recall the sample we saw in Chapter 1: YUTS A LADE YET FEHEG AD HE KOT FLEPR. ("Once a lady went fishing and she caught Flipper.") This sample fits the pattern we have just described: Every letter in the sample stands for a sound, and no letters are supplied unnecessarily. Let's try to determine why the child chose the letters she did to represent the sounds in those words.

Notice the spelling YUTS for "once" and YET for "went." Why the letter Y for the sound we normally represent with a letter W? The answer lies in the name by which each letter is known. The letter Y is called "wye" and W is called "double-yu." Which name sounds more like the beginning sound in "once" and "went"?

The child who wrote YUTS A LADE . . . is apparently using a letter to spell a sound if the name of the letter closely resembles the sound. This technique for spelling has been called the *letter-name strategy*.[1] The letter-name strategy accounts for the spellings of almost all the letters in YUTS A LADE YET FEHEG AD HE KOT FLEPR.

Two factors influence the use of the letter-name strategy in determining which letters will represent what sounds in a word. The first factor is the availability (or lack) of a good letter-name-to-sound match. The English alphabet has twenty-six letters, but the English language has forty-four standard sounds, or phonemes. Some of the sounds children wish to spell have ready matches in letter-names. For others, no direct letter-name matches exist. In these latter cases, children will select the nearest fit and have good reasons—albeit subconscious ones—for the selections they make.

The second factor involved in the choice of letters for spellings has more to do with the sounds in words themselves. As we noted above, when speech sounds come together in words, some odd things happen to them. Some sounds are changed around, and children perceive changes that we don't and tend to spell what they hear. Some are overshadowed by others and not heard distinctly. Let's consider a range of possible sound and letter combinations and see what happens when children put the letter-name strategy into practice.

Initial Consonants

As Daryl's sample shows (Figure 5–3), initial consonants—consonants that come at the beginning of a word—usually find close matches to letter names. The name "ell" has in it the first sound in the word "live." "Tee" for "Texas" is clear enough, as is "em" for "my." Note that "gee" does not match the initial consonant sound in "Goliad," which begins like "gold." Neither does the letter name "aitch" sound anything like the beginning sound of "house." Daryl has learned that letter G represents the beginning sound of "gold" and that the letter H represents the "huh" sound in the beginning of "house."

The letter N in Daryl's sentence stands for the word "in"—a reasonable procedure since the name of the letter sounds the same as the word.

A sample of Daryl's writing taken a month later shows the initial consonants still being unambiguously represented and his words filled out in other ways, too (see Figure 5–4).

In this sample, the G's and the H's are used correctly—not as letter-name matches, but for their representational value.

What sort of problems do beginning consonants present young spellers? Which ones work by letter name and which ones by an arbitrary presentational relationship?

Table 5–1 lists all the consonants that have a stable and predictable letter-name match.

FIGURE 5–3
Daryl
Grade 1
Early invented
spelling

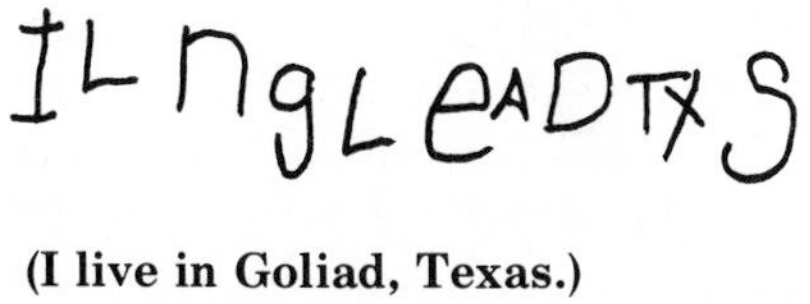

(I live in Goliad, Texas.)

FIGURE 5–4
Daryl
Grade 1
Later invented
spelling

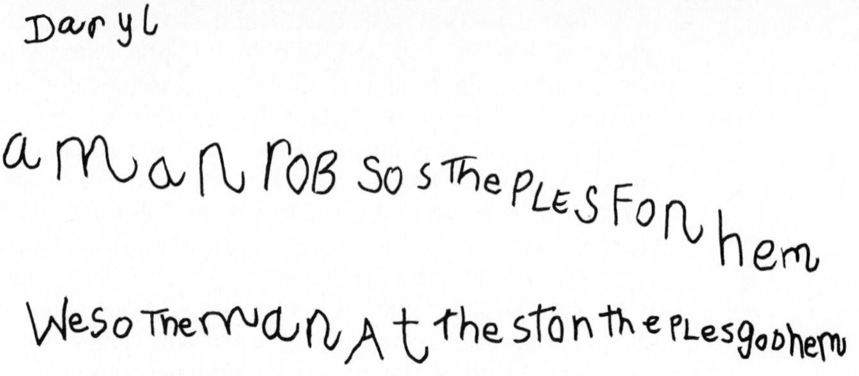

Daryl

a man rob sos the ples for hem

Weso ther man At the ston the plesgoo hem

(A man robbed shoes. The police found him. We saw the man at the store. The police got him.)

TABLE 5–1
Letter-name
matches for
consonants

Sound	Letter	Examples
b as in bat	B	BBGON (B B gun) BABE (baby) B (be) BEG (big) BLW (blue)
p as in pat	P	PEC (pick) PAT (pet) PLAG (playing) POGOSTECK PANS (pants)
f as in fat	F	FEH (fish) FES (friends) FEN (friend) FOWS (flowers) FAS (face) AFTR (after)
v as in very	V	HAV (have) LUV (love) LEV (live) VOT (vote)
m as in man	M	MI (my) HOM (home) MENEKDE (manicotti) GAM (game) MOTR (mother)
n as in note	N	NAM (name) NIS (nice) EN (in) BLON (balloon) NAW (now)
t as in tan	T	TXS (Texas) TIM (time) DOT (don't) WUT (what) SURT (shirt)
d as in Dan	D	DOT (don't) GLEAD (Goliad) DESES (dishes) TODA (today)
s as in sun	S	BICS (bikes) HAS (house) SCIEY (sky) SIK (sick) SUMS (swims)

Sound	Letter	Examples
k as in kick	K	SIK (sick) WRCK (work) KAT (can't) SKIY (sky) SEK (sick) TAK (take)
j as in joke	J	JOPT (jumped) JEP (jeep)
z as in zoo	Z	PLEZ (please) ZB (zebra)
l as in lay	L	LETL (little) LAS (last) PLES (police) PLANS (planes) BLON (balloon) LAT (let)
r as in ray	R	RETTE (ready) RAD (red) GRAON (ground) STOR (store)

Other consonants, like G and H, do not have a letter-name match with the sounds they normally represent. Nevertheless, they regularly represent one sound, and they appear frequently enough to be learned easily by children. Table 5–2 shows these *representational* consonants.

Spellings like WRRX for "works" and HAWS for "house" are so strange to the eye it is safe to conclude that the children who created them were not imitating anyone else or dimly remembering a standard spelling they had seen somewhere. These are 100 percent original! Yet as far from standard spelling as they are, they do employ the consonants C, G, H, W, and Y to represent their standard sound values. So the children must have learned something about spelling from someone outside of themselves; these relationships cannot be invented.

TABLE 5–2
Representational consonants

Sound	Letter	Examples
k as in kick	C	CENT (can't) PEC (pick) CUM (come) CLAS (clouds) CADY (candy)
g as in good	G	GUD (good) GAM (game) GLEAD (Goliad) GOWE (going) GIT (get)
h as in hay	H	HOO (who) HED (head) HEM (him) HAS (house) HORS (horse)
w as in way	W	WUT (what) WET (went) WEO (will) WERRE (wearing) WEH (with) WRRX (works)
y as in yes	Y	YALO (yellow) YOR (your) YASEDA (yesterday) YIU (you)

Another type of consonant representation that children have more difficulty mastering is the spelling of consonant digraphs.

Consonant Digraphs

Anyone who trains as a reading teacher comes across the terms *consonant blend* and *consonant digraph.* After a few years of teaching, though, a person is likely to have forgotten the difference between them. Knowing the difference between a blend and a digraph is probably not necessary to successful reading instruction. But digraphs do present serious challenges to young spellers.

The word digraph comes from the Greek, meaning "double writing." It describes a single sound spelled with two letters. The "ph" in "digraph" is a digraph, since the two letters together spell a single sound, which is often represented by the letter F.

The *gr* sound in the word "digraph" is not a digraph but a blend. Blends occur when the letters that represent two or three distinct consonant sounds are pronounced closely together. *Cl* in "closely" is a blend, as is the *bl* in "blend." Blends differ from digraphs in that it is possible to hear each of the sounds that make up a blend, if you pronounce the blend slowly. The same is not true of digraphs. No matter how slowly you pronounce the word "digraph," you will never hear separate sounds for the p and h.

Young spellers seem to perceive correctly that digraphs represent one sound. What they do not know is that digraphs have to be spelled with two letters and not one. So inventive spellers are forced to puzzle out which individual letters are best suited to represent digraphs. Note in Figure 5–5 what one first grader did with the digraphs.

The digraph *th* received three different spellings. "The" was correct, but it is likely that Joey had memorized the spelling of this word as a whole. In "they" he spelled it T, twice. In "each other," IHOVR, he spelled it V; and he used the same spelling for *th* the second time he wrote "the."

Note, too, his spelling of the digraph *ch* in "each other," IHOVR. In both digraphs, *th* and *ch,* Joey's tendency was to represent the single sound with a single letter.

On what basis did he choose the letters to represent the sounds? Again the basis seems to be the similarity between the sound to be represented and the name of a letter of the alphabet. The spelling of the H in IHOVR is an interesting example of this. Say to yourself the letter-name H ("aitch"). Note

FIGURE 5–5
Joey
Grade 1
Note spellings
of th

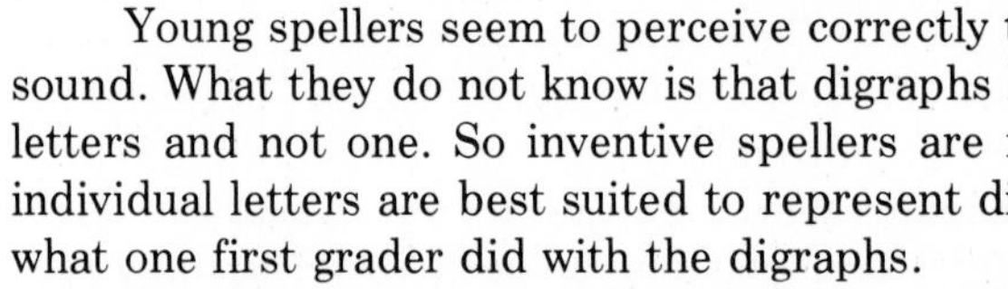

FIDI I SOR THE BLA AJLS
TA R APRLNS TACRT IHOVR
AO FOL UP NTU VE CLALS

(Friday I saw the Blue Angels. They are airplanes. They crossed each other and flew up into the clouds.)

the *ch* sound contained in that name. If you sound out the names of all the letters of the alphabet, you will not find another that contains the sound *ch*. Of all the single letters that could spell the digraph *ch,* the letter H is the best choice.

There is no such clear candidate to represent the digraph *th*. The child made two inventive entries: T and V. In order to understand why those two consonants are good choices to represent the sound of *th,* we must digress for a moment to explore the question of how we make consonant sounds.

HOW WE MAKE SPEECH SOUNDS: A LONG BUT NECESSARY DIGRESSION

To begin, it won't surprise anyone to hear that breath is the substance of speech. But there is more to speech than breathing. We direct our breath through the vocal bands in the throat, and the resulting vibration of these vocal bands makes the sound that we call our voice. Stretching or loosening these bands makes the pitch of our voice go up or down.

Breath and vocal bands, however, still do not give us speech. The activation of those two alone will enable us to (1) cry and (2) ooh and ah. (No wonder these are children's first utterances!) But we still cannot *say* anything without adding something more.

What we add is the *shaping* activity of the tongue, lips, teeth, mouth, and nasal passages. How do all these so-called shapers work together to form speech sounds, like the ones represented by the letters B, Y, A, Z, CH, and so on?

When we breathe through our vocal cords and set them vibrating, and then allow the sound to pass uninterrupted through the mouth and out into the air, we have produced a vowel. Say "ahhhh" and you will see that this is so. All spoken languages employ several vowels. We produce different ones depending on the position of the tongue when the vibrated air passes through the mouth. After saying "ahhh" say "eeeee"; if you pay attention to your tongue, you will see that this is so. We will say more about vowels later.

Consonants are made when we use the shapers in the mouth to interrupt the flow of vibrating air through the mouth. For example, when we say "ahhh," and then open and close the lips repeatedly, we produce a series of *b*'s: "Abababababab . . ." If we stop the air flow by repeatedly raising the back of the tongue against the roof of the mouth, we get a series of *g*'s: "Agagagag." And if we stop the flow by hitting the tip of the tongue against the fleshy ridge right behind our upper front teeth, we get a series of *d*'s: "Adadadad." Try it and see.

Consonants are produced by interrupting the flow of vibrated air through the mouth. But *which* consonant we make depends on three further concerns: (1) the *place* in the mouth where we make the interruption; (2) the *manner* of the activity that produces the interruption; and (3) whether or not the vocal cords are vibrating while the interruption is being made (*voicing*).

The three consonants we just produced, *b, g,* and *d,* were alike in the *manner* in which they were made: All three temporarily stopped the air flow— in linguistic parlance they are therefore called *stops.* They were also alike in that the vocal cords were vibrating as we made them—they are therefore said to be *voiced.* They differed only in the *places* they were made: the *b* on both lips, the *g* between the back of the tongue and the rearward roof of the mouth, and the *d* between the tip of the tongue and the ridge behind the front teeth.

Now let's try some variations. Hold your fingers over your Adam's apple and say "Abababab" again. With your fingers still in place, now substitute *p*: "Apapapap." Notice the difference? The sound of the letter *p* is like *b* in both *place* and *manner;* it differs only in being *unvoiced*—that is, the vocal chords don't vibrate as it is made. Try alternating "Agagagag" with "Akakakakak"—*g* and *k* are alike except that *k* is *unvoiced.* The same is true of *d* and *t, z* and *s, ch* and *j,* the *th* in "thin" and *th* in "their." All of these pairs are alike in the *place* and *manner* in which they are made, but different in *voicing.* These facts have consequences for children's spelling.

Try another variation. Say the sound of the letter D—"duh." Notice the spot on the fleshy ridge behind your teeth where your tongue tapped. Now hold your tongue just short of touching that spot and blow air out through the constricted space over your tongue. You should hear a sound like that of the letter S. Now, if instead of blowing out, you say "ahhh" while you raise your tongue to that same spot (raise it until you hear a whistle, but don't let it touch), you should hear a sound like that of z. You will be saying "ozzzzzz . . ." Two points: First, we have demonstrated that the sounds of *s* and *z* are alike except for *voicing.* Second, we have demonstrated another manner of making consonants—by restricting the air flow so that we hear a sort of whistling friction.

The name *fricative* is applied to consonants made in this manner. Let's make some others. Say "ozzzzzzzzzzz" again. While you are saying it, slide your tongue forward and down, until it is behind the upper front teeth themselves and almost—but not quite—touching them. You should hear the sound *th* of "*th*en." If you'll leave off saying the "ahh" part and just whistle air through that space, you will hear the other *th* of "thin." The two *th*'s, *th*en and *th*in, are voiced and unvoiced fricatives, respectively.

Here's another pair of fricatives. Place your lower lip against your upper teeth in Bugs Bunny fashion. Now say "ahhh" again, and you should hear a *v* sound: "Ahhvvvvvv . . ." If you turn off the voicing and just blow air out through the space, you should hear a long *f* sound. The sounds of *f* and *v* are alike in the *place* and *manner* in which they are made, but different in *voicing.*

There are other manners in which consonants are made and other places also. But our brief exploration should enable us to answer an important question: Suppose a child wants to represent a sound in spelling a word, but he cannot find a perfect fit with a letter name. He chooses a near fit—a letter name that is *somewhat* like the sound he wants to represent. In what specific ways can sounds of letters be *like* each other or *unlike* each other?

Our discussion of consonants provides a way of answering. Speech sounds—for instance, sounds of consonants—can be like each other in the *place* and *manner* in which they are made, and perhaps in *voicing*. With these features in mind, let's return to our examination of digraphs.

A Return to Digraphs

Digraphs present a special problem in invented spelling because children don't accept the notion that two letters can represent one sound. So they are forced to search for a single letter whose name sounds most like the sound they wish to spell, a sound that adults represent with a digraph. This sometimes causes them to make some strange-looking substitutions.

In Figure 5–5, Joey represented the *th* sound of "then" (the *voiced* sound) five times. He spelled it once correctly in "the," a word he probably had memorized. Twice he spelled it with the letter T, and twice with the letter V. His inconsistency is strange, but his choice of letters makes sense.

Remember that the *th* sound is made by placing the tongue behind the front teeth and vibrating (fricating as linguists would say) forced air between the tongue and the teeth. To make the sound *t,* we touched the tongue to the fleshy ridge just behind the front teeth—a place very close to the place where *th* is made. The sound of *t* stops the air, though, and it is unvoiced. But we can say *t* is quite similar to *th* in the *place* where it was made.

The letter V for the sound of *th* appears to be a stranger choice. But recall that the sound of *v* is made by a frication, just as *th* is, and that it is voiced just as *th* is. These two facts, plus the fact that *v* is made in the forward region of the mouth, make the sound *v* fairly similar to *th* and hence justify the spelling V for the *th* sound.

The sound represented by the digraph *sh* gets various spellings in children's inventions. The spelling S for it, in Figure 5–6, is frequently offered. The letter S seems to be a natural choice, first because it is one of the letters of the digraph *sh* and the child may have remembered seeing it in other words. But the letter S is a good choice, too, because it is identical in *voicing* and *manner* to the sound of *sh* and very near it in the *place* in which it is made. If you make a long hissing stream of S's, then change to make the *shhhh* sound without stopping the air flow, you'll find that your tongue simply moved back a fraction of an inch along the roof of your mouth while you continued to blow the air through.

When children invent spellings, they virtually always come up with something other than standard spellings for consonant digraphs. Table 5–3 shows some frequently offered inventions for them.

FIGURE 5–6
Susie
Grade 1
Note spelling of
"dishes"

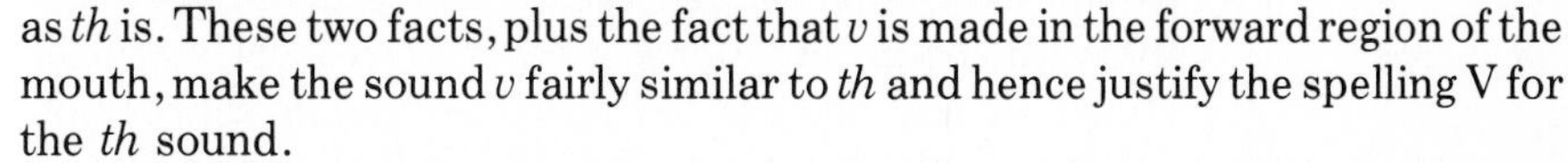

(I got Baby Alive and some dishes and a pogo stick.)

TABLE 5–3
Digraph consonants

Sound	Letter	Examples
ch as in chip	H	HRP (chirp) IHOVR (each other) TEHR (teacher)
sh as in ship	H	FIH (fish) FEH (fish) HE (she)
sh as in ship	S or C	SOS (shoes) COO (show) SES (she's)
th as in the	T	BATEG (bathing) TA (they) MOTR (mother) GRAMUTR (grandmother)
th as in the	V	IHOVR (each other) VE (the) VU (they)

"But," you may ask, "surely children do not deliberately set out to find consonants that are alike in place, manner, and voicing—what five year old ever used these terms?"

Let us remind you of our earlier discussion of language development. There we said that children learn to talk by developing a system of language rules that enables them to understand and produce speech. We see evidence, for example, in the three year old's statement, "I got tiny foots," that the child has formed a *rule* to the effect that plurals are formed by adding the letter S to a noun. We doubt, though, that a three year old would give you a definition of the word "noun" or "plural" or even "word." Nevertheless, on some level she knows what a noun is because she only pluralizes nouns—not adjectives, adverbs, or prepositions. We conclude that she knows some things about language on a working level that she can't explain.

The same is true of spelling. If you watch a youngster invent spellings, you will see and hear him exaggerating the production of speech sounds: whistling her S's, stabbing repeatedly at her D's, choo-chooing her H's. On a working level she is exploring place, manner, and voicing. But if you ask her what she's doing—"Writing you a letter," she says!

Nasal Consonants: The Letters N and M

When children invent spelling they do so by breaking a word into its individual sounds and finding a letter to represent each sound. This point, we hope, has been made abundantly clear. But if children represent sounds they hear, how do we account for the peculiar case of N and M? These sounds quite often go unspelled, even by children who have otherwise demonstrated a keen ear and an inventive hand. Note, for example, the omission of the N's in

YUTS A LADE YET FEHEG AD HE KOT FLEPR.

Surely a child resourceful enough to think of using the letter Y for the sound *w* and the letter H for the sound of *sh* could find a spelling for an *n* sound if she wanted to. Notice, too, that *n* and *m* sounds are often spelled by children in some words. Sometimes on the same paper *n* and *m* will be spelled in one spot and left out in another, as in Figure 5–7.

What factors might there be in the *position* of the *n* and *m* sounds in words that would lead to their being spelled in one place and not spelled in another? Study Figure 5–7 again and see if you can answer this question. The factor that decides whether an *n* or *m* sound will be spelled or not is what follows it. If a vowel comes after an *n* or *m* sound or if either comes at the end of a word, these consonants will be spelled. Accordingly, the sound of *n* is spelled in NIS ("nice"), SNAK ("snack"), and the M is spelled in SMIL ("smile").

On the other hand, when the sounds of *n* or *m* are followed by some other consonant, they often go unspelled. Thus, the letter N is omitted from YET ("went"), AD ("and"), FEHEG ("fishing"), and YUTS ("once"). Knowing where the N's and M's are omitted, however, does not explain why they are. We might venture a guess that the following consonant somehow overshadows the N or M, so that the child doesn't *hear* it, and hence, omits it. But is it the case that he doesn't hear the sound? We can easily test this out. Just ask a three year old to point to your "*lap*," and then to point to your "*lamp*," and see if he can distinguish the two. If he can, he can hear the *m* sound. The same test could be made with the words "land" and "lad," "crowd" and "crowned," "stained" and "stayed." If the child can tell the difference between the two words, he can hear the *n* and the *m* sounds. As it turns out, children can hear *n* and *m* in these environments well before the age when they begin to create invented spellings.

If they know how to spell *n* and *m* sounds in other positions, and they can hear these sounds when they are followed by consonants, then why don't they spell them in such cases? How *do* we account for the spellings YET for "went" and YUTS for "once"?

When we pronounce the *n* sound, we place the tongue in the same spot where *d, t, j,* and *ch* are made: the fleshy ridge behind the front teeth. In fact, when the sound of *n* is followed by any of these latter consonants, it is impossible to tell from the activity inside the mouth whether the *n* is present or not. You can demonstrate this by repeating these pairs of words over and over: "witch–winch," "plant–plat," and "dote–don't."

We *hear* the *n* sound in these words, though—so how is it made? Hold

FIGURE 5–7
Melissa
Grade 1
Note omissions
of n's.

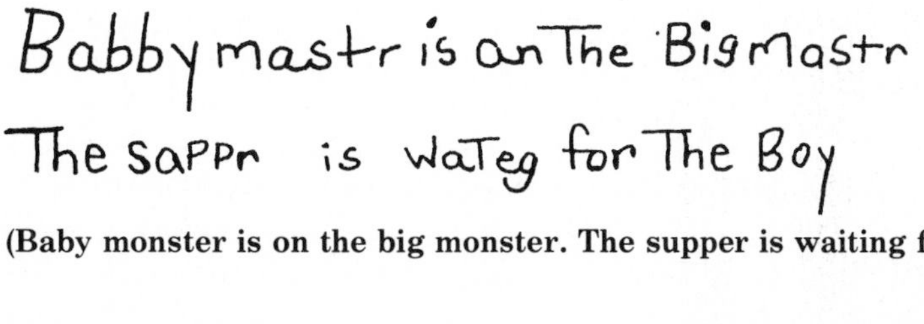

(Baby monster is on the big monster. The supper is waiting for the boy.)

your nose and say these pairs again. When *n* is present in a word, the air is resonated out through the nose while the *n* and the vowel preceding it are pronounced. When *n* is followed by a consonant made in the same place, the nasal resonance is the only feature of the *n* that is heard.

Since the nasalization is more of an influence on the vowel than on the consonant, in such cases many beginning spellers seem to assume that what they hear in "plant," "went," and "once" is a peculiar vowel, not an extra consonant.[2] As we shall shortly see, children adjust early to the idea that a single vowel letter may spell variations of a vowel sound. Thus in YET for "went," the E may be intended to stand for both the sounds of *e* and *n*.

The sound *m* works the same way, except that it is made on both lips, where *p* is also made. When *m* occurs before *p*, as in "lamp," it is typically not spelled, because the *m* then acts as a nasalization of the vowel preceding the *p*. You can demonstrate this by pronouncing "lap–lamp," "stomp–stop," and "chip–chimp."

Some common examples of omitted nasal consonants—N and M—are presented in Table 5–4.

Invented Spelling of Long Vowels

"Long vowels say their names." That useful piece of first-grade lore is true enough. Judging from their writings, though, this rule need not be pointed out to many children; they know it already (see Figure 5–8). Of course, when long vowels occur in words, correct spelling usually will not let them stand alone and still say their names. They can in "A" and "I" and also in "he," "she," "go,"

TABLE 5–4
N and M before other consonants

Sound	Letter	Examples
m	M	LAP (lamp) BOPE (bumpy) LEP (limp) STAP (stamp)
n	N	RAD (rained) WET (went) GOWEG (going) CADE (candy) AJLS (angels)

FIGURE 5–8
Ronnen
Grade 1
Note long vowel spellings

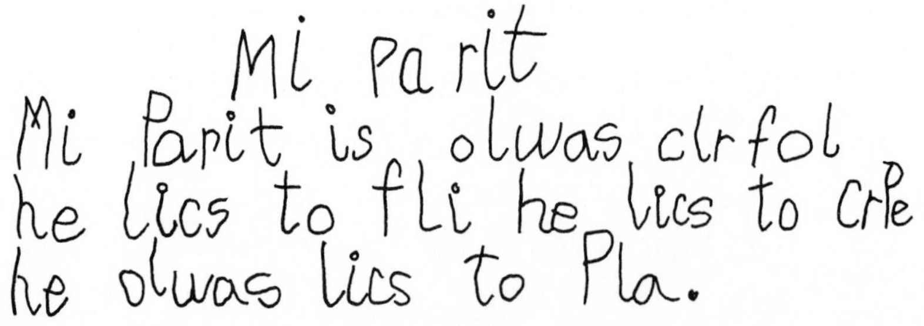

(My parrot is always colorful. He likes to fly. He likes to chirp. He always likes to play.)

and "so." But "stay," "late," "bone," "see," and the like require that the vowels be *marked* to indicate their longness. Inventive spellers leave off these markers, and this is one indication that they are inventing. The spellings that result are like those shown in Table 5–5.

Invented Spelling of Short Vowels

Short vowels do not say their own names or provide any other very good hint as to the way they should be spelled. Nevertheless, children often do figure out a consistent strategy for spelling short vowels. This strategy, like the omission of nasal consonants, reveals a surprising ability to hear and to make judgments about speech sounds.

In the samples in Figure 5–9 and 5–10, how are the children solving the problem of spelling the short ĭ sound? These two children consensed on a spelling of E for the ĭ sound. Why did they?

The best explanation for children's representing the ĭ sound with the letter E is provided by Charles Read.[2] Read's explanation starts with the letter-name strategy for matching speech sounds with written letters. When children spell "fish" FEH, they use the letter E for the sound of the letter's name, which is long—ē. They use the letter name E because they perceive a similarity between the *long sound of ē* and the *short sound of ĭ*.

	Sound	Letter	Examples
TABLE 5–5 *Long or "tense" vowels*	ā	A	LADE (lady) PLA (play) TA (they) NAM (name)
	ē	E	PLES (police) MNEKDE (minicotti)
	ī	I	MI (my) FLI (fly) TRID (tried) SLIDEG (sliding) BIT (bite)
	ō	O	JOD (Jody) DOT (don't)
	ū	U, O	SOS (shoes) NTU (into)

FIGURE 5–9
Jody (left)
Grade 1
Note spelling of ĭ

FIGURE 5–10
No Name (right)
Kindergarten
Note spelling of ĭ

JoD

ETS S prng.

(Jody. It is spring.)

The LaTiSoGeKeG

(The lady is drinking.)

Let's see how inventive spellers solve the problem of spelling the short ĕ sound. As in the word "pet," the short sound of ĕ does not have an exact match in the names of any letters of the alphabet. Actually it *is* contained in the letter names for F, L, and S; but children rarely use consonants for vowel sounds in this way. Note in Figures 5–11 and 5–12 how these children spelled the short sound of ĕ. The letter these children used, we see, was A. Again our hypothesis is that they used the letter A for the long sound in its name.

In children's invented spelling, short vowels are sometimes spelled correctly, presumably because children learn or are told their correct spellings in some words. But when they are spelled incorrectly, the most frequent substitution is E for short ĭ, A for short ĕ.

These substitutions create spellings that look very little like adult spellings for the same words. They sometimes lead us to the erroneous conclusion that children don't know what they are doing when they produce spellings like ALVADR for "elevator." What are they thinking? By what process do they arrive at these spellings? Again we must consider the way speech sounds are made, and again our source is Charles Read.[2]

HOW VOWELS ARE PRODUCED

This time, let's consider vowels. If you open your mouth wide and vibrate your vocal cords, you will make a vowel, probably "ahhhh." If you pronounce a

FIGURE 5–11
Susie
Grade 1
Note spelling
of ĕ

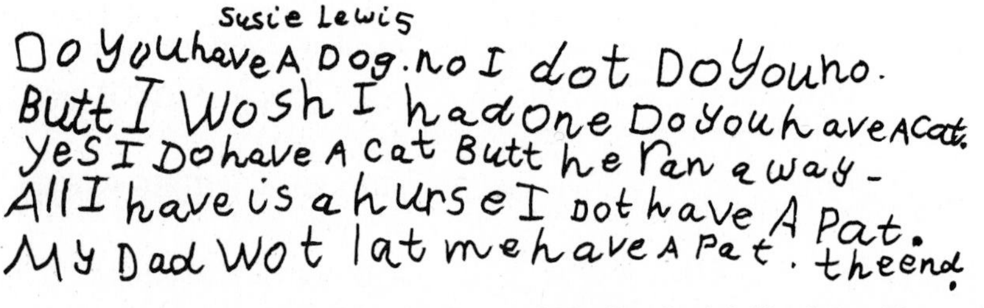

(Do you have a dog? No, I don't. Do you? No. But I wish I had one. Do you have a cat? Yes, I do have a cat but he ran away. All I have is a horse. I don't have a pet. My dad won't let me have a pet. The end.)

FIGURE 5–12
Brian
Grade 1
Note spelling
of ĕ

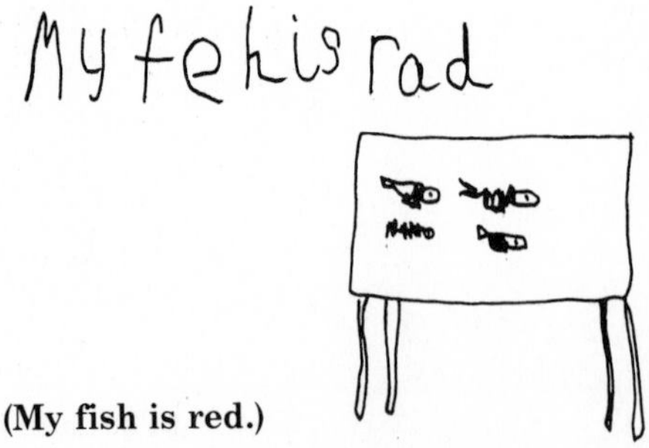

(My fish is red.)

drawn out "ahhhh" and switch abruptly to "eeee," note what happens in your mouth. You may be aware of two things: first, your jaw raised slightly on "eeee," but even more obvious was the raising of the tongue in the front of the mouth. Now try this: pronounce "aaahh," and then change *very, very slowly* up to "eeee." You probably heard some other sounds you could recognize as vowels in between. What were they? Where was the tongue when they were made?

Pronounce the *u* sound of "fruit," stretching it out. Then shift to "eeee" again. Now back to *u*. What does your tongue do? You may have noted that it went up at the front of the mouth for "eeee," but that it went up at the *back* of the mouth for *ū*. If you didn't feel it go up in the back for *ū*, try saying *ŏŏ* (as in "took") in alternation with *u* (as in "new"): *ŏŏ–ū; ŏŏ–ū; ŏŏ–ū*. This should help you become aware of a movement of the back of the tongue up toward the back of the roof of your mouth.

We make vowels by holding the tongue in certain positions as voiced air passes through the mouth. Essentially, the placement of the tongue is along two planes—it can move from front to back and from high to low; or into intermediate positions between high and low and front and back. We could diagram the positions of the tongue with a grid, as in Figure 5–13.

Let's demonstrate the *front* vowels. Try saying these sounds, gliding smoothly from one to the other: *ē* (as in "beet"), *ĭ* (as in "bit"), *ā* (as in "bait"), *ĕ* (as in "bet"), *ă* (as in "bat"): *ē, ĭ, ā, ĕ, ă*. Do it three times and pay attention to what your tongue does. Now try it in reverse: *ă, ĕ, ā, ĭ, ē*. You probably noticed your tongue started high and went low in the first series, and that it started low and went high in the second series. You also may have noticed that this move-ment took place in the front of the mouth (although *ē* is somewhat further forward than *ă*).

FIGURE 5–13
A diagram of tongue positions as different vowels are produced

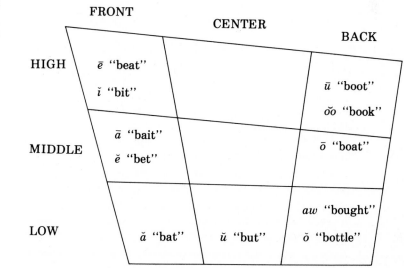

Note that the sounds $\bar{e}$ and $\breve{\imath}$ were positioned next to each other—that is, from $\bar{e}$ the next position you came to in the first series was the $\breve{\imath}$ sound, as you went from high to low. The sounds of $\bar{a}$ and $\breve{e}$ were also quite close in the position of the tongue. In the vowel grid in Figure 5–13 these vowels appear close together.

Actually, they are even closer than the vowel grid makes them appear. The sounds of $\bar{e}$ and $\breve{\imath}$ are formed in almost the same place in the mouth. They differ in what has been called tenseness/laxness. Hold your fingers against the flesh on the underside of your jaw and alternate pronouncing the vowels, $\bar{e}$–$\breve{\imath}$, $\bar{e}$–$\breve{\imath}$, $\bar{e}$–$\breve{\imath}$. You may feel the muscles in the floor of your mouth becoming tense with the pronunciation of $\bar{e}$, and lax with pronunciation of $\breve{\imath}$. You should feel the same tensing and laxing with $\bar{a}$ and $\breve{e}$, respectively. Some language scientists consider $\bar{a}$ and $\breve{e}$ to be alike in the place in which they are sounded, and different mainly in tenseness and laxness.[3] That is, they are tense and lax versions of the same vowel. The same is said of $\bar{e}$ and $\breve{\imath}$. The child who wrote FEH for "fish," and LATR for "letter" must have sensed this pairing of the tense and lax vowels by position.

Let's quickly recapitulate the argument. Remember that children who are inventive spellers represent sounds in words according to the similarity between the sound in the word and the sound of the name of some letter of the alphabet. All of the vowel letters of the alphabet have long vowel sounds in their names. All of these long vowels, it turns out, are produced by tensing the tongue and floor of the mouth. Therefore, all the vowels you think of as long are also tense: $\bar{a}$, $\bar{e}$, $\bar{o}$, $\bar{u}$—we'll get to $\bar{\imath}$ in a minute! No short vowel sounds have *exact* matches with the names of any vowel letters, for a good reason. All short vowels are *lax*—produced by relaxing the tongue and floor of the mouth—while the sounds of all vowel letter names are *tense*. If you are getting confused, pronounce these sounds and check for tenseness:

$$\bar{a} \qquad \breve{e}$$
$$\bar{e} \qquad \breve{\imath}$$
$$\bar{o} \qquad \breve{o}$$
$$\bar{u} \qquad \breve{o}\breve{o}$$

The vowels marked long should have felt tense, though $\bar{o}$ and $\bar{u}$ tense the tongue more than the floor of the mouth. The vowels marked short should have felt lax.

When children seek to spell a long or tense vowel, they have no trouble finding a letter to represent it, as we have seen, because the names of the vowel letters A, E, I, O, U are long or tense themselves. But when they want to spell a short or lax vowel trouble ensues because there are no short or lax letter names. The strategy most children employ in such a case is to *find the long (tense) letter name that is made in the same place in the mouth as the short (lax) vowel they wish to spell.*

This is sometimes called the vowel pairing strategy, so-called because it pairs in spelling the tense and lax vowels that are pronounced in the same position in the mouth. It results in some other strange matches beside $\bar{e}$–$\breve{\imath}$ and $\bar{a}$–$\breve{e}$, although these two are the most consistent. Another match that is often seen is o for $\breve{u}$: as in BBGON ("BBgun"). Still stranger is the case of the long $\bar{\imath}$ sound.

The long $\bar{\imath}$ is actually made up of two sounds: $\breve{o}$ and $\bar{e}$. If you pronounce it slowly, you will feel your tongue start low and back and then move high and front while the vowel is still being made: $\breve{o}$–$\bar{e}$. Children sometimes notice this "short" $\breve{o}$, or broad $\ddot{a}$ (as in "ahhhh" with a physician's tongue depressor) element contained in the letter name I, and make use of it to spell $\breve{o}$ (as in BIDM for "bottom" and WIS for "wants").

Why do the spellings produced by children's vowel pairing strategies ($\bar{a}$ with $\breve{e}$, $\bar{e}$ with $\breve{\imath}$, etc.) appear strange to us? For a very good reason: Although standard spelling pairs vowels, it pairs them differently from the matches that inventive spellers work out for themselves. Standard spelling pairs "long" and "short" A: $\bar{a}$, as in "bay," with $\breve{a}$, as in "bat." It pairs "long" and "short" I: $\bar{\imath}$, as in "bite," with $\breve{\imath}$, as in "bit." It pairs them because they are represented in spelling by the same letter—not because they sound the same, or because they are made in the same place in the mouth. The pairing of $\bar{a}$ and $\breve{a}$, $\bar{\imath}$ and $\breve{\imath}$, $\bar{e}$ and e are second nature to us adults, simply because of our years of reading and writing experience. But this system of pairing vowels does not seem natural to beginning spellers.

Table 5–6 summarizes the vowel pairings that Read identified, with examples from writings we have collected from children.

Syllables without Vowels

Children who produce invented spellings often show surprising acuity not only in learning speech sounds but in categorizing them together on the basis of very subtle features. Why is it, then, that they leave out so many vowels, as in Figure 5–14?

We note two things in the circumstances of the vowel omissions: They happen before certain consonants—L, R, M, S—and they happen in certain

TABLE 5–6
Pairing of lax (short) vowels with letter names

Sound	Letter	Examples
$\breve{e}$	A	FAL (fell) RAD (red) PAT (pet) TALUFO (telephone)
$\breve{\imath}$	E	FEH (fish) HEM (him) BET (bit) VESET (visit)
$\breve{o}$	I	WIS (wants) BIDM (bottom)
$\breve{u}$	O	JOPT (jumped) MOD (mud) SOPR (supper) FOTIME (funtime)

The girl's went to The Zoo
Thay Saw A Got and An Alagadr

(The girls went to the zoo. They saw a goat and an alligator.)

places, mostly the ends of words, in unstressed syllables. The consonants before which vowels are omitted sound much like vowels themselves. The sound of r is made without any complete closing of the shapers in the mouth and consists largely of the vibration of the vocal cords to make themselves heard. The sound of l is made with the tongue against the roof of the mouth; the vibrated air is passed around the sides of the tongue for the l. The sounds of m and n both close off the mouth, but pass the vibrated air out through the nasal passage. All of these consonants are *voiced*; that is, the vocal cords vibrate while they are being made. All of them also allow the vibrated air to pass uninterrupted out of the mouth or the nose. Hence, of all the consonants, they are the most like vowels—because vowels are uninterrupted passages of voiced air.

When vowels occur in syllables that are unstressed, they are said to be *reduced*. Say these words aloud: "table," "wonderful," "lentil," and "infernal." The last syllables you probably pronounced all the same way—$\breve{u}l$—even though they were written four different ways. In normal speech, the individual vowels in these unstressed syllables are unrecognizable—they are all reduced to a common *uh*.

When the vowellike consonants occur in these unstressed syllables where one cannot hear any distinct vowel, children tend to let the vowellike quality of the consonant serve for whatever vowel is needed. By children's logic, any vowel letter that they *did* write in such a place would say its name clearly—giving us "litteel" if they wrote LETEL or "bottoam" if they wrote BIDOM. This is not what the children intend, so they leave the vowel out. Some common examples of syllables without vowels are given in Table 5–7.

	Sound	Letter	Examples
TABLE 5–7	$\breve{u}l$	L	LETL (little) BISECL (bicycle)
Syllables			TABL (table) AJLS (angels)
without vowels			
	$\breve{u}r$	R	TEHR (teacher)
			GRAMOTR (grandmother)
			PECHRS (pinchers)
			SOPR (supper)

Choo Choo Chran

Sometimes invented spelling diverges from standard spelling because children perceive oddities of pronunciation that adults do not. Words like "tree," "train," and "trick" are commonly pronounced as if they began with "chr." We read *tree* and say "chree"—but we adults don't believe we say "chree" because we have seen the "tr" in print and we have a strange hidden conviction that what we've been seeing is what we've been saying. But children are not easily taken in. They will sometimes spell *tr* CHR.

They will do a similar thing with *dr*. When we pronounce "drink," "drive," and "dragon," we often say "jrink," "jrive," and "jragon." When children spell these words the way they hear them, they often use letters G or J at the beginning of the word.

Often, too, they omit the letter R after the T or D. Children seem to have a bias toward simplicity in their pronunciation.[4] They *say* "jink" for "drink." It may be that the bias for simplicity carries over into spelling, too. We notice that many consonant blends get reduced to a single letter even when they *could* be puzzled out by the letter-name strategy.

Figures 5–15 and 5–16 show some samples where the sounds of *dr* and *tr* have been dealt with imaginatively by the children.

THE DEVELOPMENTAL DIMENSION OF INVENTED SPELLING

We have covered the most important aspects of children's invented spelling with the letter-name strategy. The spellings we saw in this chapter are of the most inventive sort that children produce. The children who wrote them were acting mostly on their own intuitions about spelling; learned spellings showed up less frequently than invented ones. In the next chapter this condition will be reversed. Learned spelling will dominate the children's writing, though invention will still be in evidence as children employ learned spelling patterns

FIGURE 5–15
Carrie (left)
Kindergarten
Note spelling of
"drinking"

FIGURE 5–16
No Name (right)
Grade 1
Note spelling of
"trained" and
"drive"

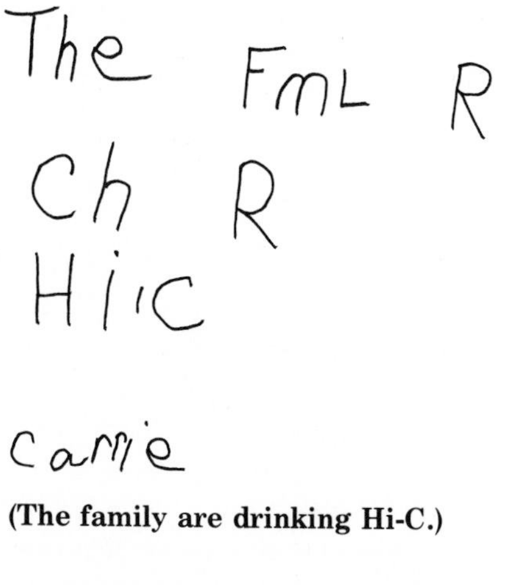

The FmL R

Ch R

Hi'C

Carrie

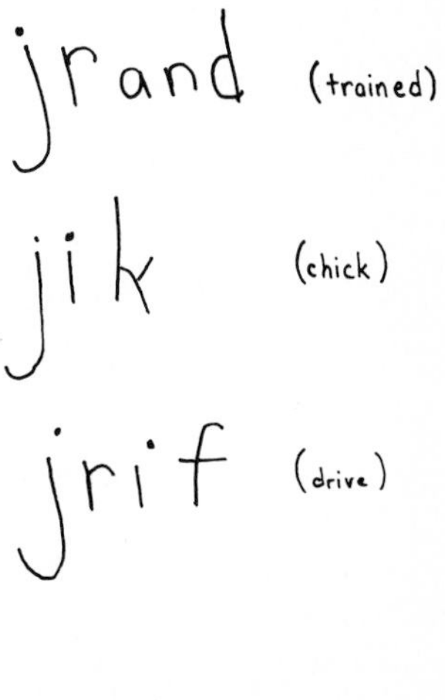

(The family are drinking Hi-C.)

jrand (trained)

jik (chick)

jrif (drive)

in novel ways. The result will still be spelling errors, but the errors will be influenced more by learning and less by intuition than those we encountered in the present chapter.

The next type of spelling, which we will call *transitional* spelling, is a developmental step beyond the letter-name spelling. On that subject, however, there is a developmental aspect of letter-name spelling that has been lurking in the background of the present discussion. The reader will have noticed that some of the spelling samples displayed in this chapter were more complete, more filled out, than others. Consider again the following two samples by Daryl. The first was written in September of his first-grade year, the second, two months later.

1.   I L N GLEAD TXS ("I live in Goliad, Texas")
2.   A MAN ROB SOS THE PLES FID HEM. ("A man robbed shoes. The police found him.")

Daryl used the letter-name strategy to produce invented spelling in both sentences. But in the second one he represented considerably more speech sounds with his letters than he did in the first. This reflects a widely observed characteristic of children's invented spelling: Early in their career as spellers, children represent far fewer speech sounds or phonemes with their letters than they do later in their development.

As we see in Figure 5–17, when a child begins to spell by phonemes, he does not advance instantly to producing well-formed spellings. Spelling words phoneme by phoneme, or *phonemic spelling,* at first seems to restrict the quantity of a child's written production. Whereas before he may have scribbled volubly, and produced pages of mock writing, his first efforts at phonemic spelling yield only a trickle of production—usually only a letter or two for each word he wishes to spell. Clearly this reduced production indicates that the task of phonemic spelling is hard for the child and that he must really work at it. What is so hard about phonemic spelling?

FIGURE 5–17
No Name
Kindergarten
Early phonemic
spelling

(This is spring.)

There are at least three sources of difficulty: the need to segment words into phonemes, the need to have a stable "concept of word," and the task of choosing a letter with which to represent the phonemes.

Segmenting Words into Phonemes

To anyone who can read this book, the idea of breaking a word down into its smallest sounds or phonemes may not seem to be an unusually difficult task. Our experience with reading written words over the years has made it natural for us to see words as bundles of phonemes—if we understand phonemes to be the sounds to which individual letters correspond. Certainly there are exceptions in the correspondences, but the very fact that we can recognize exceptions and irregularities in the match between letters and speech sounds is an indication that we have a working sense of the sound units to which letters correspond.

Our experience with print may be misleading, however, because even though letters on the page are distinctly recognizable units, the speech sounds to which they correspond are not. When we say "bat," we do not say "buh," "ă," "tuh" rapidly together. No matter how quickly we pronounce those three sounds, we can never run them together to say "bat." Laboratory experiments have been conducted to test this point. Using sophisticated hardware, scientists have taken words like "bat" and mechanically broken them into their smallest components. Then they have tested to see if people could recognize the parts of the word. Invariably, people had no difficulty recognizing the vowel sound, but when the vowel sound was removed from either consonant, the consonant was unrecognizable—people reported hearing a "chirping sound" instead of a consonant![5]

The explanation is that we produce many phonemes together when we speak in a process called *coarticulation*. If we are able, on reflection, to separate phonemes out of the speech we hear, it is only because we have a sense of what we are looking for; the phonemes do not come to us separately. The task of recognizing the individual phonemes that make up a word—called *phonemic segmentation*—is more of a complex perceptual operation than it appears. It does not simply consist of recognizing separate items; it also includes the act of deciding how they might be separated.

For children, segmenting words into syllables is not very difficult. But segmenting words into phonemes usually is.[6] In any group of five year olds, there may be a few who are able to segment phonemes, a larger number who can distinguish only one or two phonemes per word, and a like number who cannot break a word down further than a syllable, if that.

The Concept of Word

In order to spell, a child must develop a concept of what a word is and the ability to think about words.[7] Like phonemes, words come to us all run together in undifferentiated strings. There is not usually any clue in the speech stream we listen to as to where one word leaves off and another begins. As in the case of phonemes, we usually attend to the meaning of words rather than to their sounds. Thus, a bilingual person may not be able to remember in what language a particularly interesting comment was made to her. The idea will be remembered but the words somehow fall away.

But for the child to be able to spell a word, the word must have some reality for him as a unit; he must be able to make it hold still in his mind while he operates on it. For in order to spell a word, the child must:

1. say the word mentally to himself;
2. break off the first phoneme from the rest of the word;
3. mentally sort through his repertoire of letters and find one to match with that phoneme;
4. write down the letter he has decided on;
5. recite the word again in his mind;
6. recall the phoneme he has just spelled, subtract it from the word, and locate the next phoneme to be spelled; and
7. match that phoneme with a letter of the alphabet, and so on, until all of the phonemes are spelled.

The child must have a very stable image of the word in his mind to be able to switch back and forth between the sound of the word, its phonemes, his repertoire of letters, and the motor act of writing each letter.

We can illustrate the importance of the concept of word in carrying out the tasks of spelling with an analogy. Suppose that your first assignment in an astronomy class is to make a chart of fifty stars in the sky. You go outside on a starlit night, armed with drawing paper and pencil, and look up. You spot a bright star. You look down at the paper to see where its mark should go. You look up to verify its position, but alas! Which star is it? So it goes—every time you isolate a star from the thousands of others, you lose your place in the transition from sky to paper and back.

But suppose later on you studied the constellations. Now when you looked into the sky you could quickly orient yourself to the patterns of stars in the sky. Every time you looked down at your paper you could quickly reorient yourself by the constellations.

For the beginning speller, we expect that a concept of word is akin to our ability to recognize constellations. It serves the same important orienting function when he attempts to spell.

LETTERS TO REPRESENT SOUNDS

After phonemic segmentation and the concept of word, the third source of difficulty for a beginning speller is deciding which letters should represent the sounds she has isolated in a word. At first, inventive spellers are very creative in finding these letter-to-sound matches. And although they are capable of sophisticated thinking in deciding on these matches, they are also largely unconcerned with being correct. The experience of reading, however, shows them again and again that their inventions are not the ways of the adult world, and they begin to be aroused to the need to spell words in a standard fashion. There is one strain of continuity in this new concern with standard spelling: The inventive speller continues looking for patterns of regularity—for rules that will enable her to generate standard spellings for words—in the same way she was able to generate letter name spellings for them during the beginning stages we have just considered. The task of coming to grips with standard spelling is the topic of the next chapter. In it we learn more about both children's learning processes and the written language they are trying to master.

CONCLUSION

All of the spelling forms and spelling stages we have considered in this chapter have one important feature in common: they result largely from children's invention, from their untutored assumptions about the way spelling works. In succeeding chapters we will see what happens as children begin to learn the patterns of standard spelling. For now, a pair of questions remain to be answered about invented spelling.

Do all children invent spelling? If every child spontaneously wrote out invented spelling at the kitchen table, the phenomenon would be as widely known a writing behavior as baby talk is a speech behavior. But they don't and it's not. Many children do not explore writing before they enter school, and there they usually practice writing only words they have memorized. However, if these children were ever to write words whose spellings they had not memorized, it is probable that they would employ the strategies we have described in this chapter.

Should all children invent spelling? We raised this question in the first edition of this book in 1982. At that time our answer was, "Yes, children will learn to spell and write fluently if they are encouraged—but not forced—to express themselves in writing as soon as they feel the urge, and as best they can." We based that answer on our teaching experience and on anecdotal evidence from many teachers. The educational community has had much more experience with invented spelling since 1982, and virtually all of it supports the value of encouraging children to invent spellings for words.

REFERENCES

1. James Beers. "Developmental Strategies of Spelling Competence in Primary School Children." In Edmund H. Henderson and James W. Beers (eds.), *Developmental and Cognitive Aspects of Learning to Spell*. Newark, Del.: International Reading Association, 1980.

2. Charles Read. *Children's Categorization of Speech Sounds in English.* Urbana, Ill.: National Council of Teachers of English, 1975.

3. Ronald Langacre. *Language and Its Structure, Some Fundamental Concepts.* 2d ed. New York: Harcourt Brace Jovanovich, 1973.

4. Jill DeVilliers and Peter DeVilliers. *Language Acquisition.* Cambridge: Harvard University Press, 1979.

5. A. M. Liberman, F. S. Cooper, D. Shankweiler, and M. Studdert-Kennedy. "Perception of the Speech Code." *Psychological Review* 74 (1967): 431–461.

6. I. Y. Liberman et al. "Explicit Syllable and Phoneme Segmentation in the Young Child." *Journal of Experimental Child Psychology* 18 (1974): 201–212.

7. Darrell Morris. "Beginning Readers' Concept of Word." In Edmund H. Henderson and James W. Beers (eds.), *Developmental and Cognitive Aspects of Learning to Spell.* Newark, Del.: International Reading Association, 1980.

6/ Learning Standard Spelling

Susie wrote the writing samples shown in Figure 6–1 during the fall of her first-grade year. The writing in Figure 6–2 she wrote in the spring. The difference between her spelling at the two times is striking. Her first efforts are strange to the eye, while her later ones are familiar; she seems to have moved out of some exotic, foreign way of writing and into English writing. Her later words look like they *could* be English words.

How do we account for the difference? It does not reside in the way she sounded out the words she spelled. In both types of writing each word appears complete with all of its phonemes represented. What is different is the *way* she represented the phonemes in the word. She has largely given up her original letter-name basis for spelling. In its place she has begun to employ features of standard English spelling. But although she has begun to notice and employ features of standard spelling in her writing, she does not use them correctly. She is in a stage of experimentation with standard spelling forms, a stage which we call *transitional spelling.* With practice and learning, she will move directly from this stage into correct spelling. But for now she must come to grips with the system of generalizations that make up standard spelling.

FIGURE 6–1
Susie
Grade 1
Susie's letter-name spelling

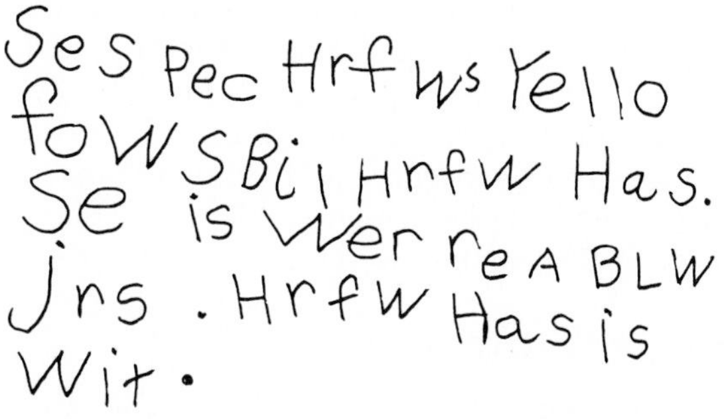

Ses Pec Hrf ws Yello
fowSBil Hrfw Has.
Se is Werre A BLW
Jns . Hrfw Has is
Wit.

(She is picking her flowers. Yellow flowers by her flower house. She is wearing a blue dress. Her flower house is white.)

FIGURE 6–2
Susie
Grade 1
Susie's
transitional
spelling

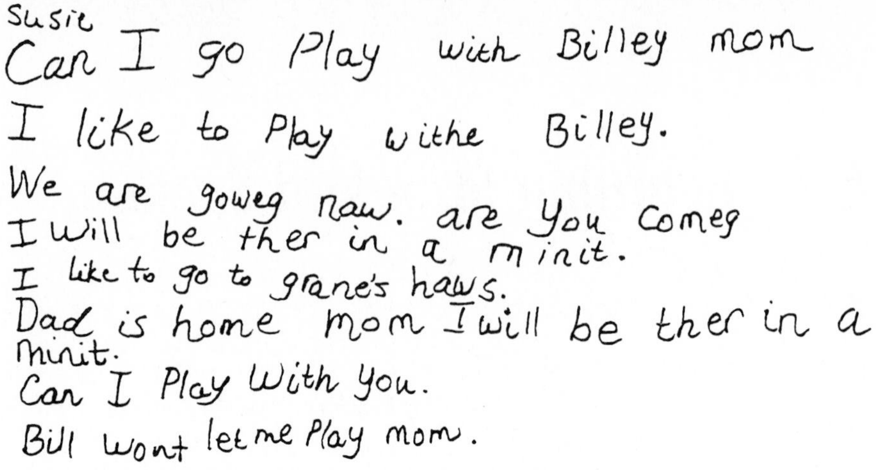

Susie
Can I go Play with Billey mom
I like to Play withe Billey.
We are goweg naw. are You comeg
I will be ther in a minit.
I like to go to grane's haws.
Dad is home mom I will be ther in a minit.
Can I Play With you.
Bill wont let me Play mom.

(Can I go play with Billy, Mom? I like to play with Billy. We are going now. Are you coming? I like to go to Granny's house. Dad is home Mom. I will be there in a minute.
Can I play with you?
Bill won't let me play, Mom.)

What system of generalizations are we talking about? English spelling often draws complaints for being *un*systematic because it frustrates the expectation of simple letter-to-sound relationships. The letter A, for example, can represent a dozen different sounds, and the sound *ā* can be spelled as many different ways. The patterns of regularity in English spelling are complex, but they do exist, nevertheless.

The patterns that relate English spelling to the spoken language necessitate recourse to such things as *marking systems,* in which combinations of letters, some of them silent, represent sounds of words; *grammatical considerations,* in which parts of words that contain grammatical information, such as verb tense markers and noun plural markers, are spelled in one way while they are pronounced in several ways; considerations of *pronunciation,* which copes with the normal changes that speech sounds undergo when they occur next to other speech sounds; and finally, patterns that stem from spelling changes made by medieval scribes.

Before we describe these aspects of English spelling in detail, and then discuss the ways that they show up in children's spelling, we should say a word about how English spelling came to take its present form.

HOW ENGLISH GOT ITS STRANGE SPELLING

The alphabetic system of writing was introduced into England by the Romans. They spoke and wrote Latin, of course, but their writing system and alphabet were put to early service of the Anglo-Saxon or Old English language that was spoken on the island. Old English manuscripts have been found dating back to the eighth century, A.D.[1]

England does not occupy a large piece of geography, nor are there many natural barriers on the island. But early peoples living in different regions had very limited contact with each other. Thus each region had a markedly different dialect of English. When speakers of these dialects occasionally came together, their dialects influenced each other in strange ways to give rise to new ways of speaking. Gradually, the whole language was propelled forward with changes of speech and usage unevenly spread across the land. By the time the printing press was imported to England, the language had evolved into what is called Middle English—the language of Chaucer.

There were great varieties in Middle English, but we know that in general when Middle English was written down most letters, especially vowels, had one pronunciation; and almost all the letters that were written in a word stood directly for a sound.

It was in 1476 that William Caxton set up the first printing press in England. Up until his time each scribe had had his own style of spelling. With printing that changed. The printer became the final arbiter of spelling, and variations of spellings for individual words greatly diminished. Caxton selected the London dialect of Middle English as the basis of his spelling, and succeeding printers usually followed his example.

In the few centuries before Caxton, England had been invaded and ruled by the French from Normandy. Though French was widely spoken, Latin was the language of the church, the school, and of the court. Through the seventeenth century, literate people read more Latin than they did English, and also a good deal of French. At this time, when occasional attempts were made to reform the spelling of English, the reforms actually moved spelling away from sound so that English words would look more like their Latin and French cousins. *Dette,* for example, was changed to "debt" in order to make it resemble the Latin form *debit.*[2]

To complicate matters further, it seems that many of the early printers were from Germany and Holland. Some were not good speakers of English or French, and so they introduced several peculiarities into our spelling out of error! They gave us "yacht," for example, for *yotte.*

From the fifteenth century through the eighteenth, the English language changed so much that a speaker from the later period could not have understood a speaker from the earlier one. But spelling changed relatively little during the same time. The seventeenth and eighteenth centuries saw several efforts to reform English spelling along phonetic lines. The most influential man of letters of the eighteenth century, however, would have none of it. Dr. Samuel Johnson published his famous *Dictionary* in 1755 and established from that time to this the historical, or etymological, basis of English spelling instead of the phonetic.

English spelling is today considered "historically phonetic": it is spelled roughly the way it sounded 500 years ago. In all these years many differences have occurred between spelling and sound. There are two such differences that stand out above all of the others.

One source of difference between spelling and sound is the Great Vowel Shift. In Old English there was not the same distinction between long and short vowels (by which we really mean tense and lax) that we have today. But in Middle English, vowels came to have relaxed pronunciations when they occurred in unstressed syllables. The letter E was at that time pronounced $\bar{a}$ in stressed syllables and $\breve{e}$ in unstressed syllables. Thus the word "bete" would have been pronounced "bāteh." The letter I was pronounced $\bar{e}$ in stressed syllables and $\breve{\iota}$ in unstressed ones, giving bēteh for "bite." The respective pronunciations for the letter A in stressed and unstressed syllables were *ah* and $\breve{a}$.

Between the fifteenth and sixteenth centuries a very peculiar thing happened: The pronunciation of each of the above vowels in stressed positions were changed around, while the unstressed vowels kept their original pronunciations. The stressed letter E went from $\bar{a}$ to $\bar{e}$; stressed letter I went from $\bar{e}$ to $\bar{\iota}$; and stressed letter A went from *ah* to $\bar{a}$. Thus, the two vowel sounds that were represented by each vowel letter became remote from each other, as we can see in pairs such as "mate–mat," "bite–bit," and "Pete–pet."

The second major change that occurred in the relation between spelling and pronunciation was the appearance of silent letters. Words in Old and Middle English had almost no letters that did not stand for some sound. Thus "bite" was pronounced "beeteh," and "light" was pronounced "lixt," with the *x* having a sound akin to the *ch* in "loch" and "Bach." But with changes in pronunciation, the last vowel sound in "bite" dropped off, and the *x* sound in "light," "right," "bright," "sigh," and similar words ceased to be sounded. The spellings for these silent sounds stayed on, however. They came to indicate that the preceding vowel had its long or stressed pronunciation, since the first syllable in a two-syllable word was always automatically stressed. Today they serve as *markers*—letters that are silent themselves but serve to indicate the pronunciation of neighboring letters.

SOME LEARNABLE PATTERNS OF MODERN ENGLISH SPELLING

To account for the relationship between spelling and sounds of words in modern English, it is necessary to consider the historical background of the relationship. But that does not mean that children must become historians of language. Rather, it means that they must be able to sense patterns of spelling that are old in origin, but that can be perceived today as generalizations governing the relation between spelling and sound.

In the modern English spelling we can identify four separate types of patterns, all of which emerging spellers must contend with as they seek to learn the system. We will refer to them as *rules*, though we must emphasize that they were never deliberately planned as rules, and they are rarely explicitly taught in the fashion in which we will describe them. The patterns we will treat are *marking rules, phonological rules, scribal rules,* and *morpheme conservation rules.*

Marking Rules in English Spelling

As we noted in the previous section, the system of cues that tell us which pronunciation to give vowels and certain consonants was not deliberately designed as a system. Nevertheless, the result is a highly general, and, hence, learnable, set of patterns that can be summarized as follows:

1. *Vowel + consonant.* When a vowel is followed by a consonant, that vowel has its short (or lax) pronunciation. *Example:* mat.
2. *Vowel + consonant + e, i,* or *y.* When a vowel is followed by a consonant, followed by either of the above three vowels, the vowel has its long (or tense) pronunciation. The same is true when two vowels are written before a final consonant. *Example:* sale, sail.
3. *Vowel + consonant + consonant + e, i,* or *y.* A vowel can be insulated from the marking influence of e, i, or y by doubling the intervening consonant. *Example:* mat, matted versus mat, mated.

While it is true that some reading and spelling curricula teach these rules explicitly to young children, children who approach learning to write as a process of discovery find the rules out for themselves, as we shall presently see. As they do, they encounter three kinds of challenges. First, they must discover that there are some letters that make no sounds of their own and serve as markers. Second, they must discover how these markers work. Third, they must learn to coordinate the adding of grammatical inflectional endings with the marking rules; that is, word endings such as *-er, -est, -ing,* and *-ed* have the effect of marking the preceding vowels long. A child who is learning to add these onto words for grammatical reasons may not realize that they function as markers, too.

To make matters still more complicated, some consonants—notably *c* and *g*—also have variant pronunciations that are signaled by markers (e.g., *sag, sage*). Inflectional endings, of course, have a marking effect on these consonants as well (hence, *wag + -ing* goes to *wagging* and not *waging*).[3]

Children and Marking Rules. To use marking rules correctly, spellers must coordinate several things at once. To be able to spell "mat," for example, they must

1. remember that the letter A in English spelling properly spells the sound *ă;*
2. recognize that a vowel letter occurring before a word-final consonant will have its short pronunciation; and
3. recognize that if the first two above conditions are met, then no further marking is necessary.

Beginning spellers do not always coordinate all three considerations at one time. In Figure 6–3 note the spelling of "pick" is PIKE. Elaine correctly paired the vowel sound ĭ with the letter I (she has moved beyond the letter-name match, by which she would have paired the sound ĭ with the letter E). She also demonstrates an awareness of markers—hence, the silent E she places after the K. But she appears not to know precisely when she should use markers and when the environment (i.e., the two consonants around the vowel) can do the work of marking for her.

But the reader may see that there is another problem. PIK does not spell "pick" (except in advertisers' spelling!). The letter K in word-final position

FIGURE 6–3
Elaine
Grade 1
Note vowel
marking
problems

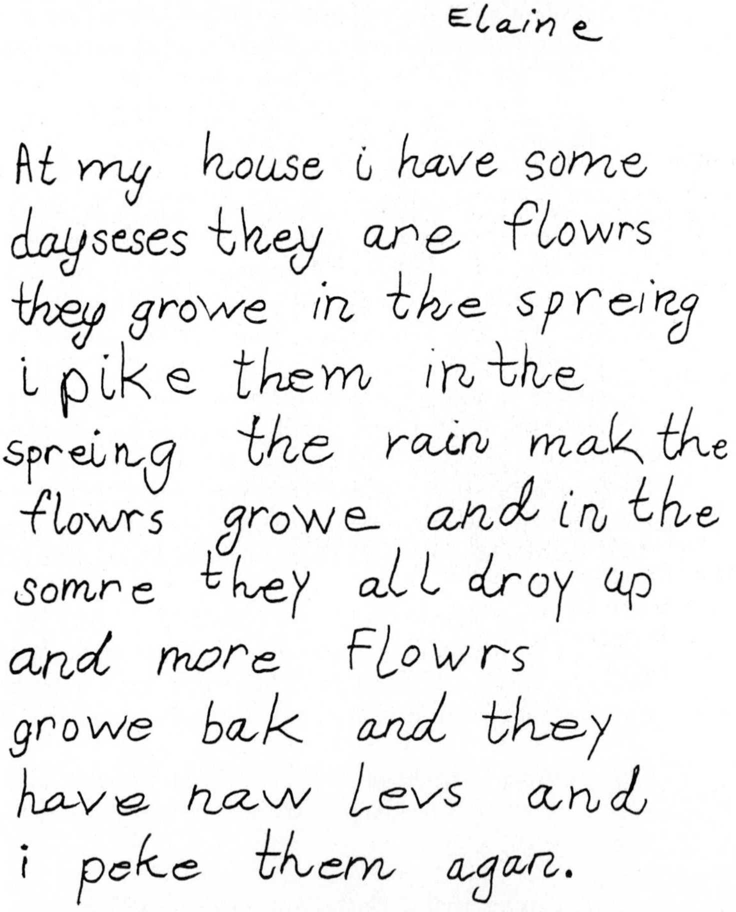

Elaine

At my house i have some
dayseses they are flowrs
they growe in the spreing
i pike them in the
spreing the rain mak the
flowrs growe and in the
somre they all droy up
and more flowrs
growe bak and they
have naw levs and
i peke them agan.

(At my house I have some daisies. They are flowers. They grow in the spring. I pick them in the spring. The rain makes the flowers grow and in the summer they all dry up and more flowers grow back and they have new leaves and I pick them again.)

follows a scribal rule: K can never stand alone after a single vowel without a vowel following. We cannot have PIK, or BAK, or LOK, or DUK. The letter K needs to be accompanied by a preceding C in all such cases. The reason for this goes back to the Middle Ages. At that time it was standard practice to double final consonants after a preceding *short* vowel—"egg" and "ebb" still follow that pattern. But the scribes of the period had an aversion to writing the two letter K's together (we don't know why). So they developed the device of substituting CK for KK. The practice of doubling final consonants to mark a short vowel is long past, but CK is still with us, as a *scribal rule.*[2]

Elaine may have seen that PIK was not what she wanted, and she may have therefore been put in search of a way of marking PIK to make it right. It would be logical, though incorrect, for her to arrive at PIKE.

GROWE is another interesting extension of the silent letter E marker. By a certain logic, she is well motivated to put it there. The letter W is, after all, a consonant whose influence on the word is easily felt in the rounding of the lips. By the normal pattern, a vowel between two consonants GR-O-W would have the *short* pronunciation without a final E-marker. So Elaine's E, by this logic, is marking the O long.

Teri has overextended the marking strategy, too (see Figure 6–4). But her overextension is just the reverse of Elaine's. She has correctly noted the common juxtaposition of the letters C K, but she employs it for the long vowel marker instead of the short one. This pattern is apparently strong with Teri, since she uses it both for FLACKS (flakes) and MACK (make). The word WENE, on the other hand, has been given a long vowel marker, even though the E is short.

Figure 6–5 shows another by Elaine. She shows very clear signs of experimenting with marking as a strategy in invented spelling. It is not just a half-remembered feature from some other words. From her handwriting, it appears that she first wrote DUCK, and later appended an E to it—perhaps to make it look more like the words that followed! DREKE is a move toward institutionalizing the omission of N before other consonants. With the N omitted, the spelling DREKE probably comes closest to standard spelling of what is left. WOTTRE is another case of an earlier invented spelling that has an overlay of standard practice. At an earlier stage, the letter R would have represented the final syllable by itself. Elaine seems to have sensed that a consonant cannot spell a syllable by itself, so she has inserted a vowel—but in a secondary position, which is what she may have thought it deserved. Meanwhile she seems to recognize the need to double the consonant at the syllable boundary in order to keep the preceding vowel short.

Note that "take" is marked the reverse of the correct way, TACK. Note, too, that this marking business is still not second nature: She spells "straight" by the old letter-name strategy: STRAT.

Marking rules develop as a concept. The concept is applied very generally as a strategy for spelling words when the spellings have not previously

FIGURE 6–4
Teri
Grade 1
Note the marking
of ā

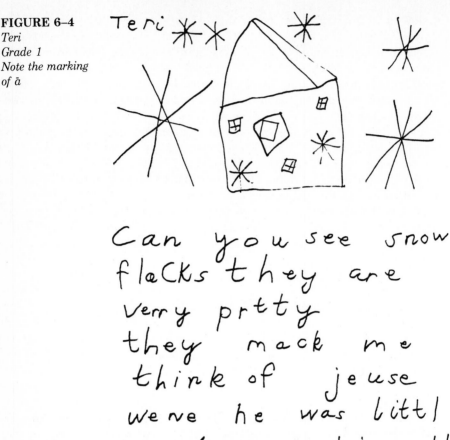

(Can you see snow flakes. They are very pretty. They make me think of Jesus when he was little and Mary, his mother.)

been memorized. Sometimes these markers create spellings that can quite easily be read and understood by adults.

For example, Darla's paper (Figure 6–6) is easily readable, but she shows some uncertainty with marking patterns. RASCULES (rascals) and PEPPLE (people) are marked in a fashion just the opposite of standard spelling.

Scribal Rules in English Spelling

Even when marking rules are taken into account, there are many words in English whose spellings appear to violate the normal relation between letters and sounds.

These irregularities can often be traced back to the influence of the medieval scribes. The scribes, acting as the manual forerunners of the printing press, had a monopolistic influence on spelling, just as printers were to have

FIGURE 6–5
Elaine
Grade 1
Note marking
problems

Elaine

I have a ducke. I can drcke wottre. She has baby ducklings. Theye foloe her in a strat line. Theye leve ina barine. Thoye are yellow. Theye can tack a bathe and The sun is out. and we play a lot with Theme.

(I have a duck. I(t) can drink water. She has a baby ducklings. They live in a barn. They are yellow. They can take a bath and the sun out and we play a lot with them.)

later. Occasionally, they made spelling changes to reflect changes in pronunciation. Sometimes their changes moved spellings toward greater consistency across classes of words. HWIC (which) and HWAT had their initial letters reversed to conform to the CH and SH spellings of words like "church" and "ship."

The scribes made some spelling changes to correct confusions among words brought about by the peculiar style of handwriting used in formal documents during the Middle Ages. The Gothic style of the period stressed a repetition of heavy vertical strokes, which reduced the means of discriminating between letters. An example can be seen in the text reproduced in Figure 6–7.

The spelling of the word "love" demonstrates the effects of two scribal changes. "Love" violates our expectations of regularity in two ways. First, it has a letter E at the end. This E looks like a marker for a preceding long vowel; but the vowel heard in "love" is short. The second irregularity is the sounded vowel: The vowel we hear in "love" is usually spelled by U, not O. How do we account for these anomalies?

FIGURE 6–6
Darla
Grade 1
Note marking
problems

Darla

here are the dogs

Once a pon a time we bote a
little kitten and you no how
they are win there little
They are little rascules.
But this one loved to climb
tree and scach pepple He was
a mean rascule.

(Once upon a time we bought a little kitten and you know how they are when they're little. They are little rascals. But this one loved to climb trees and scratch people. He was a mean rascal.)

FIGURE 6–7
Gothic script u's
are difficult to
distinguish from
M *or* N

Beloved, let us love one
another: for love is of
God; and every one that
loveth is born of God,
and knoweth God.

I John 4:7

The final letter E is there because since the early Middle Ages it has been unallowable for an English word to end in a letter V. This strange prohibition came about in the days when the letters U and V were not regarded as separate letters. Until the seventeenth century, the letters U or V could be written interchangeably for the vowel or the consonant sound. But confusion could be avoided if word-final V, when it stood for the consonant, were followed by the letter E. Thus "you" was spelled YOU, or YOV. But "love," which had earlier been spelled LOU or LOV, came to be spelled LOUE or LOVE. In the seventeenth century, the vowel *u* and the consonant *v* were each stably identified with its own letter, but by then the silent E after V had become so entrenched that it is still with us 300 years later.

But what of the letter O in "love"? This vowel and the same vowel in "above," "some," "son," "one," "come," and "none" took its present form as a direct result of the Gothic script. In Old English, "love," "above," "some," and the others were spelled with the letter U.

The evolutions of their spellings were as follows:

Year			
A.D. 1000	lufu	bufan	sum
1200	luue	buuen	sum
1300	lou	abuue	summ
1400	love	above	somme
MODERN	love	above	some[4]

It seems that in all of these words the letter U was changed to O deliberately, because in the Gothic script, with its repetition of bold vertical lines, the letter U was difficult to distinguish from M, N, and, of course, from V. In the example of Gothic script in Figure 6–7 this difficulty is easily observed.

The Gothic script stayed in active use for centuries. Later typefaces alleviated the discrimination problem, but by the time this occurred, the letter O before V, N, and M was a solid fixture of English spelling.

Children and Scribal Rules. Like the vowel pairings ($\bar{e}$–$\breve{\imath}$; $\breve{a}$–$\bar{e}$) we saw in Chapter 5, the presence of scribal rules in English spelling leads to divergences between children's invented spellings and standard forms.

These are apparent in spellings involving a final letter V, as we see in Figure 6–8. This child's spelling of the word "of" lays bare some of his thinking on this problem. His spelling UV by itself would be phonetically regular, but his addition of a final letter E shows he is aware that V's never occupy the word-final position without an E.

The scribal rule concerning U/O and V is a central issue in Michelle's paper (Figure 6–9). She, too, had arrived at the spelling UVE for "of," showing

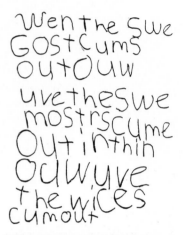

I like thee rivrs
and i likekande
thisis wut iLuve
mykusos i wi will
witthere nomes
kimma tt faikie
this is wut I
hattobsis
wiltihai

Wen the swe
gostcums
out ouw
uvetheSwe
mostrscume
out inthin
ouw,uve
the wices
cumout

(I like the rivers and I like candy. This is what I love, my cousins, I will write their names: Kim, Matt, Frankie. This is what I hate: to be . . .)

(When the swamp ghost comes out, all of the swamp monsters come out and then all of the witches come out.)

at once the tendency to spell the vowel phonetically with the letter U and remembering to "cover" the letter V with the following letter E. She used that spelling twice.

"Come," however, she spelled two different ways: CUM and CUME. The first of these spellings is phonetic. The second, strangely, contains the final letter E, perhaps because Michelle remembered seeing an E in the correct spelling.

Phonological Rules in English Spelling

Sometimes words change their pronunciation when they change their part of speech. Note the shift between "bath" and "bathe," between "teeth" and "teethe," between "strife" and "strive." These differences in pronunciation are reflected in spelling. But other such changes are not. Note the difference between "produce" (as a verb) and "produce" (as a noun; e.g., vegetables), "contract" (as a verb) and "contract" (as a noun; e.g., a document), "recess" (as a verb) and "recess" (as a noun).

Some sounds in words change their pronunciation when they occur next to other sounds. Say this sentence aloud, as you would to a friend: "I bet you can't eat the whole thing!" Chances are the end of "bet" and the beginning of "you" ran together as something like "betcha."

There are *phonological rules* that govern these sound changes. They work within words, too. When the sounds of *t* or *s* are followed by the sound *y*, the sounds blend to *ch* or *sh*. Thus we write *initial* but say "inishul." We write *special* but say "speshul." We write *fortune* but say "forchun." It is the coming together of the *t* or *s* and *y* sounds in each of those words that gives way to *sh* or *ch*. And that is a *phonological* phenomenon.

It is often the case that spelling is tied to a careful, overprecise pronunciation of a word. An accurate speller may need to work back from a relaxed pronunciation to an overprecise pronunciation and from there to the spelling.

It is one thing when the difference between the actual pronunciation and the spelled pronunciation is the same for everyone, as is the case with "special," "nature," "initial," and the like. The situation is more complicated when dialects are involved. Inhabitants of different regions and members of different social and ethnic groups sometimes have pronunciation patterns that differ strikingly from each other. These pronunciation differences have interesting effects on spelling.

Children and Phonological Rules.   Young spellers have no way of knowing that "speshul" is a compact way of saying "spessyal" and that it's "spessyal" that the spelling is tied to. Nor do they know that "nachure" is a compact way of saying "natyure," and it's "natyure" that we are supposed to spell. So it is not surprising that their first untutored approaches to these spellings are phonetically based and incorrect.

Note how Stella (see Figure 6–10) went about spelling "nature trail." The affricated (*ch*) sound of *t* and *r* rapidly produced was discussed in Chapter 4. Not surprisingly, she heard the *ch* in "nature" also.

Stephanie's spelling of "especially" is also interesting (see Figure 6–11).

FIGURE 6–10
Stella (left)
Grade 1
Note spelling of
"nature trail"

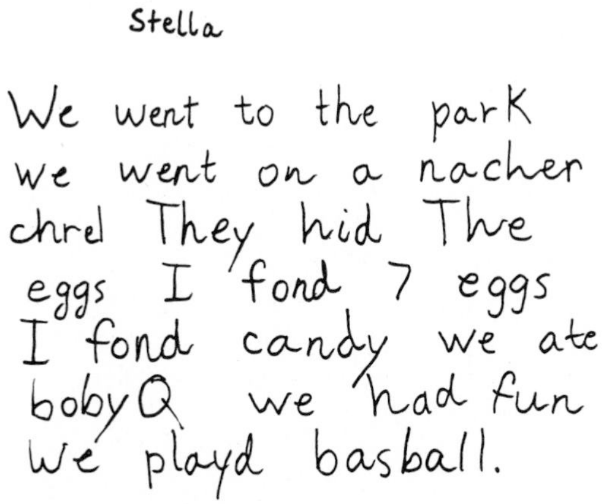

FIGURE 6–11
Stephanie (right)
Grade 1
Note spelling of
"especially"

Stella

We went to the park
we went on a nacher
chrel They hid The
eggs I fond 7 eggs
I fond candy we ate
boby Q we had fun
We playd basball.

I like
school espeshely
when we have
Art

(We went to the park.
 We went on a nature trail. They hid the eggs.
I found 7 eggs. I found candy. We ate barbecue. We had fun. We played baseball.)

(I like school, especially
when we have art.)

To include the first syllable in "especially" indicates a careful attempt to spell the word, but the C and I in the middle of the word is simply not available even to the most careful reflection.

"Grocery" is another word whose individual sounds are often compacted and changed in normal speech. The letter C is often fricated (see Chapter 5) to yield GROSHRY.

Susie's spelling of the word indicates the pronunciation usually given in southern Texas (see Figure 6–12).

Susie's SH in "grocery" and Stella's CH in "nature" were clever, but not surprising. We adults may sometimes forget what these words really sound like—seeing print biases our ears—but the children hear the sounds in words very acutely as they are spoken. GROSHRY and NACHUR are good renderings of what these children hear in those words.

In Figure 6–13, Susie shows that her knowledge has gone a step further. In her spelling of "jewelry box" she demonstrates that she is aware that the sounds of *j* and of *dy* may alternate with each other. This awareness goes beyond having an acute ear for sounds. Her spelling demonstrates an awareness of phonological rules and of their relation to spelling.

A fine example of the influence of regional dialect on spelling is seen in Figure 6–14. This, too, comes from southern Texas.

Morpheme Conservation Rules in English Spelling

Morphemes are words, or else they are parts of words, that have meaning yet cannot stand alone. "Word" is a word, and a single morpheme. "Words" is also a word, but is composed of two morphemes: *word* and *–s*. The letter S has meaning of a sort, because it shows that there is more than one of whatever it is attached to. There are dozens of these *bound morphemes*, thus called because they cannot stand alone: *–ed, –ing, –ly, –er, –ness, –ful, –ity, –ation, un–, re–, dis–, anti–* are some examples.

FIGURE 6–12
Susie
Grade 1
Note spelling of
"grocery"

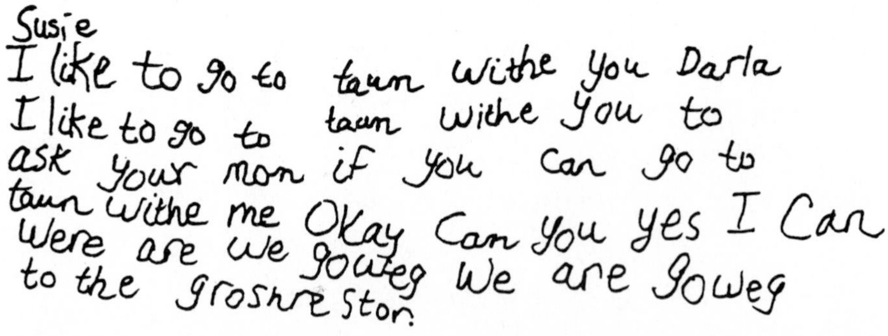

Susie
I like to go to taun withe you Darla
I like to go to taun withe You to
ask your mon if you can go to
taun withe me Okay can you yes I can
Were are we goweg We are goweg
to the Groshre stor

(I like to go to town with you, Darla. I like to go to town with you, too. Ask your Mom if you can go to town with me. Okay. Can you? Yes, I can. Where are we going? We are going to the grocery store.)

FIGURE 6–13
Susie
Grade 1
Note spelling of
"jewelry"

On the holaday.
I went to my gramows house
and we went to mexeco and
I got a dyolreybox and I
honeted ester egg and I got
elevn and my bruther fawd
three and my sistder got elevn.

(On the holiday. I went to my grandma's house and we went to Mexico and I got
a jewelry box and I hunted Easter eggs and I got eleven and my brother found
three and my sister got eleven.)

FIGURE 6–14
No name
Grade 2
Regional dialects
affect spelling

Onece there was two dogs
he chood on the sofa
and inee thang he can
git a hode uv.

(Once there was two dogs. He chewed on the sofa and anything he can get a
hold of.)

Morpheme conservation gets to the heart of the issue morphemes raise for young spellers. The problem is this: Because of speech habits, some morphemes are pronounced in a variety of ways. But because the different pronunciations all *mean* the same thing, they are usually spelled one way. In these cases we say that letter-to-sound regularity is ignored so that the identity of a morpheme may be conserved or maintained. And that is the *morpheme conservation rule*.

Let's return to *–s*. The *–s* actually represents two morphemes. One is a plural marker, as in "one duck/two ducks." The other indicates the number of the verb, as in "I duck/she ducks." But note the different sounds these morphemes can have:

Nouns	*Verbs*
cats	stacks
dogs	folds
foxes	presses

There are three possible sounds in *–s: s, z,* and *iz.* Which one it takes depends on the ending of the word it attaches to.

There is a phonological rule, that is, a rule of sound relationships, that summarizes the conditions under which *–s* will take its various sounds.

- Generally, *–s* takes the sound *s* after words ending in the sounds of *f, k, p,* or *t*.
- It takes the sound *z* after the sounds of *b, d, g* (as in "bag"), *l, m, n, r, v, w,* and all vowels.
- It takes the sound *iz* after words ending in the sound of *j* (such as "page"), *ch, sh, s,* or *z.*

This rule is well known on an unspoken level to all native English speakers. (It is devilishly tough, though, for foreign speakers of English!) To demonstrate, try pluralizing these nonsense words:

- one *barch,* two _____
- one *pog,* two _____
- one *bort,* two _____

You undoubtedly produced the correct sounds for *–s*. The curious thing is that we can do this sort of thing automatically, without being conscious of knowing or using a rule. We may even be surprised that *–s* has three sounds. Is this because the three sounds of *–s* are psychologically the same to us, or because we have so often seen them share a single form in print? It is difficult to say. The task for children, however, is to learn that the various spoken forms have a single written form.

The past tense marker *–ed* is another morphemic ending. Like the ending *–s*, it has one usual spelling, but three pronunciations. The pronunciations depend on the sounds of the word ending to which the *–ed* is attached.

To demonstrate for yourself the three pronunciations of *–ed*, put the following nonsense verbs into the past tense: Today I will *blog* my yard. Yesterday I _____ my yard, also. Today I *trock* my grass. Yesterday I also _____ my grass. But I won't *frint* the leaves. I _____ the leaves yesterday.

The three endings, as we hope you discovered, are *–d*, *–t* and *–id*, respectively. Here is a summary of the distribution of the sounds represented by *–ed*.

1. Generally, *–ed* takes the sound of *d* after endings in all vowels, and after the sound of *b g* (as in "beg"), *j*, *l*, *m*, *n*, *r*, *v*, *w*, *z*, and all vowels.
2. Usually *–ed* takes the sound of *t* after endings in the sounds of *f*, *p*, *s*, *ch*, and *sh*.
3. Similarly, *–ed* takes the sound of *id* after endings in *d* or *t*.

Children and Morpheme Conservation Rules. Since the sounds of *s*, *z*, and *–iz* all mean the same thing, it is convenient for readers that they be written in a standard way, with a letter S. Children, however, may not be aware that spelling in this instance ignores the various sounds of the *–s* element in favor of its meaning. Thus, they will spell the *–s* ending in a variety of ways that honor the sounds. Examples of this are found in Figures 6–15 and 6–16.

As readers, we have become accustomed to seeing written words ending in *–ed* whose endings are pronounced different ways. We may even be surprised that these endings *are* pronounced different ways, since we have learned to associate them with one written unit: *–ed*. Children who have not learned that different pronunciations are associated with this one written unit,

FIGURE 6–15
Ginger
Grade 1
Note spelling of
"hugs"

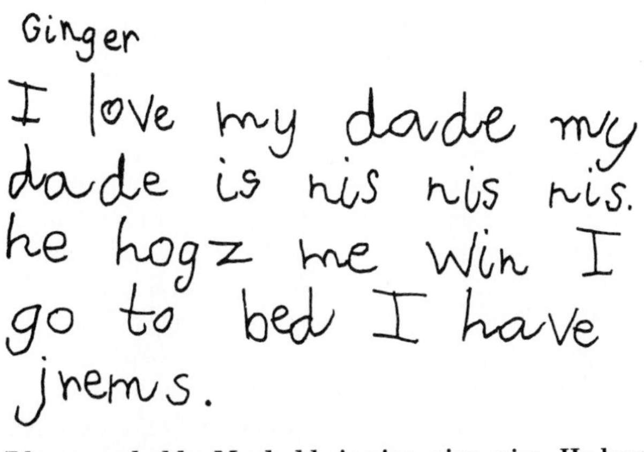

(I love my daddy. My daddy is nice, nice, nice. He hugs me when I go to bed. I have dreams.)

FIGURE 6–16
Elaine
Grade 1
Note spelling of
"tadpoles"

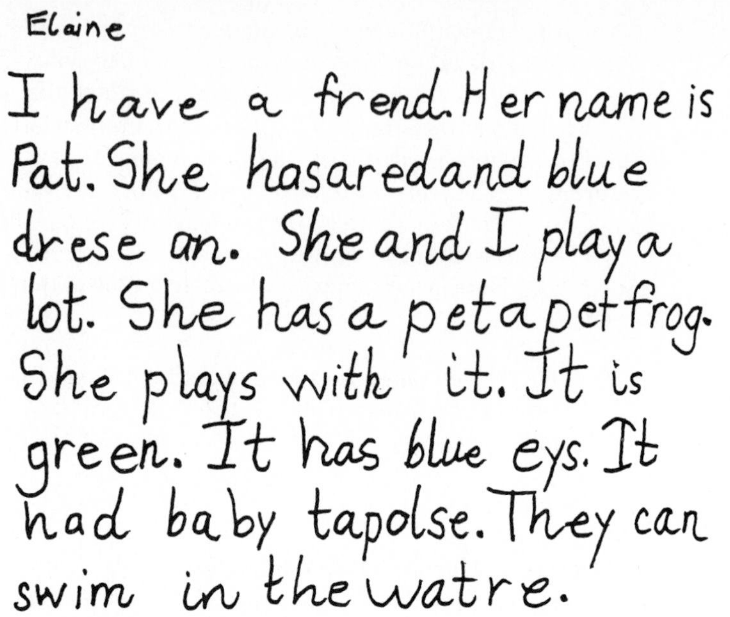

Elaine

I have a frend. Her name is
Pat. She hasaredand blue
drese on. She and I play a
lot. She has a petapetfrog.
She plays with it. It is
green. It has blue eyes. It
had baby tapolse. They can
swim in the watre.

(I have a friend. Her name is Pat. She has a red and blue dress. She and I play a
lot. She has a pet, a pet frog. She plays with it. It is green. It has blue eyes. It
had baby tadpoles. They can swim in the water.)

however, are likely to spell these endings different ways. Note in Figures 6–17
and 6–18 how these children treated the endings.

Teri shows that she has become aware of *–ed* as a morphemic unit that
must preserve its *—ed* spelling. She has not figured out how to graft it on
properly to the rest of the word, though (see Figure 6–19).

CONCLUSION

When children first begin to spell, they seem to perceive their task as one of
breaking down their spoken words into individual speech sounds and
matching each sound with a letter. As they move toward mature spelling, they
must abandon the relatively simple phonetic approach to spelling and take on
the complex patterns that are at work in our spelling system. Marking rules,
scribal rules, phonological and morpheme conservation rules are involved in
some of the more important patterns.

Children become aware of these rules and patterns through experimenting with spelling and comparing their productions with correctly spelled
words. When children reach the stage of transitional spelling, well-considered
teaching can help, too. This is the topic of the next chapter.

FIGURE 6–17
Ginger (left)
Grade 1
Note spelling of
"pushed" and
"rode"

GingerLee

FIGURE 6–18
JoBeth (right)
Grade 1
Note spelling of
"lived"

I Wet to The prK.
I SUEG on TheSUEg.
I Slide on The SlSe.
I posht ThemiErgou
and I Rod my bik.
ten I Spetonit at th
es has ten I camt
Schoo.

(I went to the park.
I swing on the swing.
I slide on the slide.
I pushed the merry-go-round and I
rode my bike.
Then I sped on it at my house. Then I
came to school.)

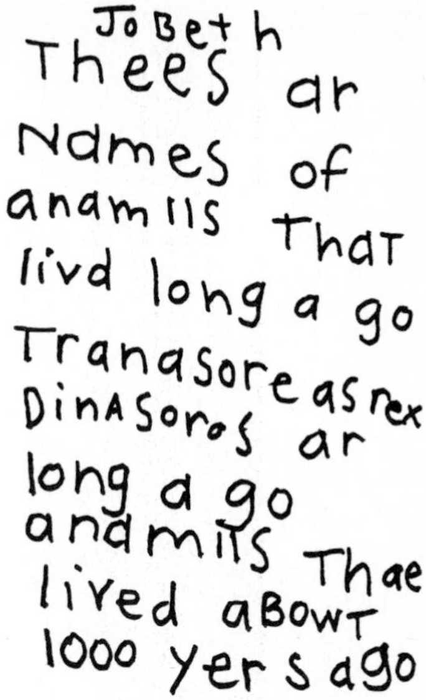

JoBeth

Thees ar
Names of
anamils That
livd long a go
Tranasore as rex
DinASoros ar
long a go
anamils Thae
lived aBowt
1000 yers ago

(These are names of animals
that lived long ago. Tyran-
nosaurus Rex. Dinosaurs are
long ago animals. They lived
about 1000 years ago.)

FIGURE 6–19
Teri
Grade 1
Note spelling of
"told"

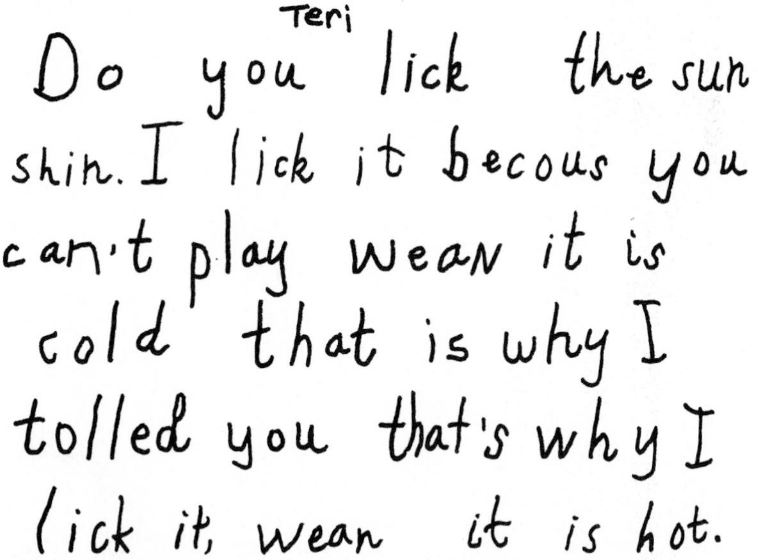

Teri

Do you lick the sun
shin. I lick it becous you
can't play wean it is
cold that is why I
tolled you that's why I
lick it, wean it is hot.

(Do you like the sunshine? I like it because you can't play when it is cold. That
is why I told you that's why I like it when it is hot.)

REFERENCES

1. G. L. Brooks. *A History of the English Language.* London: Norton, 1958.
2. G. H. Vallins. *Spelling.* London: Andre Deutsch, 1965.
3. Richard Venezkey. *The Structure of English Orthography.* The Hague, Netherlands: Mouton, 1970.
4. *The Oxford English Dictionary.* 13 Volumes. Oxford: Oxford University Press, 1933.

7/ Making Progress in Spelling

Children's invented spelling changes as they get older. Early spelling strategies give way to later ones, and the changes in strategies are reflected in the way words are spelled. Observe in Figures 7–1 and 7–2 spellings of the words "dragon" and "purred" offered by five children at different levels of maturity.[1]

FIGURE 7–1 *Developmental changes in spelling*	*Lorraine* *2nd grade*	*Joyce* *2nd grade*	*Chris* *1st grade*	*Angela* *Kindergarten*	*Brian* *Kindergarten*
	DRAGON	DRAGUN	GAGIN	J	MPRMRHM

FIGURE 7–2 *Developmental changes in spelling*	*Lorraine*	*Joyce*	*Chris*	*Angela*	*Brian*
	PURRED	PURD	PRD	P	BDRNMPH

Though these spellings were taken at one time from different ages of children, it is probable that any one of them could have passed through different stages of spelling in the order suggested here. That means that if we were to watch Brian over a period of about two years, we would see his spelling change so that it would resemble first Angela's, then Chris's, then Joyce's, and finally Lorraine's.

To give these spelling strategies names, we would call Brian's spelling *prephonemic.* We would call Angela's spelling *early phonemic.* Chris's spelling we call *letter name,* and Joyce's spelling we call *transitional.* Lorraine's spelling is, of course, correct.

Our purpose in this chapter will be to place these stages of spelling in developmental perspective and to explain how you may accurately determine where a child is in his spelling development. Then we will describe the instructional goals that seem appropriate for a child at each stage of development and suggest several learning activities that have been found helpful at each stage.

THE STAGES OF SPELLING DEVELOPMENT

Let us begin by fixing the stages of spelling development firmly in mind.

Prephonemic Spelling

The characters in Figure 7–3 are examples of *prephonemic spelling.* They were written by Kurt at age five. At that time he formed letters accurately and wrote voluminously, but he had not yet discovered how spelling works. He had not discovered the phonetic principle, which is the notion that letters represent the speech sounds or phonemes in words. Hence, his letter strings *look* like writing, but they do not *work* as writing works.

When children string letters together without attempting to represent speech sounds in any systematic way, they are spelling prephonemically. This is the sort of spelling Brian produced in Figure 7–1 and Figure 7–2.

Prephonemic spellers usually have not learned to read, but they appear to know a lot about written language. They know how letters are formed and that they are supposed to represent language, some way, as we see in the following anecdote.

Four-year-old Emily wrote what is shown in Figure 7–4 and said, "This *can* say Lauren—for make believe." (Lauren is her friend.) Then her mother wrote what is shown in Figure 7–5.

"*That* can't say Lauren," Emily objected.

FIGURE 7–3
Kurt (left)
Age 5
Prephonemic
spelling

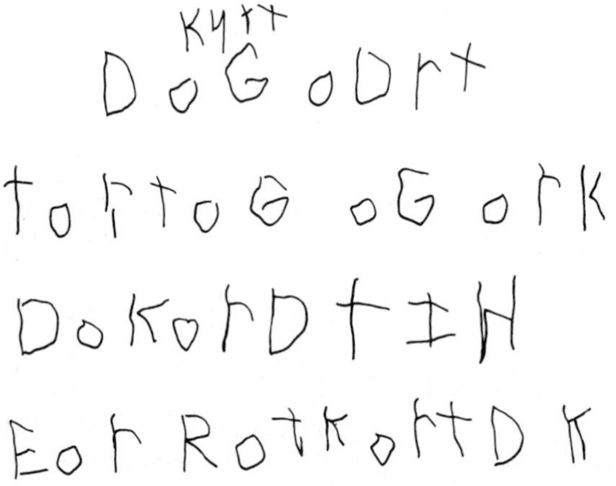

FIGURE 7–4
Emily (right)
Age 4
*"This could say
'Lauren'"*

FIGURE 7–5
Ruth
Age 35
"This couldn't"

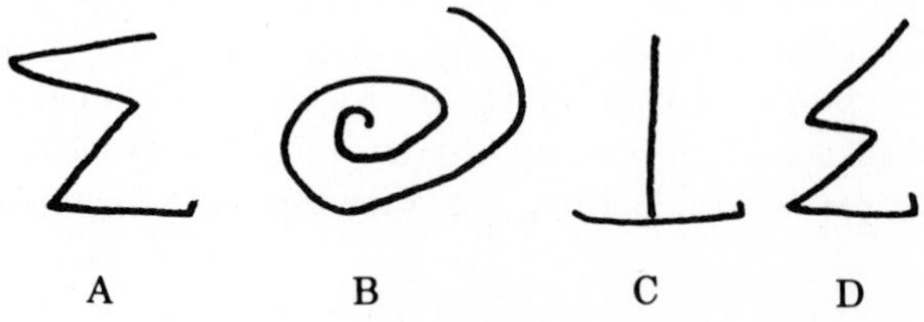

A   B   C   D

"Why not?" asked her mother.

Pointing to the first letter, Emily said, "That's wrong." Pointing to Figure C, "That's upside down." Pointing to Figures A and D, "They're upside down."

Thus we see that Emily, a prephonemic speller, knows that letters can represent words, but only allowable letters can do this.

Early Phonemic Spelling

Figure 7–6 shows examples of early phonemic spelling, so called because the children have attempted to represent phonemes in words with letters. These children have discovered the phonetic principle—they know basically how spelling works. But there is a curious limitation to early phonemic spelling. The children write down letters for only one or two sounds in a word, then stop. Thus, spelling in which letters are used to represent sounds, but only very sparsely, is called early phonemic spelling. Sometimes children in the early phonemic spelling stage will identify and spell one or two phonemes in a word and then finish the word out with a random string of letters, as in Figure 7–7.

The limitation seems to be related to the stability of the speller's concept of what a word is. The early phonemic speller cannot make words "hold still in his mind," while he examines them for phonemes and matches the phonemes with letters.

The transition from early phonemic spelling to the next stage, *letter-name spelling,* appears on the surface to be a matter of degree. A child

FIGURE 7–6
No name
Kindergarten
Early phonemic
spelling

MBEW WML Int

My Baby was with me last night.

VL†∧ DAL ISOM†hR

Valentine   Day   is almost   here.

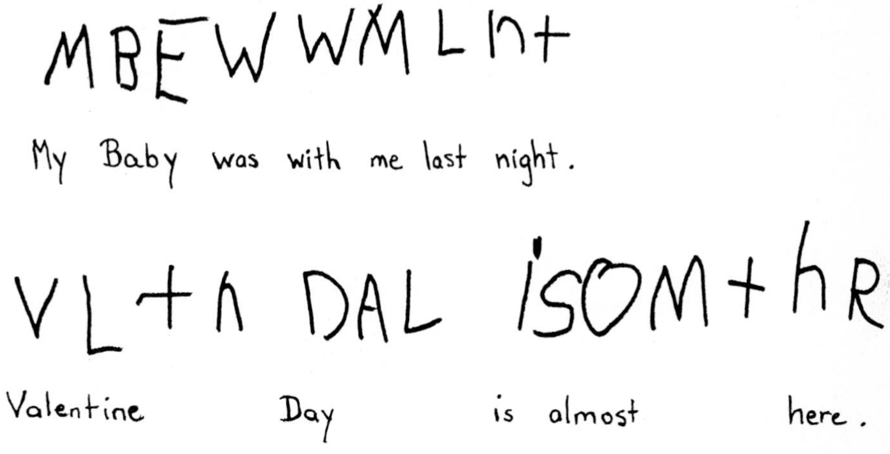

FIGURE 7–7
Daryl
Grade 1
Daryl in October

ILNgLEᴬDⳤS

represents more and more phonemes with letters until he is representing most of them. But the transition takes place rapidly. One month a first grader is producing early phonemic spelling, like Daryl's. Two months later he produces letter-name spellings (see Figure 7–8). The abruptness of this progress seems to be the result of an underlying factor: Most likely the concept of word has stabilized between the early stage and the later one.

Letter-Name Spelling

Letter-name spelling is the practice of breaking a word into its phonemes and representing the phonemes with letters of the alphabet (see Figure 7–9). The

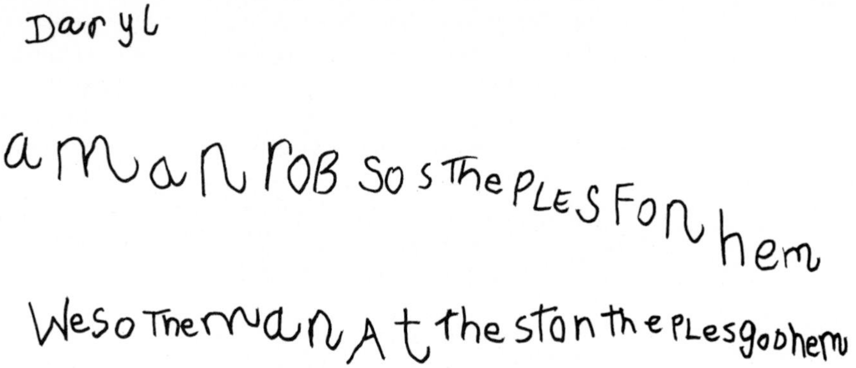

FIGURE 7–8
Daryl
Grade 1
Daryl in
December

Daryl

a man rob so s The PLES For hem

Weso ThermanAt the ston the PLesgoohem

FIGURE 7–9
Daryl (no
relation)
Age 5
Letter-name
spelling

He had a blue clth. It trd in to a brd.

(He had a blue cloth. It turned into a bird.)

letters are chosen to represent phonemes on the basis of the similarity between the sound of the letter names and the respective phonemes.

Letter-name spellers often are not yet readers. That is, they may begin producing letter-name spelling before they are able to read. But the concept of word, and the ability to identify phonemes in words are important prerequisites for reading. Thus, when a child begins producing letter-name spellings he usually begins to read soon after. For a time he will read words written in standard spelling and write words in letter-name spelling! This leads, not surprisingly, to confusion when a child reads his own writing.

Before many months have passed the experience of reading will present the letter-name spellers with differences between their way of spelling things and standard spelling. When their spelling begins to change as a result of this influence, they pass to the next stage.

Transitional Spelling

Figure 7–10 shows *transitional spelling*. Words spelled by transitional spelling look like English words, though they are not spelled correctly. Transitional spellings employ many of the features of standard spelling—the silent letters for markers, scribal rules, and the rest—but employ them uncertainly. The conventional spellings for short vowels are normally employed at this stage, with occasional throwbacks to the letter-name strategies for spelling vowels. Words with irregular spelling patterns are usually misspelled by the children, and sometimes the misspellings have the effect of making the spelling of the word look the way it *should*.

Transitional spellings will be mixed in with correctly spelled words whose forms the children have either accurately invented or memorized.

FIGURE 7–10
Susie
Grade 1
Transitional
spelling

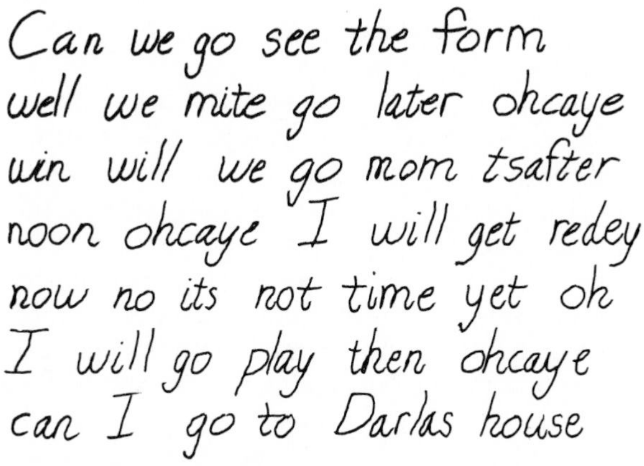

Can we go see the form
well we mite go later ohcaye
win will we go mom tsafter
noon ohcaye I will get redey
now no its not time yet oh
I will go play then ohcaye
can I go to Darlas house

(Can we go see the farm? Well, we might go later. O.K. When will we go, Mom? This afternoon. O.K. I will get ready now. No, it's not time yet. Oh, I will go play then. O.K. Can I go to Darla's house?)

Children who produce transitional spellings often demonstrate that they have become aware of *features* of standard writing; particularly marking rules, scribal rules, phonological rules, and morpheme conservation rules. But they have not yet integrated all of these features into a systematic understanding of English spelling that works. In most cases, they will do so with practice.

Transitional spellers are readers. The source of the features, the generalizations about spelling that they are beginning to manipulate, is in the print they see around them. The path to correct spelling lies through more reading, more writing, and more attention to the way words are put together.

Correct Spelling

Few of us spell everything correctly. All of us resort at one time or another to a dictionary for the spelling of a troublesome word. Still, most literate adults have an accumulated body of knowledge about English spelling that enables them to spell an immense quantity of words with hardly a second thought. We couldn't have memorized them all. Most of the words we write we were never directly taught. Many of them we have occasion to write no more often than once every two or three years, yet we still spell them correctly without hesitation.

Moreover, we can write and read words nobody ever saw before (Figure 7–11). We couldn't do this unless our knowledge of spelling were based on generalizations or rules about the structure of words. We couldn't do it at all if what we had in our heads was simply a catalog of all the words we knew how to spell and read. The mature literate person's knowledge of spelling is a complex system of rules that relates phonemes to letters, and relates to phonemes a multitude of concerns: the parts of speech of the words, the sound changes they go through, other words to which they are related, and even the old language—Latin, Greek, French, or Anglo-Saxon—from which they passed into English. Yet this knowledge exists only on a working level. The person may not be aware that he has it or is using it.[2]

You may wonder how it is that children make progress through the spelling stages if so many adults know so little about what they are doing! It does not seem that we could lead them to understand things that we are not conscious of ourselves. Clearly, children's learning of spelling concepts is largely self-directed. We teachers and the environment in general provide the wealth of information about written language through books, spelling lessons, reading instructions, and the like; but the children rather selectively attend to aspects of that information that they can use at any one time.

This does not mean that teaching has no role in children's learning about

FIGURE 7–11
How can we read this?

GLIGHLY DE BROMBLY SLOM GLARMED FROT
DE FLOOZLE, ERMULLY, GLUGLISS, BOD
GERFLIMANED DO LANG AY WHISS MOUT.

print, however. It is true that children make progress in spelling if they are surrounded by print and encouraged to write. Their progress, nevertheless, can often be improved and confusion avoided if they are provided with encouragement, modeling, and instruction that is directed toward their current level of thinking about print.

If our teaching is to engage their thinking about spelling most directly, then we must have some means to determine where their thinking is. In the next section we will explain two procedures for assessing a child's level of spelling development. Then in the final section of this chapter, we will suggest instructional activities that are best suited to children at each level of spelling development.

ASSESSING CHILDREN'S SPELLING DEVELOPMENT

In order to tell what children's spelling strategies are, we need to have them write words they have not been taught—words they have not memorized. That is because our object is to see the fruits of their spelling concepts, rather than to test their ability to memorize words. If children spell words correctly, there is no way to tell if they produced the spellings from their own concepts or carried them over from some other source—a memorized spelling or one copied from somewhere in the room where they were writing. So we need to set up circumstances where children will spell words incorrectly because we may safely assume that incorrect spellings are neither copied nor memorized.

There are two ways to get children to spell words that they cannot always spell correctly. One is simply to invite children to write about some favorite topic, taking care to invite them to use whatever words they wish, spelling them as best they can. With some children this works easily. With others, using motivating topics like those suggested in Part Three will get them writing freely and producing creative spellings. But many children are too inhibited for either approach to yield freely spelled words. These children will write words they are completely sure of and few others. For them we can use an assessment test like the one Gentry and other researchers at the University of Virginia used to sample their ideas about spelling. This structured prompting is just what some children require before they will take the risk of spelling words they are not sure of.

A recommended word list for such an assessment test is found in Figure 7–12.

| **FIGURE 7–12**
Experimental
spelling list | 1. *late*
2. *wind*
3. *shed*
4. *geese*
5. *jumped*
6. *yell* | Kathy was late to school again today.
The wind was loud last night.
The wind blew down our shed.
The geese fly over Texas every fall.
The frog jumped into the river.
We can yell all we want on the playground. |

7.	*chirped*	The bird chirped when she saw a worm.
8.	*once*	Jim rode his bike into a creek once.
9.	*learned*	I learned to count in school.
10.	*shove*	Don't shove your neighbor when you line up.
11.	*trained*	I trained my dog to lie down and roll over.
12.	*year*	Next year you'll have a new teacher.
13.	*shock*	Electricity can shock you if you aren't careful.
14.	*stained*	The ice cream spilled and stained my shirt.
15.	*chick*	The egg cracked open and a baby chick climbed out.
16.	*drive*	Jim's sister is learning how to drive.

When you administer the word list, it is best to follow these steps:

1. Explain to the children that they are not expected to be sure how to spell many of the words. You want to see how they *think* the words are spelled. They should do their best, but they will not get a grade for their work.
2. If they are stumped by a word, they should try to figure out how it begins, then try to figure out its middle, then its ending.
3. Read the word, then the illustrative sentence, then read the word again twice. Give the word its normal pronunciation—don't exaggerate any of its parts.

Scoring the children's spellings is a matter of deciding which category the child's spelling of each word falls into. As you examine the way the children wrote each word, you

- give the word a 0 if it is *prephonemic*;
- give the word a 1 if it is *early phonemic*;
- give the word a 2 if it is *letter name*;
- give the word a 3 if it is *transitional*; or
- give it a 4 if it is *correct.*

You must assign each word a category according to the descriptions given in the previous section.

In Figure 7–13 we have scored a child's paper according to this system. If you are not sure how we categorized the spelling of each word, go back and review the early part of this chapter where the categories were described.

There are two ways to tabulate the children's scores—you can find the average or the mode. The mode is the single score that occurs most frequently. To find the average, you add up the scores for the individual words and divide the sum by the number of words. The average for Figure 7–13, for example, is 2.2. The average, however, is subject to some distortion. If the child happened to know the spelling of several of the words, the accumulation of 4's could raise his average to make it appear, by this way of reckoning, that his strategy was

FIGURE 7–13
Scoring a
spelling list

L a t	2
W n d	2
S e a d	3
G e e s	3
G o u t	2
u L	2
c u t p	2
L o s	2
L d d	2
S u f	2
t r a d	2
t e r	2? 3? (The *y* spelling is learned.) Call it 2.
S o c K	3
S a d	2
c e K	2
d r i f	2

more advanced than it really was. Thus it is safer always to calculate the *mode* as well as the average. In the example in Figure 7–13, the mode was 2. What this means is, most of the child's spellings fell into the letter-name stage of spelling. Since the average and the mode were in the same range, we may trust this conclusion.

HELPING CHILDREN MAKE PROGRESS IN SPELLING

Once we know the stage of spelling development in which a child is functioning, what can we do about it? Conceptual learning—and this includes learning how to spell—resists direct teaching. It is not very profitable merely to tell a speller that he is wrong when he makes a mistake. It is not much more effective to require him to memorize the spellings of the words he will have to write. There are too many of them to memorize; and in any case, what we are after is that the students develop a set of concepts about spelling that will enable them to write thousands of words.

Conceptual learning has to run its own course, as children make discoveries, operate according to a particular hypothesis for a time, and then revise it as they find information that challenges that hypothesis. But as teachers we *can* encourage this process along by offering children opportunities to write and steering children's attention to things that matter about the writing system.

In the following pages we will list goals around which to organize the spelling instruction of children at each stage of spelling and illustrate activities that develop children's spelling ability.

For the Prephonemic Speller
Goals for prephonemic spellers are concerned with orienting children to the writing system. Books, magazines, and other written material should be a source of pleasure. Parents and teachers, both, should read to these children. It is especially helpful to read certain books several times and then leave them around so the children can talk their way through them.

Parents can read the feature articles from the newspaper aloud to children and point to the caption words. They can also share comic strips that are easy to understand, and let children develop the habit of following them from day to day and Sunday to Sunday.

When parents take their children to a restaurant, they should read the placemat aloud to their children. They should read the menu, too, and point to the words as they tell the child the choices available. Parents can read cereal box cartoons and captions at the breakfast table.

Children should learn that writing communicates. Parents can point out to their children the messages communicated by other examples of writing around them. They can

- read aloud the road signs the family passes that have words on them: "stop," "yield," "speed limit 55," "school zone," and so on.
- read words that are flashed on the TV screen, such as show titles and cast of characters.
- read labels on items around the house, such as toothpaste, cereal, spices (salt, pepper, mustard, catsup), and foodstuffs (flour, sugar, and so on).
- write letters and other messages to, for, and with their children. For instance, parents can encourage children to dictate a message, write it down, and read it back. Then the parent can go over the message with the child and see if he thinks it is right. The beginning writer will not know, of course, but by raising the question the parent suggests to the child that it is reasonable for him to concern himself with the print. Then the children can sign the dictations to make them theirs. Ask children to label their art work, and then explain why they used the letters they did. Label rooms or things around the house (or for teachers, around the classroom). Around the house these might be the bathroom, the television set, the refrigerator, the child's own room. At school these can be children's desks, lockers or clothes hooks, reading or science centers, pencil sharpeners, blackboards.

For the Early Phonemic Speller

Early phonemic spellers have discovered that letters spell phonemes, but they cannot spell more than one or two phonemes per word.

Instructional goals for these children include the same general goals as for the prephonemic spellers. We should continue to surround them with print: read to them, encourage them to identify particular books that they enjoy, that they can learn by heart and recite while they turn the pages. Also, we should continue to have them experiment with writing. Give them plenty of opportunities to put down what they can by way of spelling out words.

We have some more specific goals for early phonemic spellers, too. One is to encourage them to develop a stable concept of what a word is. The way to do that is to call the children's attention to words in print as we—or they—are saying words out loud. James Moffett has a procedure for this, which he calls the Lap Method.[3] You hold a child on your lap, read to her a book with which she is very familiar, and point to each word in the text as you read it aloud. Gradually, you can get the child to try to point to words as you read them, and read words as you point to them. But the goal is to direct the child's attention to a written word at exactly the instant that the word is being read aloud. With this kind of support, the information that links a printed word with a spoken word is brought into focus for the child. Aspects of this information are things like the fact that a word in print is a configuration of letters bound by spaces on both ends, that they are arranged from left to right, that more than one syllable may be a single word, and that individual letters they recognize may resemble individual sounds they hear in words.

There are several successful variations of the Lap Method. One is done with a poem or a song that the child has memorized. The teacher and the child sit down with a written version of the poem or song, which is ideally four to six lines in length. They read each line chorally, as the teacher points to each word. Then the teacher points to a single word and asks the child what it is. The teacher points to the first word in the line, then the last, then one in the middle. It is not likely that the child will be able to recognize the words pointed to. Instead she will have to recite the line to herself and guess what each word must be by its order in the written line. This gets her thinking about words as units of writing and gives her practice matching a word in her head with one in print.[4]

Taking dictated experience stories, a part of the language-experience approach to reading and language arts instruction, also helps develop the concept of words in print. Dictated accounts are done either with individuals or in groups. After the children have undergone an interesting episode— perhaps an encounter with baby rabbits or a field trip to the post office—each child is invited to dictate one sentence to the teacher as part of a group composition. A number of reading activities usually follow the dictation: The group reads all the sentences chorally several times; individuals volunteer to read words or sentences; the teacher points to a word in the line and asks a child to read it. In cases where the child knows by heart what the line says but cannot recognize the word, he is likely to work his way through the line, matching memorized words with units of print until he makes a match with the word in question.

The shared book method, as developed by Don Holdaway in New Zealand,[5] is nicely suited to helping young readers and writers learn about the relationships between print and speech. Holdaway's method uses big books, yard-high versions of children's books that are read through in the children's presence by the teacher, who uses a pointer to touch each word as she reads. After several passes through the big book in the group setting, the children are handed regular sized versions of the book to read through on their own. Holdaway and his colleagues began by creating their own big books, out of whatever books were likely to be favorites with their particular children. Following their lead, commercial publishers (notably Holt, Rinehart & Winston [Canada] Limited and the Wright Group in California) have begun to offer printed versions of big books for sale.

Many early phonemic spellers write their own names correctly, as well as the names of their friends, brothers, and sisters. Names can be used in learning activities to establish the concept of word. Write the child's name several times on a strip of paper without leaving any spaces between the names. Then ask the child to help you separate the names. The child spells her name first, pointing to each letter. When she comes to the end of one spelling, she cuts the name apart from the one that follows. When she has cut the names apart, she may paste them on another piece of paper, leaving spaces between them (see Figure 7–14).

A similar procedure, involving whole sentences, is suggested by Marie Clay.[6] Have the child dictate a sentence to you, write it down, and read it back to him. Then read the sentence with him, until he can read the sentence by himself. As you read the sentence each time, point to the words. When the child is able to read the sentence by himself (he is able to do this by memorizing, of course, not by actual reading), write the sentence a second time on a strip of paper. Now cut the words off the strip, one at a time, reading the sentence aloud minus the severed word each time. As a next step the child can match the cut apart words with those in the sentence that was left intact. A fairly easy task is for the child to arrange the cut apart words on top of the words to which they are matched. A more difficult exercise is to arrange the words into a sentence several inches below the sentence left intact.

Emily thought this activity up when she was not quite four. She put pieces of thin paper on the covers of her favorite books and traced the titles. A sample of her work is found in Figure 7–15.

Another specific instructional goal we have for children who are early phonemic spellers is that they grow in their ability to segment spoken words into individual phonemes. The most natural practice is to continue to spell the

FIGURE 7–14
(left)
*Establishing the
concept of word*

FIGURE 7–15
(right)
*Tracing book
titles*

parts of the words of which they are more certain. Thus their spellings may look like this at first: I W __ T D __ N __ E P ___ ("I walked down the path"). But in time, there will be fewer blanks left and more letters filled in as children gain practice in segmenting phonemes.

The final instructional goal we have for early phonemic spellers is that they be more willing to take risks. We have seen abundant evidence that making errors is a necessary part of learning to spell. We want children to pay attention to the print around them and see how it is put together and how it works. But we want just as much for them to produce their own writing, in which they try out spelling the way they think it is. We want them to formulate ideas about written language and act on them; then they will know what to do with the information they gain from examining other people's written language.

Unless children take risks and unless they are willing to make errors, their progress as spellers will be slow and inhibited, and their delight in making their own messages in print will be small. Children who are willing to invent spelling for words usually become correct spellers in a reasonably short time— and they also become fluent writers in the process.

Whether or not a child is a risk-taker depends on a number of factors. His personality, the expectations of his parents, and the atmosphere of his classroom all contribute. There are several steps the teacher can take to help a child gain self-confidence and take risks:

1. Provide many opportunities to write, which will not be graded—at least not for spelling. If you have a spelling program and teach word lists and give tests on them, you need not also grade spelling on other writing that the children do. Many kinds of writing need not be graded at all. For example, the child may put messages for the teacher in a message box or tack them on a bulletin board or write them to other children.
2. Talk to the children and praise them for what they *know* about writing. If some children have discovered that writing goes left to right across

a page, they may be congratulated for this discovery. If some have discovered that words have letters in them, and that the letters are mixed, this is something that the teacher can discuss with them. And if some have discovered that words are spelled by matching letters with individual sounds, this is a realization worthy of an adult's attention. Having an adult express interest in these issues as the children investigate them adds to the children's sense of accomplishment, and reassures them that their efforts are worthwhile.

3. Parents and teachers should both understand the value of encouragement, practice, and freedom to make errors in learning to spell. If the teacher encourages invented spelling at school but does not share her position with the parents, confusion may result. Parents may be alarmed that children bring home papers with uncorrected spelling errors, or that children enthusiastically produce writing with spelling errors at home. Unless the teacher enlists the parents' understanding and support, they are likely to say discouraging things to their children, with the best of intentions. They may even question whether the teacher is doing her job, mistakenly equating the teacher's encouragement of early writing and invented spelling with a lax attitude that leaves errors uncorrected.

For the Letter-Name Speller

Children who produce letter-name spelling have developed a system of spelling that can be read by others who understand the system. Letter-name spelling represents the high-water mark of the children's intuitive spelling development, and their spellings during this period are their most original. From this point on, children will become increasingly aware of the details of standard spelling, and their spelling will grow closer to that of adults.

By now their concept of a word in print is beginning to stabilize, but exercises to develop this concept still further will continue to be helpful—both for their spelling and for their reading. Their ability to separate individual phonemes out of words has become highly productive. What they do not yet know is all the business on the other side of the sound-to-letter representation issue. They are just beginning to explore the rules by which letters represent phonemes.

They can find the phonemes, but so far their ideas of how these phonemes should be spelled stick closely to the names of the letters. They use letter names as if they themselves were pieces of sound—building blocks out of which words can be constructed. They have not yet realized the complexity that exists in rules for choosing letters to represent words.

If the disparity between their system and the complexity of standard spelling is pointed out to them too suddenly or too harshly, many children will lose confidence. If this happens, their progress into standard spelling will be delayed because they will not experiment with new forms enthusiastically. The greatest amount of progress may be gained if children at this stage are encouraged to continue writing—indeed, if they are given a steady agenda of interesting writing tasks. Their writing can be taken seriously for the sake of its message. The teacher and the parents can talk about what the child wrote and not just her spelling—focusing on the message is likely to be more motivating than dwelling on the spelling.

If the letter-name speller is exposed to a good supply of interesting print, this should provide him with data from which he can draw new conclusions about spelling at his own pace. We should continue to read to him. We should continue to help him find favorite books, read them to him frequently, and encourage him to read them to himself. Read-along books can be highly beneficial at this stage both for reading and for writing. Language-experience teaching—dictated stories that are reread together—begins to bear even more fruit at this stage, both in the children's ease at finding words by the voice-to-print matching method, and in the number of words the children can learn to recognize after a dictated story. They will now recognize words in the story days after they were dictated, a feat they could not do before.

Having children build a word bank—a collection of word cards for the words they recognized during the reading of a dictated story—is good practice. It's a good idea to check each child's word bank occasionally, and see if she can still read all the words in her word bank. Any words that she cannot read should be taken out, placed in a separate envelope, and reviewed at a later time. The children can be encouraged to use their word-bank cards when they are writing because they are always spelled correctly, and so constitute a source of correct spellings.

Teaching spelling by means of word lists begins to be helpful at this stage. Children need to have stores of correctly spelled words in memory. When children write freely, the correctly spelled words will not replace all or even most of the invented ones; the two types, rather, will stand side by side.

Gradually, however, children notice the disparity between their inventions and correct spellings, and then revise their spelling concepts accordingly. The revised spelling concepts will enable the children to more closely approximate standard spelling.

Learning correct spellings serves another purpose, too. It alleviates the burden of inventing *everything* and often makes children's writing more fluent. As we have maintained throughout this book, invented spelling is worthwhile activity. Nevertheless, it is hard work. An indication of the intensity with which children work at invented spelling is given in this account by Graves.[7] Using a lapel microphone and videotape equipment, he recorded the oral "sounding" a child did simultaneously with each letter she wrote during invented spelling.

Jenny's message is "all of the reindeer loved them."

Line 1:   TRACK I: luh, all, all, of, all of the, the, the all of the (sounded) reindeer

TRACK II: L   OLL   AVE   THE (written)

Line 2:   TRACK I: rein *ruh,* rein loved them, all, of, them, the
              (sounded) *muh muh*

              TRACK II: R   IENDEER   LOVE   E   M
              (written)

Children can collect words they frequently need in their writing and list
them in a spelling dictionary they make themselves. Using a small spiral
notebook, arranged alphabetically, they can write all of their words that begin
with the letter A on one page, with B on the next, and so on. This practice,
again, offers a source of correctly spelled words as grist for the mill of spelling
concept formation. It also reduces some of the burden of invention and aids
fluent writing.

Care must be taken, however, not to limit the children's writing to the
words on the spelling lists or in the spelling dictionaries. It would be sad,
indeed, if a preoccupation with these correctly spelled words undermined
their confidence in their ability to think out spellings for themselves. Their
willingness to try spelling on their own is necessary for them to move beyond
memorization and learn the system of English spelling.

For Transitional Spellers

Children who are transitional spellers are adept at breaking out phonemes for
words and finding letters to spell them. They are moving beyond the intuitive
one-sound, one-letter spelling of the previous stage. They have begun to take
note of the way standard spelling works and are trying to gain control over the
patterns they perceive in standard spelling.

As we observed in Chapter 6, the patterns of standard spelling are many
and complex. It takes time, curiosity, and much exploration for a child to
master these patterns. Children need to be led gradually to learn the patterns
at work in standard spelling, and it is best if they learn these in the context of
meaningful writing, though isolated activities are sometimes helpful.

Inductive approaches often work well for helping children learn spelling
patterns. In these, children compare the spellings of several words in light of
their pronunciation, meaning, part of speech, and origin. Then they are led to
formulate their own generalities about the patterns that appear to be at work.

Word sorts are teacher-made or home-made activities that help children
notice and form concepts about spelling patterns. Word sorts are a categorizing
exercise in which children are led to group words together that share a
common feature. This exercise gets them thinking about spelling features of
words, and it works with words the children already know.

The procedure works as follows. The teacher or the children write down a
collection of words on small pieces of tagboard. If the teacher is using the
language-experience approach, the words used are those in the children's
word banks. If he is not using the approach, then he or the children can jot

down fifty words or so from the children's sight words on word cards. It's important for all of the participants in an activity to know the pronunciation and meanings of every word used.

With an individual or small group of children, the teacher starts off the activity by dividing the cards among the participants. Then he puts a card in the center of the table. He asks the children to read it and to put any words they have in hand that *begin with the same sound* on the table below the guide word (sometimes the teacher uses a picture of an object for a guide word, so the children cannot depend on a visual match between the first letters of the guide word and the words in their hands). The teacher makes sure that the participating children have several cards in hand that match the guide word, as well as some that do not.

Besides working with beginning sounds, the activity can be centered on long and short vowel sounds; other vowel sounds, such as diphthongs and R-controlled vowels; grammatical endings, such as *–ed* or *–s*; words that end in a *v* sound; words that undergo phonological changes; words with similar prefixes and suffixes; compound words; and many other features. The activity can be directed toward any word feature—including similarities of meaning and nuance—that the teacher intends. In fact, word sort activities often bring to light interesting word features of which the students and the teacher may have been unaware.

Word sorts have the potential for helping children to construct concepts about spelling patterns and enabling them to display the concepts they already hold. (Additional reading about this activity can be found through the reference section at the end of this chapter.[8,9,10]

Children at this stage of spelling profit from games and exercises that play on the spelling patterns of words. There are many games that play on children's recognition of allowable sequences of letters—letter sequences that typically spell words. Boggle, Perquackey, and Spill 'n Spell are games of this type. In all three, the players roll out letter cubes and try to identify English words within a specified time limit out of the letters that surface. Word hunts, Hangman, and Password are more games that encourage children's efforts to think of spelling patterns in English. All are worthwhile, both in the classroom and at home.

CONCLUSION

Making progress in spelling is like making progress in playing chess. Both require enthusiastic commitment not only of the memory but of the intellect as well. It is unnatural to think of spelling this way. After all, spelling and multiplication tables are two subjects that are still learned by rote at school.

A certain amount of memory work in spelling is necessary, it seems, to spell the truly exceptional words accurately. However, the active study of words, with a mind for learning how they came to be spelled the way they are and how they resemble and differ from other words, seems to be just as necessary for accurate spelling.

Those who undertake word study are often surprised at the patterns and clues they find for predicting the spellings of words. Even when some words fail to fit patterns, they become more memorable as exceptions if the normal patterns are well fixed in mind. The memory thrives on associations; reasoning and reflecting on spellings thus makes memorization easier.

The teaching of spelling in school should therefore include plenty of discussion and exploration of words—including the patterns present in their spelling, the parts of speech they can be, and the meanings they can have. In the home, games that play on spelling patterns and word meanings should be encouraged, as should frequent trips to the dictionary.

REFERENCES

1. J. Richard Gentry and Edmund H. Henderson. "Three Steps to Teaching Beginning Readers to Spell." In Edmund H. Henderson and James W. Beers (eds.), *Developmental and Cognitive Aspects of Learning to Spell.* Newark, Del.: International Reading Association, 1980.
2. Noam Chomsky and Morris Halle. *The Sound Pattern of English.* New York: Harper & Row, 1968.
3. James Moffett and Betty Wagner. *Student-Centered Language Arts and Reading.* Boston: Houghton Mifflin, 1978.
4. Darrell Morris. "Beginning Readers' Concept of Word." In Edmund Henderson and James Beers (*ed.*) *Developmental and Cognitive Aspects of Learning to Spell.* Newark, Del.: International Reading Association, 1980.
5. Don Holdaway. *Foundations of Literacy.* Portsmouth, N.H.: Heinemann Educational Books, 1978.
6. Marie Clay. *The Early Detection of Reading Difficulties.* 2d ed. Exeter, N.H.: Heinemann Educational Books, 1979.
7. Donald Graves. "The Growth and Development of First-Grade Writers." Paper presented at Canadian Council of Teachers of English Annual Meeting. Ottawa, Canada: May, 1979.
8. Charles Temple and Jean Wallace Gillet. "Developing Word Knowledge: A Cognitive View." *Reading World,* December 1978.
9. Jean Wallace Gillet and M. Jane Kita. "Words, Kids, and Categories." In Edmund H. Henderson and James W. Beers (eds.), *Developmental and Cognitive Aspects of Learning to Spell.* Newark, Del.: International Reading Association, 1980.
10. Elizabeth Sulzby. "Word Concept Development Activities." In Edmund H. Henderson and James W. Beers (eds.), *Developmental and Cognitive Aspects of Learning to Spell.* Newark, Del.: International Reading Association, 1980.

Part Three

The Beginnings of Composition

Three-year-old Emily was intently watching her mother write. Suddenly, a pencil flew across the desk and her mother sighed over another rough draft that refused to work. "Oh, Mom," said Emily, "writing's such a cinch. All ya gotta' do is get the letters."

For Emily, and many other nursery and kindergarten children, that is what writing is all about for a while—"getting the letters." They have been exploring with pencil and paper, learning for themselves the distinctive features of alphabetic characters, and sorting out the relationship between the way words sound and their representation in print. "Getting the letters" and arranging them in some meaningful order are, in the early stages of development, prerequisites to becoming a writer.

In Chapters 2 through 7, we have explored these developmental processes in depth. In the chapters that comprise this section, we will explore the emerging patterns in the way children frame their messages—in other words, their compositions. We will look at children's movement from writing that sounds like talk to writing that sounds like written language—writing that achieves some of the purposes for which adults use it: telling a story, describing something, explaining the steps in a process, or waging an argument.

8/ The Functions and Forms in Children's Composition

Perhaps she was inspired by the stories her mother had read to her. Perhaps she was tired of being always on the receiving end of the telling. At any rate, one day four-year-old Jessie sat her mother down and told her a story. It went like this

> The rabbit was at his house and his mother told him to go to the well and fetch some water. But Bunny didn't go to the well because she was very curious. She went to the woods and picked some raspberries. So she said to herself, "Why don't I go and find Daddy? Have lunch in town and ride home with him. That will be more fun."
>
> She rided out with Daddy but then a great THUMP THUMP filled up the whole air. It was a real big air-walking giant. She really was frightened. She ran to the house and said, "Mamma, help!" And she hid them both. And they lived happily ever after.
>
> Jessica, Age 4

We can learn several things about children's composition by looking carefully at Jessie's piece. But first, let us begin by defining terms. *Composition* literally means "putting together." In this book we will define composition as *putting together the details of a message in a form that is understandable to an audience.* Now let's make some points about composition.

1. *Children can compose before they can write.* If Jessie's story is evaluated according to our definition, it is clear that she made up a composition, and she did so without writing anything down. (Even though her mother wrote down her words, we would argue that she had created a

composition even if her words had not been recorded.) Whether in making up stories, or in telling true accounts of family happenings, or in fantasy play with other children, young children compose before they write.

This point is worth making because it shows us the continuity between speech and writing. At four, Jessie is a prolific talker. She is also a fluent composer of stories, so long as speech is the medium. At five and six she will begin to write, but it will be years before she will be able to write as fluently as she can talk. Jessie's speech was a laboratory for composition before she began to write. And it should continue to serve as a laboratory as she develops writing fluency. We will want to encourage her to continue her oral composi-tions, lest the task of transcribing ideas onto paper becomes the bottle neck that chokes off her creativity. Drawing pictures and talking about them, dramatizing bits of story ideas, acting out play scenarios, and simply telling stories will keep her growing as a composer, as her skill and speed at transcribing ideas slowly develops. Later, she will be able to compose more skillfully on paper than in speech—as she learns to write, reconsider, and hone her thoughts in print.

2. *Children incorporate in their compositions bits and pieces of what they have heard and read in the works of others.* In Jessica's story, we hear echos of "Peter Rabbit," "Jack and Jill," "Curious George," "Jack and the Beanstalk," and Pete Seeger's rendition of the African folktale, "Abiyoyo." The story is her own creation, yet she created it out of images, characters, actions, and themes that came from the literature she had heard, as well as from her family life.

There's nothing unusual about the amount of borrowing she has done. Gertrude Stein once commented that the copyright law was the worst thing that ever happened to literature—it gave rise to a misleading notion of originality in writing. All writers partake freely of the literature they know. Existing literature provides the very language out of which they produce their works.

So it is with children. Children find resources for composing in the stories they hear and read—and not just stories but other catchy uses of language, too—and they learn from their peers as well as from professional writers. Michael is a second grader, but he hit on the idea of having the narrator address the reader directly, a device that so powerfully drew the audience into his work that other children noticed and readily emulated it (see Figure 8–1).

Wally used Michael's direct narrator device in his piece (Figure 8–2), on an entirely different topic.

3. *In composing, children are challenged to juggle the interests of self, audience, topic, and purpose in the writing.* Let's go back to Jessica's story for a

FIGURE 8–1
Michael
Grade 2

Hello, I am Dracula, and I want to suck your blood. Ha, ha, ha! This is my castle. Do you want to come in? You might get scared.

Do you like it? Would you like to come to my laboratory? Come on.

I make a lot of experiments here. I make them with poisonous liquids and formulas. My newest invention is the Frankenstein. I command him.

Now I will electrocute him. You will see how I do it. It's not easy.

FIGURE 8–2
Wally
Grade 2

Hello, my name is Ding Dong. Do you want to come in my house?

This is my family room, do you like it? It has a T.V., a sofa, two chairs, and a window.

And this is my kitchen. It has a stove, a
micro-wave, and of course it has me.

This is my back yard. It has a zebra, a
lion, a hippopotamus, a beaver, an anteater,
and some tigers.

moment. Although the story is ostensibly about a character called "Bunny," when the action switches from going to the woods and picking raspberries to finding Daddy in town and riding home with him, we get the sense that the fictional character is being shoved aside and Jessica, the real four-year-old girl, is taking center stage. When young writers are composing, they seem driven by a powerful urge to put themselves and their interests in the foreground.

Another challenge writers encounter lies in respecting the audience's need to know. If a child wants to write a story about Bunny, how much can she assume her readers know already? She doesn't want to tell them obvious things, like what a rabbit is; on the other hand, she *should* tell them what this particular Bunny in the story is like. These are difficult questions for young writers, presumably because their young minds cannot easily imagine other people's point of view. Piaget used the term *egocentrism*[1] to describe the young child's notion that other people know what she knows and can see what she sees. (Perhaps the best example of this occurs when a five year old says "Look at this!" yet holds his book so that only he—not you—can see it.) Young people gradually overcome egocentrism as the people around them assert their needs to be considered, especially their needs for information:

"Hold the book so I can see it, silly!"

"Wait. Who's Daddy? You haven't told us who he is or where he works."

We should note two things about egocentrism in children's composition. First, gaps in the information that writers supply readers is a sign that the writers have some maturing to do. Second, the best remedy for egocentrism in writing is to write frequently for real audiences who can ask questions and make comments about the work.

For young writers especially, writing takes time. Between putting down the first word and the last one, a child may take three trips to the pencil sharpener and one to the bathroom. Things happen to the child during this time, and other ideas—ideas that may change her focus on her topic—may occur to her. Even as she is writing, one idea may powerfully suggest another and another, until the writing veers away from the original topic.

It is clear, for example, from Warren's first sentence (see Figure 8–3) that his topic is Mr. Keller. But two-thirds of the way through the piece he digresses. He has written, "Sometimes I see him come to school," and has gone on to explain: "I am a walker." But with this mention of his own activity, Warren shifts his attention to the early morning school scenes in which Warren, not Mr. Keller, is the central figure.

In a conference, Warren asserted that his topic was Mr. Keller. The teacher asked Warren to find any sentences that did not have to do directly with his topic: Warren pointed to the two that describe the morning scene: "Then they make announcements. Then we do the national anthem and the pledge of allegiance." Then he did an amazing thing: He produced another sentence that put Mr. Keller back into his piece: "Mr. Keller always sings the loudest."

FIGURE 8–3
Warren
Grade 2

Mr. Keller is the best teacher.
If you got a chance to be in his class you would find out,

He told us he had two children.
Thier names are oder, and venisa,

He always has a smile on his face. except sometimes when he gets mad

Sometimes he likes to be funny. He's real funny some times.

FIGURE 8–3
(*continued*)

Sometimes I see him come to the school, I am a walker.

Then they they make anowmpces. Then we do the naicng lanthen and the pledge aledgent. Mr Keller always sings the loudest.

Then Mr. Keller takes etendetce and lunch counet.

Now I have told you a lot about Mr. Keller. Wouldn't you like a chance to be in Mr.Keller's cks to?

Even when writers manage to stay on the same topic, they may have trouble addressing their sentences to the same *purpose*. To use Warren's piece as an example, we see that he shifts frequently between *arguing* that Mr. Keller is the best teacher, *describing* Mr. Keller, *explaining* that the teacher has two daughters and so on. Sometimes children will announce their intention to write to one purpose, but address their whole effort to a different purpose. Tyler meant to write about Eskimos, but wrote about herself instead (see Figure 8–4).

4. *Compositions follow familiar patterns or forms.* When Jessica sat her mother down and began to talk, it was clear that she intended to tell a story. She demanded and received complete attention, her eyes twinkled, she put on a sing-song voice and an exaggerated delivery: "But Bunny didn't go to the well

FIGURE 8–4
Tyler
Age 6

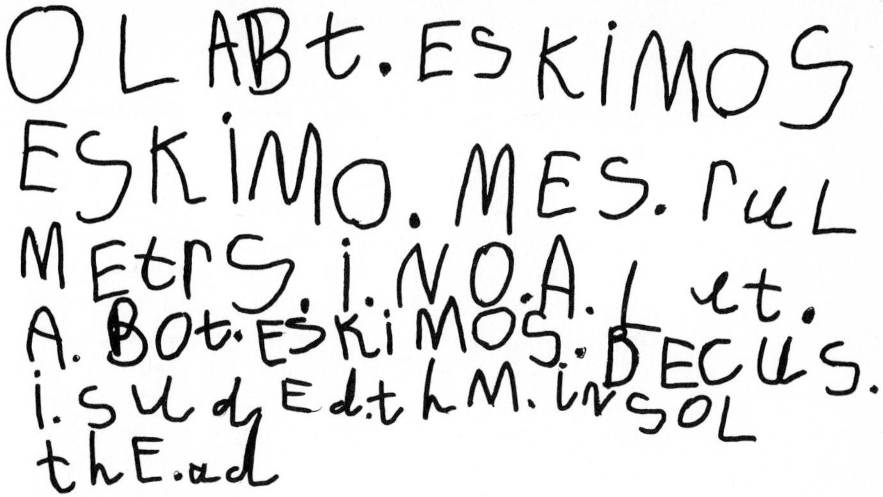

OLABt.ESKIMOS
ESKIMO.MES.ruL
MEtrS.iNOA.Let.
A.Bot.EsKiMOS.DECus.
i.SuqEdthM.iNSOL
thE.ad

(All About Eskimos
Eskimo means raw meat eater. I know a lot about Eskimos because I studied
them in school.)

because she was veeerrrry curious!" None of these signals comes through in
the written version of the story, though, and if we had been given no
introduction, we might for a moment have stayed in the dark about what sort of
writing we had before us. But by the time we reached the end of the first line, it
would have occurred to us readers that rabbits who lived in houses with talking
mothers are the stuff of fiction, and once we had used these details to
pigeonhole the work, we had a sense of what other sorts of events to expect.

The point is that readers rely on a sense of form to make sense out of what
they read. Whether the words before you are a story, a letter from a friend, a
summons to appear in court, an advertisement, or the instructions for
operating a lawn mower makes a big difference in the way you read them—not
just how attentive you are to details but the meaning you attribute to them and
the actions you expect to take after reading. In our society, the forms taken by
texts that serve these different purposes are highly conventionalized: There
are relatively few forms, used over and over, and they are, for the most part,
easily recognizable. It will be our purpose for the rest of this chapter to lay out
and describe the forms of composition that most frequently come up in
children's writing.

SELF, AUDIENCE, TOPIC, AND PURPOSE: A MENU OF WRITING FORMS

To put the self into the piece, or not? To tell the audience a lot, or a little? To
write about one thing, or many? To address our topic with an expression of
feeling about it, or as a story, or to explain or describe, or as an act of

persuasion? There seem to be many choices to make whenever we compose in written language. Those who work with young writers need some way to handle the complexity. We find such a means in the work of James Britton, an English educator who has studied and written insightfully for years about young people's development as writers.

Britton has a system for describing different acts of writing that takes into account the writer's self, her audience, her purpose, and the form she uses. The system divides acts of writing into three major categories, for which we will use the term *modes*[2]: the *expressive mode,* the *poetic mode,* and the *transactional mode.* Figures 8–5, 8–6, and 8–7 provide examples of each. (Britton used the term *voice* for what we are calling *mode.*)

The sort of writing in Figure 8–5 seems to come naturally to young writers. The author has put herself directly into the piece, in center stage. The reader, if any is contemplated, might be assumed to be anyone who is interested in the author: the piece is written as if to a friend. The purpose of the piece seems to be to *express Jo Beth's likes and dislikes.* We may say that JoBeth has written in the "expressive mode," about which we will say more later.

Figure 8–6 shows a piece of writing with a clearly different purpose. In this piece the writer is in the background; it is the topic as well as the reader that are brought most prominently into the piece. Something is expected of the reader: he is supposed to learn how to ride a bicycle. Britton calls writing of this kind *transactional* because it conducts or transacts some real-world business between the writer and the reader.

FIGURE 8–5
JoBeth
Grade 1

FIGURE 8–6
Missy
Grade 2

Missy

firstyou get on your bicyle and put your left hand on one bar. And you put your right hand on the other bar. Then put your left foot on one pedle. And your other foot on the other pedle. And then you put your but on the seat and you know how to ride a bike.

In the transactional mode the writer may wish to persuade, describe, explain, or give directions. The writer may assume that the reader is interested in her message itself, rather than in the writer's personal life. She may also assume that the reader can consider her message for its truth value or usefulness in the real world: The reader may say, that's right or wrong, worthwhile or not worthwhile.

Note that it doesn't matter who the writer is in Missy's piece in order for the piece to achieve its purpose. Moreover, the truth of the statements can be verified by simply getting on a bike and seeing if, by following her directions, we can ride the thing.

The third mode of writing in Britton's scheme is the *poetic.* The term "poetic" is a little misleading here. It comes from a Greek word *poeien,* which means "to create." Hence, poetic writing is not limited to poetry but is any written work whose function is to stand as a product of creativity in itself—as a work of art or as a verbal object to be admired. As in the case of the transactional mode, when a writer uses the poetic mode we are not usually concerned with *who* he is. A story is a story, regardless of the teller. But the reader does not respond to this kind of writing in the same way he does to writing in the transactional mode. It is not appropriate to criticize a story by asking whether it is literally true or not—that is, how well it matches (at least the surface details of) the real world we know. Instead, we ask whether it is whole, consistent within itself and to its type, or "storylike." In other words, does it have all the elements a good story should have?

FIGURE 8–7
Annabrook
Grade 1

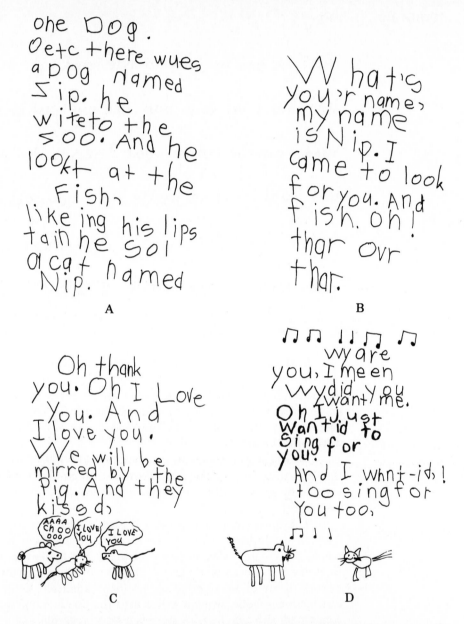

one Dog.
Oetc there wues
a Dog named
Sip. he
witeto the
soo. And he
lookt at the
Fish,
like ing his lips
tain he sol
a cat named
Nip.

A

What's
you'r name,
my name
is Nip. I
came to look
for you. And
fish. oh!
thar ovr
thar.

B

Oh thank
you. Oh I Love
You. And
I love you.
We will be
mirred by the
Pig. And they
kissd,

C

wy are
you, I meen
wy did you
want me.
Oh I Just
wantid to
sing for
you. for
And I whnt-id!
too sing for
You too,

D

Consider the piece in Figure 8–7. The work is not intended to express the writer's likes and dislikes, at least not directly. The story does not stand or fall on the readers' knowledge of or interest in Annabrook. Nor is its truth or falsehood meant to be tested in the real world. The function of this piece is to stand as a work of delight, much like a picture hung on the wall.

As Britton explains it, the reader of a poetic piece is placed in the role of *spectator,* rather than *participant.* For example, one of the authors recently saw a performance of Thornton Wilder's *Our Town,* which was performed in a church in Middlebury, Vermont. At one point, an actor, dressed as a priest, climbed the steps to the pulpit and delivered a short sermon. Had a visitor wandered in at that moment and taken the scene at face value, he would have seen a priest delivering a sermon to us, the congregation. But in reality, we were an audience, not a congregation: We applied the priest's words not to our own lives but to the actions and themes of the play. We were spectators, not participants; and the sermon was a piece of a poetic work, not a transaction.

The three major categories of writing that we have discussed have been succinctly outlined recently and are listed below.

1. *The expressive mode.* This is language that is close to the self, used to reveal the nature of the person, to verbalize his consciousness, and to exhibit his close relation to the reader. Expressive language is a free flow of ideas and feelings.
2. *The transactional mode.* This is language concerned with getting things done. It involves giving information or instructions, and attempting to persuade and advise others.
3. *The poetic mode.* Poetic language is a verbal construct, fashioned in a particular way to make a pattern. Language is used in the poetic mode as an art medium.

Britton's three modes capture the basic varieties of young children's writing fairly well. In terms of children's development as writers, it appears that most children write first, and continue to write most easily, in the expressive mode. Gradually they also gain control over transactional writing and poetic writing.

As we shall see, a child's writing may fall in transitional points between expressive and transactional and poetic. Before we explore these, however, let us begin with expressive writing and see how it works, and how a child moves out from it.

THE EXPRESSIVE MODE

Writing in the expressive mode can sound a lot like talk. It is even common for children to put dialogue into their early writing, apparently because the give and take of dialogue is more familiar to them and easier to maintain than a long message by a single speaker. Sometimes the other partner in the dialogue is the writer's intended audience. Sometimes it is some other character. Figures 8–8 and 8–9 are examples of both.

In any case, most writing relies on monologue, not dialogue, and for many children this represents a profound shift between two very different ways of using language. Children may need experiences in drawing language out by themselves, without an interlocuter. Some researchers urge teachers to en-

FIGURE 8–8
John
Grade 2

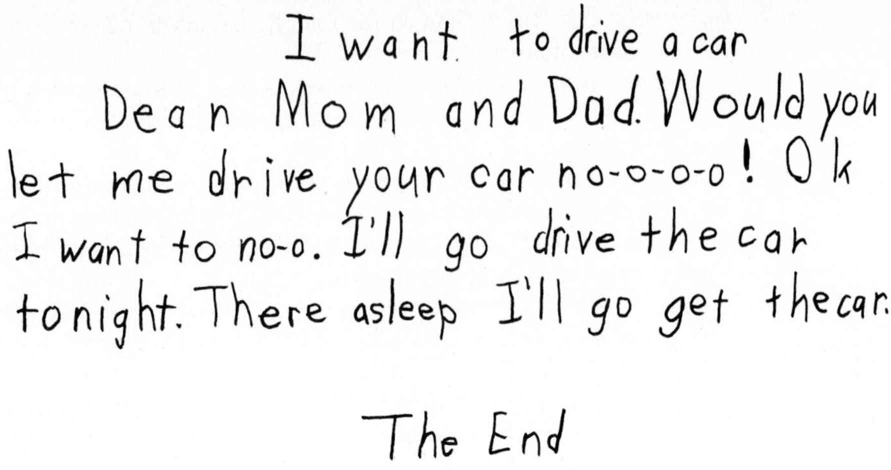

I want to drive a car
Dean Mom and Dad. Would you
let me drive your car no-o-o-o! Ok
I want to no-o. I'll go drive the car
tonight. There asleep I'll go get the car.

The End

FIGURE 8–9
Susie
Grade 1

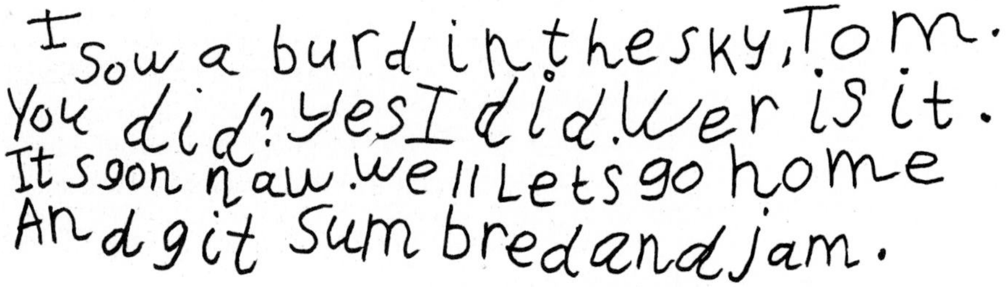

I sow a burd in the sky, Tom.
You did? Yes I did. Wer is it.
It soon naw. Well Lets go home
And git sum bred and jam.

courage children to engage in dramatic play in the classroom because this allows children to practice language that is decontextualized from the here-and-now reality, in which language relies heavily on gesture. Hence, such play requires them to elaborate, as we do in writing: "No, you're a princess. See? This is your crown." At the same time, language use within dramatic play is supported by more than one interlocuter, making it a sort of intermediate activity between conversation and the monologue of writing.[4]

James Britton encourages teachers to draw out children's contributions to conversation by asking questions: "Yes, and then what happened?" "Was there anything else you saw?" and so on.[2] Having children write in a journal is another means of drawing out monologue. Even first graders can be encouraged to keep journals. Figure 8–10 shows an example of one first grader's monologue. JoBeth, a first grader, entered this piece in a diary that she and the rest of her classmates were keeping at school.

Another loose form expressive writing may take is what Susan Sowers, a researcher at the University of New Hampshire, called an *inventory*.[5] Inventories are collections of things a child has or knows or likes. Tyler's first piece (see Figure 8–11) lists all the books she likes just now, and Figure 8–12 lists what her friends can turn into in their sleep.

FIGURE 8–10
JoBeth
Grade 1

Sant PdTriks
day is comeing in
to weeks. my
Teachr hasdnt
GoT a chance
To PuT up The
Pichers for it.
I Like it
Becose We Get
to edT Goas
and Turky BuT
The Best Part
is. you GeT TO
GeT Fat.

A

Boy is this
boring.
S.t. Paterics
day is in two
Months if you
Thank thats
not Boring
Tell Me What is.

B

No Geting
To eat turcky.
No Pillgrims.
No indeins
No inethang.
Like I say
if you Dont thank
thats Not Boring Whdt
is

C

FIGURE 8–11
Tyler
Age 6

i.LiC.the.BFG.i.LiC.it.BiLoS.
than.is.A.Lit.uLL.GuLLN.it
NADeSoFI.ioSO.LiC.COOKIEMON
STERS STORYBOOK.i.LC.it.BICS
iLiC.CUiS.ioSO.LiC.SiR.
CEDRIC.RiDES.AGAiN.
ad.hels.A.NO.thr.StrE.iLiC.
S.tart.thEad

(I like the B.F.G. I like it because there is a little girl in it named Sophie. I also like Cookie Monster's Storybook. I like it because I like cookies. I also like Sir Cedric Rides Again. And here's another story I like: Stuart. The End.)

FIGURE 8–12
Tyler
Age 6

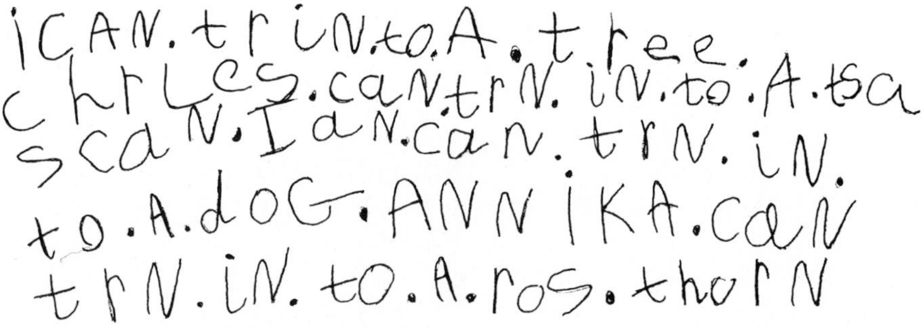

iCAN.triNto.A.tree.
ChrLeS.caN.trN.iN.to.A.tsa
scaN.IaN.caN.trN.iN.
to.A.doG.ANNIKA.caN
trN.iN.to.A.ros.thorN

(I can turn into a tree. Charles can turn into a trash can. Ian can turn into a dog. Annika can turn into a rose thorn.)

TRANSITIONAL WRITING: EXPRESSIVE TRACES IN THE OTHER TWO MODES

Many children's first compositions are written in the expressive mode. With these children, the features of expressive writing may linger in their work even when they intend to write in other modes. The loosely structured conversational tone, and the tendency to put the self and the self's interests on center stage, may pop up in pieces that might have been expected to tell stories, give explanations, or make arguments. When this happens, we call the result *transitional writing*. Note, for example, the piece written by Debbie in response to the challenge by her teacher to write an argument (see Figure 8–13). Debbie's intention was to write an argument. She clearly succeeded; yet the language she used has the give-and-take structure and bouncy rhythm of conversation, as if she had rehearsed her speil by arguing with herself in the mirror. Whether children are writing directions for hatching hens' eggs or creating a story, their delight in authorship may lead them to come out from behind the pen and enjoy the limelight of being read; and suddenly the reader's attention will be shifted away from the topic or the plot onto some deeply felt emotion or new awareness of the author's.

Movement away from these expressive outbursts may be slow. Children, and adults for that matter, approach the transactional and poetic modes only as they begin to think about the things their audience—the people who read their work—may need to know, and as they begin to consider the structural requirements of the different forms of written composition. Britton points out that young children will not be able to comply fully with all the expectations readers of transactional or poetic writing have of the writer. It is by *attempting* to meet these expectations that children gradually gain control over the different modes of writing.[2]

In any case, the fact that young writers put themselves visibly into their writing and use direct conversational language shows that they are keeping alive their own *voice,* the expression of their own personal stake in their topic.

On this point, consider the writing style of any syndicated newspaper columnist—James Kilpatrick, Ellen Goodman, Russell Baker, or William Safire. Each one serves up a goodly portion of personal opinions and experiences in the course of getting her or his message across. Consider on the other hand the dead prose of the college student who has deliberately kept his own beliefs out of his writing at all costs: "It is indeed a truism that the world

FIGURE 8–13
Debbie
Grade 2

Debbie Belyeu
Age 7

I wish I had high-hill-shoes but my mother things I'm to young but who kers. Because I like to wer them and they make people pretty and if you are smoll they make you tall and I like the flep-flop ones. The just look pretty to me.

today requires, without a doubt, perspicacity of the highest order." Teachers of writing at the college level spend much of their time trying to persuade skeptical students to put personal expression back into their papers!

As Debbie, the author of the "high-hill" composition, shares her work with teachers and peers, and as her writing efforts and reading experience help her become aware of her audience and the various structures that may shape written composition, Debbie will produce more consistently structured examples of the transactional and poetic modes. For now, remnants of the expressive mode come into her writing, even when she is trying to address other purposes. When they do, her writing will have plenty of personality, but a slightly disorganized and digressive style. Some of these features may come up in the teacher's conference with Debbie, just as they did in the conference with Warren (see Figure 8–3). As they do, with each succeeeding work this child will learn to stick to one topic and purpose in each piece.

THE TRANSACTIONAL MODE

We have defined the transactional mode as writing designed to get things done. But there are several things writing can do, and teachers of writing usually differentiate three other forms within the category we have called transactional. It will be helpful to look at the three forms in some detail here.

Exposition

Exposition explains its subject. It is used to tell what a thing is, how it functions, its history, how its parts are related to each other, or how it is related to other things. Aliki Brandenberg's discussion of how dinosaur bones turned into fossils is an adult example of one type of exposition.[6]

> When the dinosaurs died, they were covered with sand and mud. They were buried for millions of years.
> The sand and mud turned into rocks, and the dinosaurs' bones became fossils.

Simple directions are expository as well, and most classrooms abound with hundreds of examples. Just open any mathematics workbook and undoubtedly an example will pop out at you.

Most young children are capable of writing expository prose. Consider Figure 8–14, which shows an informative piece by JoBeth, a first grader whose work we met earlier in this chapter.

The last sentence says, "And that's all on the 6 o'clock seen (scene)." Although she calls this piece the planet *story,* she is obviously aware by the end that she is informing and not storytelling. Her sign-off is proof of that.

Expository prose can be used to give directions. Young writers can handle this purpose, too. Figures 8–15 and 8–16 are the responses of two second graders to the assignment, "Tell us how to float on your back."

FIGURE 8–14
JoBeth
Grade 1

the planit
Story.
the forthist
Planit away from
the sun is plooto.
the Nerrist to the
Sun is Venas. And moon
thats All on theColor

FIGURE 8–15
John
Grade 2

John

How to float on your back
I laya on my tumme and sta
stell for a wile and move very slo
And the water ceps me up.

FIGURE 8–16
Rachel
Grade 2

Rachel

You Prtend theat You are
Laying on a bad and you
Jost lay back.

Description

Description is discourse that helps us visualize. It focuses upon the appearance or the nature of an object. "In description, we see vividly and concretely; we perceive the object with a kind of fullness for which exposition does not strive."[7] Readers of descriptive prose expect the writer to display a subject's unique or characteristic appearance. When writing describes a familiar face, for example, the reader expects information about style and color of hair, color of eyes, skin tone, general expression, and so on, rather than a list of facial subparts.

A paragraph from Jean Henri Fabre's essay about the praying mantis is a fine adult example of descriptive prose.

> Apart from her lethal implement (the forelegs), the mantis has nothing to inspire dread. She is not without a certain beauty, in fact, with her slender figure, her elegant bust, her pale-green coloring and her long gauze wings. No ferocious mandibles, opening like shears; on the contrary, a dainty pointed muzzle that seems made for billing and cooing. Thanks to a flexible neck, quite independent of the thorax, the head is able to move freely to turn to the right or left, to bend, to lift itself. Alone among insects, the mantis directs her gaze; she inspects and examines; she almost has a physiognomy.[8]

Children are also capable of writing descriptive prose. Some first-grade students wrote descriptions of people they know or pets they have. Notice in Figure 8–17 how Angie has sensed the requirements of description, and how she focuses on her subject's individual, rather than general, characteristics.

Argumentation

Argumentation, or persuasion, offers evidence in support of a statement. Sometimes it is concerned with establishing a statement's truth value: for example, *Bricks make better houses than boards.* At other times argumentation is concerned with matters of "what ought to be": for example, *Children should obey their parents.*

FIGURE 8–17
Angie
Grade 1

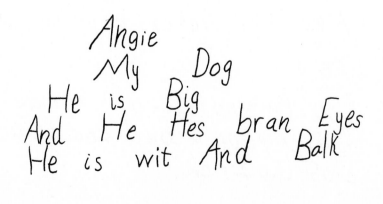

Angie
My Dog
He is Big
And He Hes bran Eyes
He is wit And Balk

Both the structure and content of an argument are crucial, as children, to the amazement of their parents, know all too well. Figures 8–18 and 8–19 are examples of children's arguments.

FIGURE 8–18
Lois
Grade 2

Lois

Dear Mother,

Why can't I play in the rain? When it rains there is nothing to do. When it rains I want to put my shorts and my short sleve shirt on and go out side and play in the rain. One time I played in the rain cause daddy said I could.

FIGURE 8–19
No name
Grade 2

Dear Mom,

why can't I jump on my bed? It's so, so fun it does'nt make to much noise down stares. Oh please let me jump on my bed it's like a tranpalene. I could learn how to do flips and other things. Please, please, please!

THE POETIC MODE

Writing that is done in the poetic mode is meant to stand as a verbal object—something to be admired as a whole. Though the name "poetic" suggests that this mode is limited to poetry, it includes stories, plays, songs and the like. In this book, we will be concerned mostly with stories.

What is a story, anyway? Consider the following lines:

MERMAID

Once there was a boy who was always adventurous. He loved going into the woods nearby, and he loved the ponds. But out of everything he liked, his dream was to go out in the ocean and find a mermaid.

His mother thought it was really weird. She said: "There's no such thing as a mermaid." She said: "If you don't stop talking about mermaids I'm going to send you to bed without your dinner."

But Joe kept on talking about mermaids and as his mother said, he went to bed without any dinner. In the night he was really hungry and he couldn't get his mind off his dream. Then he got an idea: He could run away from home. He thought about it for a while and he got in his clothes and started walking away from his home.

After a while Joe came to a hut. He had four dollars with him and he wanted to buy a boat if he could. He knocked on the door and a man came out. Joe said: "Do you have a boat for sale?"

"Yes. I do. Please come in." The old man showed Joe some boats. Joe said: "I'll take the boat that's fifteen feet long." The old man said "Fine." and took his money, and Joe thanked him and left. The boat came with a wheelbarrow so he could bring it to the ocean. Joe walked for a long time. When he got to the ocean he was really excited. But he needed to get some sleep. He curled up under some leaves.

In the morning Joe got up and stretched and then pushed his boat into the water. He was missing his mother, but Joe thought: "I've come this far and I'm not going back now. Anyway she'd probably take my boat away so I couldn't go to the ocean again." Joe jumped in the boat and pulled the sail up.

Joe had been sailing for eight hours and was very sick. In the distance he saw an island. He headed for it. He landed on shore. He pulled his boat up beside him on the ground. Joe went to sleep on the sand.

When Joe woke up he was very hungry so he went into the jungle to get some food. He came back with a lot of fruit and started eating. In the middle of eating suddenly he heard someone saying "Help!" So he went to see what was the matter. He saw a mermaid stuck between two rocks. He ran back to his boat and went to help her. When he got there he pulled her out.

"How did you get caught in those rocks?" said Joe.

"The current pushed me into them, and I've been there ever since. I'm Elenor."

"Elenor, I have to go home now."

"Sure" said Elenor, and she swam away.

Joe missed Elenor, but Joe said: "I found what I wanted, so I'm going home." So he took off in his boat.

The End

Paul, Age 8

Unlike, say, the paragraph that preceded it, Paul's story doesn't represent the world in any direct way. We don't take Paul's story as proof of the existence of mermaids, or of the courage or sailing prowess of eight-year-old boys. No, stories do not point to the real world; rather they invent a world of their own, and take us into it. Since this is a world in which we aren't expected to do anything (unlike the world created by transactional text, in which we might be expected to fix a leaky faucet or vote Republican), James Britton suggests that poetic writing such as Paul's puts us in the *spectator's role* (rather than the *participant's*).[2]

How does Paul create this other world? In two ways. First he weaves it out of bits of stories he has heard,[9] plus a generous dose of his own imagination. We hear whispers in "Mermaid" of Maurice Sendak's *Where the Wild Things Are* and of Jean de Brunhof's *Babar and Zephir,* both of which Paul knew and liked. Those of us who know Paul recognize his love of boating (he is doubtlessly out sailing on Seneca Lake as we write this).

Secondly, he uses a particular weave, a particular pattern of language that honors the conventions we recognize in our culture as constituting a story. We are referring not only to his use of "once" and his describing magical events, but also to his introduction of a character in a setting, with a problem that leads him to set a goal, which inspires attempts to reach the goal, and outcomes of those attempts, a conclusion, and the character's reaction to what happened to him. These elements in approximately this order are common features in most of the stories we read.[10]

Younger children than Paul grapple with the same patterns Paul included in his story. Figure 8–20 is a sample written by Claudia, a first grader.

Claudia managed to include in this piece all of the elements we just mentioned: There are characters, there is a problem to be overcome and a goal, there is action toward achieving the goal, and there is success in its achievement. She fell short of success, only when it came to ordering those elements. The story would have had a clearer line of development and a bit more suspense had she put the goal toward the beginning of the story, rather than at the end.

Stories are such familiar forms to children that as teachers we often underestimate how difficult they are to produce. As Claudia's piece makes

FIGURE 8-20
Claudia
Grade 1

This stry is aBowt Wen
a man Co ld up The old
man it was a rany Day
he askt if He cooe
wrcke for him The old man
Sad yes I Do want To
wrke for you. The old man
and woman wer So happy
now we will not Be pore
The nex Day The old man
went to wrck in the
ev ng He came Bake with
Two Dolrs the old womin
was so Happy and The old
man Side He liked his work
He Began giting more and
more monny and Soon tha
wernt pore any more and
That is the end of my Story
 aBowt the old man and
The old womin By Clavia

clear, the successful story writer must set forth at least four different types of
story elements and arrange them in a certain order. That is a more complex
task than writing descriptions, or explanations, or arguments, or works of
expression.

CONCLUSION

In this chapter we described five basic forms of composition: expression,
description, exposition, argumentation, and story. To produce these forms, a
writer works in three rhetorical *modes:* the expressive, the transactional, and
the poetic. These can be displayed in diagram form, as shown in Figure 8-21.

FIGURE 8–21

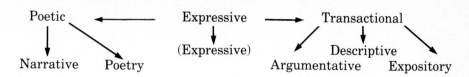

Children write most naturally in the expressive mode. As we shall see, their attempts to write in either the poetic or transactional mode—and the corresponding rhetorical forms—take some time to develop. In chapters 9 and 10 we will take a closer look at children's untaught efforts to compose in the poetic and transactional modes. Then, at the end of each chapter, we will discuss some examples of responsive teaching that have been tried to help children develop this ability.

REFERENCES

1. Jean Piaget. *The Language and Thought of the Child.* New York: New American Library, 1974.
2. James Britton. *Language and Learning.* Harmondsworth, England: Penguin Books, 1970.
3. Lawrence Sealy, Nancy Sealy, and Marjorie Millmore. *Children's Writing: An Approach for the Primary Grades.* Newark, Del.: International Reading Association, 1979.
4. Lee Galda. "Narrative Competence: Play, Storytelling, and Story Comprehension." In A.D. Pellegrini and T. Yawkey (ed.), *The Development of Oral and Written Language in Social Contexts.* Norwood, N.J.: Ablex, 1984.
5. Susan Sowers. "Young Writers' Preference for Non-Narrative Modes of Composition." Paper presented at the Fourth Annual Boston University Conference on Language Development, Boston, 1979.
6. Aliki Brandenberg. *My Visit to the Dinosaurs.* New York: Crowell, 1969.
7. Edwin Way Teale (ed.). *The Insect World of J. Henri Fabre.* New York: Dodd Mead, 1949.
8. Roy Weaver. *A Rhetoric and Composition Handbook.* New York: Morrow, 1974.
9. Robert Scholes. *Semiotics and Interpretation.* New Haven, Ct.: Yale University Press, 1982.
10. Jean Mandler and Nancy Johnson. "On the Remembrance of Things Parsed: Story Structure and Recall." *Cognitive Psychology,* 9 (1977): 111–151.

9/ *Writing in the Poetic Mode*

Stories are not like other forms of discourse: They are special creations that strike some essential chord in the human soul. Laurens van der Post, a novelist who grew up on a farm among traditional peoples in South Africa, finds evidence of this truth in the testament of a Kalahari Bushman unjustly imprisoned a hundred years ago in the city of Cape Town, a man who was "sick even more for stories than for home or people."

> Thou knowest that I wait for the moon to turn back, that I may listen to all the people's stories . . . For I am here—in a great city—I do not obtain stories . . . I do merely listen, watching for a story which I want to hear; that it may float into my ear . . . I will go to sit at my home that I may listen, turn my ears backwards to the heels of my feet on which I wait, so that I can feel that a story is in wind.[1]

What is it that this man longs for, more than home and friends? An experience like a trance, we would say, that at once detaches him from the concerns of the moment and tells him the truth more directly than he would otherwise ever hear it from the lips of his neighbors.

It is not surprising that children who were brought up on stories should want to write their own. But stories are enchantments, and they take some weaving. As young writers learn to weave stories, what exactly do they achieve? What qualities of story do they weave into their writing, and how does the addition of each new strand affect the whole text? These questions will concern us in the following sections, in which we will describe what we believe to be important constituents of stories, and go on to show the emergence of these constituents in the work of one first-grade boy whose writing we will follow through a whole year and one girl whose writing we will follow through second grade. Then, in the latter part of this chapter, we will look at some kinds of help teachers can offer young writers to craft finer stories.

THE SHAPE OF OTHERNESS: CHILDREN'S STORIES

Stories have a sense of otherness. When we begin reading a story, right away our attention is drawn out of our everyday concerns into a new world that has been created by the author. Sometimes this world seems pretty much like our own, as it does in Ezra Jack Keats's realistic fiction. Sometimes, though, this world is quite different—especially in fiction for young children. How do authors go about creating a sense of otherness, a separate world?

Setting and Characters

One way to establish otherness is with fictional characters in fictional places. In the storytelling tradition of the Appalachian Mountains, all you have to do is mention *Jack* and your listener will expect a tale about an unsophisticated but ultimately resourceful hero. Mention *Anansi* in the West African and Caribbean tradition, and your hearers will wait for a story about a clever trickster who often prevails by calling upon loyal family members. Mention *Smurfette*, and your hearers may expect a Madison Avenue–manipulated children's fantasy.

Animal characters or exotic settings usually mean fiction. Jessica's story in Chapter 8 (see page 118) serves as an example. Super powers or extraordinary possessions mean the same. All of these are cues to the audience that they are to receive the text as a story.

Conventional Story Language

"Once upon a time . . . ;" "Suddenly . . . ;" "a teeny tiny man . . . ;" "quick as a wink. . . ." These expressions are heard so frequently in children's stories and so rarely in other contexts that their very presence signals the narrative mode. The same is true of sequences that repeat and build, as in "First she sat in the big chair, but it was too hard; then she sat in the middle-sized chair, but it was too soft; then she sat in the littlest chair, and it was just right."

Mary Tyler wrote the line in Figure 9–1. Then she dictated the following text:

> Once upon a time there was a unicorn and she met a dragon in the woods and she married him and then all the ants, all the deer, and all the foxes gathered as much food as they could and that night they married.
> The End
> Mary Tyler, Age 5

Mary Tyler's piece uses both of the fictional devices we described above: exotic characters and a faraway setting. She also uses the conventional

FIGURE 9–1
Mary Tyler
Age 5

language of stories. She begins with "Once upon a time . . ." and also uses repetition: "All of the ants . . . , all of the deer . . . , and all of the foxes gathered. . . ." Not yet able to write the words she wants, though, she relied upon the conventional phrase, "Once upon a time," to stand for the story she wished to convey.

Focus on Topic

Story tellers create fictional worlds and stay within them. They resist the temptation of putting their own egocentric concerns ahead of relating the tale, as Jessica nearly did in her rabbit story. They resist the urge to be led away from their topic, as one thing suggests another: when the audience is told they will hear a story about a unicorn and a dragon, that is what they want to hear. It is all right to describe what all of the other animals do, so long as their actions relate to the story line about the main characters. In Mary Tyler's story, the actions of all the other animals turned out to be in preparation for the wedding of the main characters. But see what happens in another child's story:

> A carrot grew up in the garden. Then a boy came and picked the carrot and ate him. The boy played with a toy truck in the garden. Then the boy's mother called him to supper. His daddy was home. His daddy bought him a present. It was a toy tractor. The daddy is a fireman.
>
> Brad, Age 4

Arthur Applebee, who studied children's writing along with James Britton in England, has another way of expressing this requirement that the details of a story relate to the topic. He notes that the details of a story must be both *chained* (related one to another) and *centered* (related to the same character, problem, or issue).[2] For example, in Mary Tyler's story about the unicorn's romance, the events were chained, or related, in the sense that one thing led to another. The events were all centered in that everything that happened in the story was related to the romance and marriage of the unicorn and the dragon. Brad's story is chained (one event follows another) but not centered. The carrot that opens the piece is gobbled up in the second sentence and seen no more. The boy then becomes the center of attention, but quickly yields the spotlight first to his mother, then to his father.

Amanda's story is neither chained nor centered:

> The moon and a cow. The cow and a spoon. Farmer and the grass. Grass is hay. Jumping, jumping in the haystack. Edwin ran away. His mother can't find him. She's sad.
>
> Amanda, Age 3

Because the events in Amanda's story are neither chained nor centered, in Applebee's scheme of things they are the most primitive kind of story.

Chaining and centering are the two key ways children manage the complexity of story telling. Applebee found that they don't master these two tasks all at once; and he observed growth and development in children's ability to handle these concerns, some examples of which we shall see below.

The Structure of Children's Stories

The notions of chaining and centering do not suggest the complex ways in which stories relate characters and events to each other and to larger concerns. Complex as they are, though, the patterns of relationships among story elements are strikingly uniform from tale to tale. It is possible to describe these relationships using a short set of ordered terms. We will set those out directly; but first, let us trot out the story of Sam, the unlucky dog, to provide a context in which we can illustrate the terms that will follow.

> Once, there was a big brown dog named Sam. One day Sam found a piece of meat and was carrying it home in his mouth to eat. Now on his way home, he had to cross a plank lying across a running brook. As he crossed the brook, he looked down and saw his own shadow reflected in the water beneath.
>
> He thought it was another dog with another piece of meat and he made up his mind to have that piece also. So he made a snap at the shadow, but as he opened his mouth the piece of meat fell out. The meat dropped into the water and floated away. Sam never saw the meat again.[3]

A description of the structure of the Sam story in terms general enough to apply to other stories might follow the lines laid down in a story grammar developed by two cognitive psychologists, Jean Mandler and Nancy Johnson. A simple form of their story grammar would have the following elements: a *setting*, an *initiating event*, an *internal response*, a *goal*, an *attempt*, an *outcome*, a *consequence,* and a *reaction.*[4] Let us define these elements now and illustrate them, using the story of the unfortunate dog, Sam.

1. *A setting*—The main character is introduced in some place at some time.

> *Once there was a big brown dog named Sam. One day, Sam found a piece of meat and was carrying it home in his mouth to eat. Now on his way home, he had to cross a brook.*

2. *An initiating event*—There is an occurrence, or an idea strikes someone and sets events in motion in the story, or causes some important response in the main character.

> *He looked down and saw his shadow reflected in the water beneath.*

3. *An internal response*—Following the initiating event, the main character has an idea and sets a goal.

He thought it was another dog with another piece of meat and he made up his mind to have that piece also.

4. *An attempt*—The character makes some overt action to achieve the goal.

So he made a snap at the shadow,

5. *An outcome*—Another event or a new state of affairs follows as a result of the attempt.

but as he opened his mouth, the piece of meat fell out.

6. *A consequence*—Some action or new situation results from the character's success or failure to achieve the goal.

The meat dropped into the water and floated away.

7. *A reaction*—There is some emotion, some idea, or some further action that may either express the character's feelings about whether or not he achieved his goal, or relates his success or failure to some broader set of concerns.

Sam never saw the meat again.

Thus far we have looked at the ways stories do their work—how they create a different world, a sense of otherness. We have looked, too, at how writers give them shape, by centering and chaining, and by employing story elements—setting, character, initiating events, goals, attempts, outcomes, consequences and reactions—all in their conventional order.

How do children who want to write stories learn to manage all of these complexities? We get some idea by observing the development of two young writers, Joey and Sarah. We will follow Joey's story writing through his first-grade year, and Sarah's from mid-first grade to the end of her second-grade year.

JOEY'S WORKS: A FIRST GRADER LEARNS TO WRITE STORIES

Joey was a first grader in Angell Elementary School, in Berkeley, Michigan, a community near Detroit. He was a confident and prolific writer. His work folder had entries dating from the third week in September; most had big, colorful pictures and full sentence captions. He spelled some words correctly—"love," "like," "is," and "can"—and he didn't hesitate to invent spellings for other words: "dinosaur," "rocket," "blast off," and others. For the first six weeks of school, the form his early writings took were almost all expressive. He used two familiar features from this form: the *love/like inventory* that Susan Sowers noted in the New Hampshire studies,[5] and the dialogue—using the language of conversation as a model by which to structure writing. Figures 9–2 and 9–3 are examples of his early work.

In late October he began to write pieces with fictional topics (he continued to write other kinds of pieces, too—mainly expressive pieces, notes to friends, and expository and descriptive pieces). We decided to use the presence of such fictional topics as a criterion of story-ness and chose the twenty-two pieces that met this criterion for analysis.

The first piece with a fictional topic is seen in Figure 9–4. He established his (sort of) fictional topic with a nice drawing of a rocket, then went on to write "A USA rocket is taking off." But what to do next? A problem in all story writing is how to give structure to the work. By what principle does one stretch

FIGURE 9–2

FIGURE 9–3

FIGURE 9–4

out word after word to fill lots of space, as professional writers do? Joey solved the problem with the device of repetition, by reciting the count-down sequence. It doesn't take his story very far, but it is vivid and appropriate to the topic of rockets, and it fills the page nicely.

He did a similar thing in his next piece, about a turkey (see Figure 9–5). A drawing of the turkey anchored down his topic. For his structure this time he relied on the repetition of turkey sounds and a dialogue: "Gobble, gobble. Who is that turkey, big and fat? Gobble, gobble." Again, this strategy addresses the topic vividly, though it doesn't approach being a plot yet; there is nothing to propel the story forward.

There is something new in this piece: the conventionalized sentence structure of story language. "Who is that turkey, big and fat?" is not the syntax of speech, but it has the cadence of the storyteller's language.

The next piece uses a storybook character, Mr. Bump (see Figure 9–6). Here is a fictional character, taken from a series of books for children. Having introduced him, now what? Around what structure will the writer organize more sentences about him? The solution again is found in dialogue, this one between Mr. Bump and Mr. Nosy. This dialogue seems to follow its own logic, rather than to develop any story. Applebee would say that the sentences are *chained* (each one suggests the next) but not well *centered* (they don't develop to any point).[2]

The next piece introduces another character from the same book series, this one Mr. Bounce (see Figure 9–7). The structure used here is one of action, relating all of the things that Mr. Bounce does: He bounces all over the place, bounces out of the window, and has to go to the B.R. (bathroom?). But these

FIGURE 9–5

Goibal Goibal
Hiou is Taet
Takre dig and
Eat Goibal
Goibal.

FIGURE 9–6

MR BUMP.

MR. Bump I'm
MR Bump
Why are you Calling me?
MR. Noes Be Kas
I want you.
Joey

FIGURE 9–7

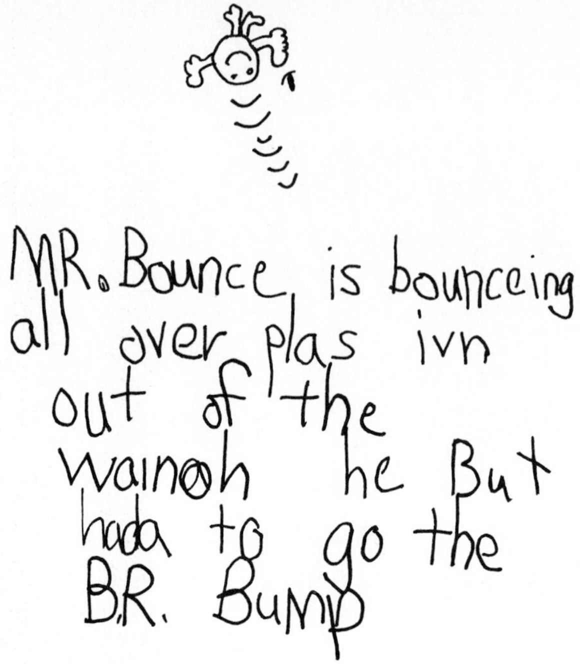

MR. Bounce is bounceing
all over plas ivn
out of the
wainoh   he But
hada to go the
B.R. Bump

actions still do not develop into a plot, and again we would say, in Applebee's terms, that the events are chained but very weakly centered—we hear of things that Mr. Bounce does, but the actions do not develop any point.

In mid-December Joey returned to the theme of rocket launching (see Figure 9–8). The last time he wrote on this topic he simply announced the topic and then wrote out the count-down sequence. This time he adds another line that uses the diction of an eye-witness reporter—"Off the rocket goes"—and then a piece of description—"In the rocket are some astronauts"—that might eventually lead into the development of a plot, but doesn't yet.

The use of description is taken much further in this next piece (see Figure 9–9). Now his use of description has become almost lyrical. "The cows are mooing, the sheep are baying. The brightest star is shining so bright, wakes Jesus up and Mary and Joseph." The details are nicely focused around the topic of the Nativity, and the little bit of action Joey has written into his piece gives it the quality of an animated tableau. But it is still a tableau, not a developed story, there is still no problem, no effort, and no solution.

After Christmas recess Joey took a giant step forward (see Figure 9–10). Joey consciously imitated the fairy tale form, and in so doing used the conventionally phrased story opener, "Once upon a time." But he did more: The undifferentiated actions that had characterized his earlier stories he now divided into a problem and an effort to solve it—"He was cold for the winter so he went to get some trees for his fireplace."

FIGURE 9–8

he is borting off
.10. 9. 8. 7. 6. 5. 4. 3. 2. 1.
bact off   So
off they go

off the rocket gos
in the rocket are
sem astronaut

FIGURE 9–9

The cios are
moing the srep
are baing
the bratis sir
is sining so brat
wozle ius up and
Miare and Joeshs

FIGURE 9–10

Wasns apon a time
thir was a giant piking
sam treesfor hisfuirplas
he was cold for the
wenter so he went
Joey to get som he gather
som more trees he was
cold

Another piece from late January showed a slighter development over his earlier work (see Figure 9–11). To this point his pieces have tended to feature action or description, but not both. But now in writing about ET's landing, he integrates good description—"His ship was big. It had many lights"—with more action—"ET was landing on earth . . . It [the spaceship] was landing that night." A pattern is emerging here: A story element will first appear in and dominate an early piece of writing before it is combined with one or more elements in another piece of writing, sometimes weeks later.

Early in February Joey appears to be consolidating his move to separate problems or causes from actions or efforts. Now it is explained that the boy is running because the ghost is chasing him (see Figure 9–12). In early February Joey wrote a Valentine piece. This is the first time that he added to the picture on the second day (see Figure 9–13). This piece shows several new developments. His first day's effort was essentially an expressive piece. The tendency to write a love/like inventory came through strongly—"I love my Dad, I love my Mom, I love my sister." On the second day he turned the piece into a story. He used himself as the character—the first time he'd done that in his fictional pieces. He also used his drawing to convey the action in the story, something he didn't do again, to such an extent, after writing this piece. Finally, in this piece he used directly quoted speech to express some of the action, before when he had quoted dialogues, these tended to digress from the direction of the story.

FIGURE 9–11

ET was landing
on erth his sihp was
big it had many laies
bt was in it it was
landing that nithe

FIGURE 9–12

the ghost was chosing
after the boy the boy
was scrared the boy
ran fast as he can.

FIGURE 9–13

I'm running too kicha a heart for my valentine I Love my Dad I Love my mom I Love my stler valentine are nice I Love tiem

oh no I'm in tralbel I don't now what to do helq, helq, helq I min tralbel yes I am, what shaed a I do helq helq me

FIGURE 9–14

A heart fairy Is coming I'm running to get a heart hi fairy can I have aheart yes you can thankyou vevrymuch, you're waelkkcome!

The next week, in his "heart fairy" piece (Figure 9–14), he again used himself as a central character, though he introduced a novel character in the heart fairy. This piece continued to observe the division between problem and solution (or we might say goal and attempt, or justification and action). It also used dialogue to carry the plot further, something Joey had not done successfully before.

The "Leprechaun" piece, again, has Joey as the central character (see Figure 9–15). The structure has become something like introductory action + problem-raising action + reaction. The actions have a definite time sequence to them: (1) "I found a Leprechaun," (2) "I touched it," (3) "I begin to turn into a Leprechaun," (4) "Oh no, look at me. I'm a Leprechaun."

This is the second piece (the first being the Valentine story of a month before) that he wrote in the first person. Before, his choosing the first person seemed to invite him to lapse into the digressive love/like inventory, that familiar feature of expressive writing. Now the expressive urge seems to have settled on the *reaction* in the piece: "Yaaaaaaaaaay, I'm a Leprechaun. . . . Good. I'm happy."

The short piece in Figure 9–16 uses the picture to portray some of the action, to show what the problem is. It also uses dialogue successfully to carry the story forward. It lacks explanation to support the dialogue.

The Cobra piece (Figure 9–17) is a further development along a line that began with the Valentine and continued with the Leprechaun. We readers are still plopped right into the middle of the action from the first sentence, an effect we have called *introductory action.* But this action, too, is broken into parts that allow some development in time—"The cobra is winning. The rattle is not . . . The cobra won."

The action, again, is followed by *reactions*—"That's great, the cobra is winning." It's not clear just who is cheering, but again this appears to be a throwback to the expressive urges in his Valentine piece.

FIGURE 9–15

FIGURE 9–16
(left)

FIGURE 9–17
(right and below)

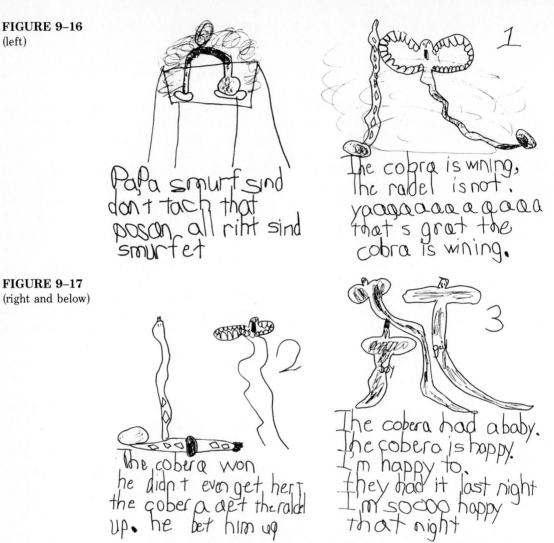

Papa smurf sind
don't tach that
posan, all riht sind
smurf et

The cobra is wining,
the radel is not.
yaaaaaaa a aaaa
that's grat the
cobra is wining.

the cobera won
he didn't even get hert
the cober a aet the raldel
up. he bet him up

The cobera had a baby.
the cobera is happy.
I'm happy to.
they had it last night
I'm soooo happy
that night

Ten days later Joey wrote the mouse piece (Figure 9–18). This piece had a nice story shape. It began with the familiar introductory action, the combination *setting* and *initiating event* of the story grammar—"My raccoon found a mouse." It continued with an *internal response*—"He liked him"—then went on to a sort of undifferentiated main action—"He invited the mouse to his home." Then followed two reactions—"The mouse was glad. The raccoon is happy."

Joey wrote only one story in April. It was about Transformers (see Figure 9–19). The topic didn't seem to inspire him, and the form of his story showed no development over what he was able to do weeks before.

FIGURE 9–18

myraccoon fond amosue
he liked him so he
invaded themosue.
to his home themosue
was glad,the raccoonis
happy.

FIGURE 9–19

by: Joey Higgins BooM!

The trace fomers won
the batle.
Of the dekeperon. the
place car shot the
bose with a lazer
gun. Trace fomers

In early May he managed to work the then-popular expression "Where's the beef?" into his story (see Figure 9–20). The rest of the piece is structured around a dialogue that strays completely from "Where's the beef."

FIGURE 9–20

The next week, still working on fitting sayings from the popular media into his writing, Joey wrote "beat it" (see Figure 9–21). This time he succeeded admirably by using techniques he already knew. He opened with his familiar introductory action, but this time, instead of using his punch line right away, he let his introduction set up a context for it—"I ran away with the radio, and some cookies." He used some descriptive detail, something else he had known how to do for months—"It was a half moon . . ." and then slipped his punch line in as part of the description—"On the radio the song was 'Beat it, just beat it.' "

With this piece, he achieved another dynamic tableau, this one with sight and sound and action. But note that he still hasn't combined his real descriptive power with plot development—the pieces with elaborate descriptive detail don't yet develop any sequence of initiating events, goals, actions, and reactions.

FIGURE 9–21

I ran away with the radio. and some cookies it was a hafe moon that night. on the radio the song was Beit Just Beit.

The next week Joey goes again to the popular media for story characters, but his piece about Care Bears—like the ones about Smurfs and Transformers—fails to take off (see Figure 9–22).

Can we make the generalization that popular media characters fail to trigger very imaginative stories? This seems to be true of one-dimensional characters—Smurfs, Care Bears, Transformers, and He-Man.

But E.T. seems to be the exception. His appearance was the occasion of Joey's experimenting with something new: integrating Rebus-like drawings into his text (see Figure 9–23). Still, the experiment didn't seem to lead him where he wanted to go. He didn't use this technique again that year.

FIGURE 9–22

FIGURE 9–23

The next week he wrote his roller coaster paper (Figure 9–24). It is the longest piece he wrote all year, with the longest text and the most detailed drawings. This piece contains a surprising number of elaborations over previous works. It has his first use of a title—"My roller coaster." His introductory action is finally split into an introductory description—"My roller coaster is a fun ride"—followed by an action—"Everybody takes a ride on it." There is specifying detail—"The kids are Toni and Justin and Fred and Malisa too"—but this time the detail doesn't overshadow the development of the story.

In continuing the story, he put in dialogue that carried his story forward ("Time to go home, kids" "Ahhh"). This time, too, it was clear who was doing the reacting; and the reaction was part of the plot: His friends expressed disappointment over going home, so Joey explained that he had to eat, and invited them back another day.

FIGURE 9–24

My roller coaster
My roller coaster
is a fun ride.
Evrey body takes
a ride on it.
The kids, are Toni
and Justin and
Fred and malisa
too. It isfun very
fun

FIGURE 9–24
(continued)

Time to go
home kids ahhh!
I have to eat.
That's bad
bye-bye kids
bye Joey.
You can play to
moyro bye-bye.

The next day,
they had lots of
fun. Thay loved the
four lops to lops
thay went on and
and on and

FIGURE 9–25

My 1 sped Dert bike
My one sped Dert bike
Is very fast.
I peldle and peldle
To go very fast.
I wender if I'll win
the Dert bike rase

me
Steve
AAP
Finsh line

The rase
The rase was finsh
I won said Steve.
I won said Lee
Joey won wow

Joey's last story turned out to be the best developed. He seemed to integrate into it almost everything he had learned about writing stories his first-grade year (see Figure 9–25).

He began with a title, and for the second time used his two-part introduction (description + action). But in this story he went on to put in a problem: He was in a race, and he wondered if he would win it. Now, he had put problems and solutions into his stories before, but this time he went a step further. He used dialogue, something he had also included many times, to *delay the solution* and hence to create suspense:

The race was finished. "I won," said Steve.

"I won," said Lee.

"Joey won. Wow!"

And he finished off with a one-word reaction.

So at the end of Joey's first year of composing, we find a piece that culminates his development very nicely. It combines in one story elements that had each made its debut alone. We saw topics introduced, followed by descriptions. We saw personal reactions. We saw problems. We saw dialogs. We saw story language. But only in the final piece do we see them all together.

SARAH'S WORKS: LITERATURE INFLUENCES STORY DEVELOPMENT

We've seen in Joey's writing over the course of the year a spirit of eager experimentalism and growth in his ability to generate longer and longer texts, by using such devices as problem + comment, problem + solution + comment, description, and dialogue. Some figures and phrases from popular culture that struck his ear made their way into his compositions: E.T., Care Bears, "Where's the Beef?," "Beat It," and "Mr. Bounce."

Let us look now at Sarah. Unlike Joey, Sarah seems to have assimilated a good deal of literature into her writing. We meet her in mid-first grade and follow her development through grade two.

In December of first grade the children in Sarah's class were passing around *Lollipop* by Wendy Watson:

> One time Bunny wanted a lollipop
> and Mom said "No"
> and Bunny kept wanting and wanting
> and Mom said "No"
> and Bunny kept wanting and wanting
> and Mom said "NO!"[6]

During writing workshop one day Sarah wrote "Julie," in Figure 9–26. "Julie" is not a close borrowing from *Lollipop,* but it does incorporate two of that story's features. The repetition of "wanting and wanting" is reflected in "nobody, nobody" and "happy, happy, happy." Also, the use of capitals to signal strong emphasis is repeated in "nobody, NOBODY," and "HAPPY HAPPY HAPPY."

Sarah wrote "The Changing Boy" (see p. 167) in the fall of her second-grade year. We can discern in it two influences from the literature she had heard and read. First, as her class was in the midst of a unit on Africa, she had listened to many African folktales, as well as parts of a story by the Nigerian novelist, Amos Tutuola, who writes in a folktale style:

FIGURE 9–26
Sarah
Grade 1

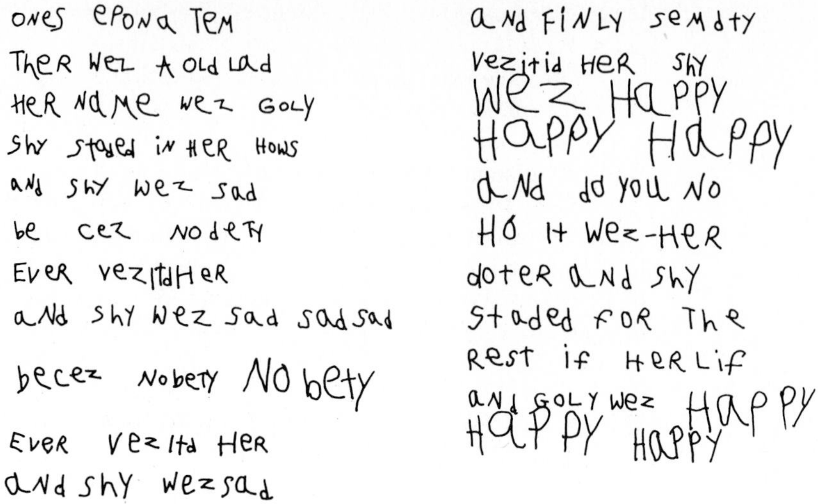

ones epona Tem
TheR Wez A old Lad
HeR Name wez Goly
shy stayed iN HeR Hows
aNd shy wez sad
be cez Nodety
EveR vezItdHeR
aNd shy Wez sad sadsad

becez Nobety No bety

EveR VezItd HeR
aNd shy Wezsad

aNd FINLY semdty
vezitid HeR shy
WEZ HaPPY
HaPPY HaPPY
aNd do you No
Ho It Wez-HeR
doteR aNd shy
staded foR The
Rest if HeRLif
aNd GoLy wez HaPPY
HaPPY HaPPY

I lay down near my bag of food. I used the bag of juju as a pillow, while I put my heavy matchet and bow and arrows of poison closely to my right hand. . . .

As I opened my eyes and sat upright with great fear, I saw a horrible black being who squatted very closely to me. . . . His head was bigger than necessary with two fearful eyes. The two eyes went deeply into his skull. The hair on his head was so long that it covered his breast. It was muddled together as if it was rubbed with a large quantity of thick grease. . . .

. . . Without wasting a sixtieth of a twinkling, I continued my journey.[7]

Tutuola's story carries on for nearly two hundred pages with a wonderful spirit of one magical thing following another, a spirit that seems to have infected Sarah's story, "The Changing Boy."

A second influence is the character who changes his identity. Such characters are commonplace in folklore. Note the following sequence from "Taleisen," one of many such tales Sarah heard that year. This segment tells of the escape of the hero, Gwion Bach, from the witch, Caridwen:

And she went forth after him, running. And he saw her, and turned himself into a hare and fled. But she changed herself into a greyhound and turned him. And he ran towards a river, and became a fish. And she in the form of an otter . . . chased him under the water, until he was fein to turn himself into a bird of the air. She, as a hawk, followed him and gave him no rest in the sky. And just as she was about to swoop upon him, and he was in fear of death, he espied a heap of winnoed wheat upon the floor of a barn, and he dropped among the wheat, and turned himself into one of the grains. Then she transformed herself into a high-crested black hen, and went to the wheat and scratched it with her feet, and found him out and swallowed him. And, as the story says, she bore him nine months, and when she was delivered of him, she could not find it in her heart to kill him. . . . So she wrapped him in a leathern bag, and cast him into the sea to the mercy of God, on the twenty-ninth day of April.[8]

Sarah seems to have adapted this idea of the metamorphosizing hero in her "Changing Boy."

The Changing Boy

It was a stormy night. I was walking home when I came to a shack. It was so stormy that I went inside and what did I see but a bag.

I was so curious that I opened it. I heard a voice say, "Thank you. I was just going to ask you to do that."

I looked inside the bag. There were lots of bones. The voice said, "Put me together."

I was very curious so I put him together. It was a huge skeleton. "Now I will eat you!"

I ran right out of the shack and into a cave and put a rock in the door. All of the sudden the light turned on. I saw a witch and a bunch of spiders.

"Here is another boy. Shall I turn him into a spider, too? These spiders were once boys, but they got turned into spiders because they did the same thing as you and I will turn you into a spider, too!"

And she pulled out of her pocket a wishbone and said

POOF!

and I felt myself change. I was a spider.

Then she fell asleep. With no sound at all I took the wish bone and ran out of the cave. When I got out I changed back into a boy.

Then a hand grabbed me and took me to a house. But it was just a hand that went down the chimney and attached to a lady. She kissed me. Oh, she stunk! We watched TV. Then she rocked me. Then a HUGE DOG came into the room and ate me. I could hear the lady yelling, "Alfred, you know little boys have to be cooked before eating!"

Then I remembered the wishbone. I said

POOF!

Finally I was home in bed and sound asleep and happy, too.

The End

Sarah, Age 7

In January of her second-grade year Sarah's teacher told the story "Don't Count Your Chickens Before They Hatch."

One summer morning a woman named Petina walked down a country road on her way to market carrying a large jug on her head, carefully set on a little cushion. She had just finished the milking and was thinking how lucky the customer would be who would buy such fresh and foaming milk. "I will ask three pennies for it, and perhaps my customer will give me one extra, because it is such a fine day," she thought. "With four pence I can buy four eggs, maybe more, and I will set them under my hens and when they hatch I can trade them for a little pig. After I fatten him up I'm sure someone will want to trade him for a young calf. When my calf becomes a fine bull he will win prizes, gold pieces with which I will buy fine gowns, and weddings for my children with musicians . . ." Petina skipped with pleasure at the thought, but alas, when she did, the jug slipped and crashed on the ground, splashing milk everywhere.

(An interesting variant of this and other familiar tales is found in Idries Shah, *World Tales*. New York: Harcourt Brace Jovanovich, 1979.)

Sarah set out deliberately to write a piece with a similar structure. She wrote "Amanda."

Once there was a little girl named Amanda. She was walking down the street with a cake on the top of her head yelling, a cake for sale! If I sell this cake I will get lots of money for it. Then I will buy myself a farm with all of the animals I like. But when everyone saw her with a cake on her head they laughed and laughed. One little boy laughed so hard he tipped over backward, dropping the eggs he was holding and knocking Amanda off her feet so there was a mess of eggs and cake. Amanda feeling very sad. Not rich. Just the same.

Sarah managed to capture both the form and the sense of the story of the milkmaid. At the same time, she put her own stamp on the plot, adding the boy whose laughter makes him drop eggs in her path and cause her to fall. The piece is derivative, but it has a complex structure and a sense of irony that are rare in second-grade writing. Sarah's imitation of the original is sufficiently different in detail to suggest that she has used the structure of it to generate her own story, rather than imitating the original detail for detail.

By May of her second-grade year, Sarah was able to sustain the writing of one story over several sessions. Her story about Rudie's adventures at summer camp we had to excerpt because it is four chapters and twelve pages long!

Rudie Goes to Summer Camp

Rudie was at school when his teacher gave him a note and said to give it to his mother. Rudie did. It said:

Dear Mrs. Vernen,
    I think you should get your son in with a few more boys by sending him to camp.

When Rudie arrived at camp . . . at cabin 15 . . . he was greeted by a man named Chip. He told Rudie he was the first one. He could have his choice of beds. Rudie picked the bottom bunk of one of the beds. Chip said he was going to go greet the others. While Chip was doing that, Rudie yanked the sheets down from up above him and draped them down over the opening.

The last one in was Mike. He walked in glumly. All the beds were occupied but the one up above the strange, mysterious bed. Mike had no choice. He climbed the ladder to the top bunk.

"Hey! There's no sheets on this bed" he yelled.

"What's going on in here? Rudie, is that you in there? Chip tore the sheets down. . . .

"Now it's supper time," said Chip. "Kids, you're at table 15."

"Ugh! That number again!" mumbled Rudie.

"What is this stuff?" asked Rudie when they got to the table.

"It's my famous stew. It's very good," said Mike, who had not even tried it.

"Since you like it so much, have mine." Rudie scraped his plate onto Mike's plate.

"Rudie, leave the table!"

"Gladly," said Rudie.

Sarah, Age 8

By now, Sarah's reading consisted of longer books, too. She was especially fond of Beverly Cleary's books about Ramona, a very normally maladjusted school girl to whom painfully funny things happen with regularity. Ramona's adventures show a child's-eye view of a world designed by well-meaning but not very perceptive adults. Without imitating Ramona's adventures point for point, Sarah uses many of those stories' features to create a story that is very much her own. The realism of the Ramona stories is there; so is the irony of having adults planning your life without consulting you. Ramona's wry verbal humor, too, seems to have rubbed off on Rudie. Even the outer form of the Ramona books—a story sustained across several chapters— is reproduced in Sarah's writing.

In these two children, Joey and Sarah, we have seen the earlier and later phases of developing story writing. In the earlier development represented by Joey, it is possible to see each feature enter into his writing and gradually become elaborated and diversified into different features. Much of this development appears to come from the inside: Joey's cognitive and linguistic development controls much of the agenda, while the influence of the writing and language he sees and hears around him are only indirectly and sporadically reflected.

In Sarah's writing, the relative importance of her conceptual development and of the influence of the texts she hears and reads have become more of a blend. Her power over the forms and features of stories has continued to grow. But her development follows no single track now. The course of Sarah's story development has diversified, and the pathways are as many and various as the stories and authors who have captured her imagination. Sarah has become able to take in the stories she hears and reads as raw materials for her own creations.[9] She has thus become an active participant in the conversation of authors, the conversation we call literature.

DEVELOPING THE POETIC MODE IN SCHOOL

Joey's and Sarah's teachers and many others have struggled to create an atmosphere and a system in classrooms where children view themselves as writers. In these process classrooms, as they are called, children are given time, encouragment, a ready audience, feedback, and occasional mini-lessons on such points as writing exciting beginnings and using quotation marks. The process approach to the teaching of writing is based on a belief that the driving force behind young children's learning is their own interest in life, coupled with their desire to express themselves. Advocates of process writing also point out that too much instruction stifles a child's urge to express herself and dissipates her learning energy and sense of purpose. Instruction is given at the point of need; in other words, a child is taught the use of a semi-colon when one is needed in her particular piece of writing.[10] The process approach to writing has been introduced into many public schools across the country and has been shown to be very successful. Because it has worked as a way of teaching writing to young children, it is taking root. We think it is one of the best things happening in schools today.

Therefore, it is with some trepidations that we include in this book the following experiments in "teaching" story-writing. In the classes where the following exercises were observed, the teacher felt that a majority of students were at a "point of need" as far as organizing and deepening stories was concerned; and she felt that instruction around these challenges would be most beneficial to children in groups, where they could learn from each other. Having carefully established writing workshop or free writing time as an opportunity for children to choose their own topics and work on their own initiative (see Chapter 11), she was reluctant to give any assignments during that time. Therefore, she established a separate writing instruction time at a different point in the day, for assignments, discussions, games, and so forth, designed to enrich the children's writing. We include these observations because they begin to answer some interesting questions.

Story Grammar

What happens when in addition to their free writing time, children are also given some exercises in inventing and shaping stories? As children progress as writers, they are sometimes frustrated by a sense that their stories are not as complete as they would like them to be, or they feel caught in a rut of sameness and begin to lose interest in writing. When several of her students seemed to be at this point, one first- through third-grade teacher, decided that sharing story grammar with them might help.

> *Teacher:* How many of you remember the story of the Three Billy Goats Gruff? Everybody? Great. [Writes the word "setting" on the board.] Who can tell me the setting of the Three Billy Goats Gruff?
>
> *Child:* What's a setting?

Child:	Like a set. A backdrop.
Child:	Mountains.
Child:	There's a stream.
Children (together):	And a bridge. And under the bridge is hiding the mean troll . . .
Teacher:	Right. You've got it. The setting is the place where the story takes place. And also part of the setting can be the time when the story takes place. When did the Three Billy Goats Gruff happen?
Child:	Never.
Child:	Once upon a time.
Child:	No. It was in the spring when the grass was high.
Child:	If it never happened you wouldn't have a story.
Teacher:	Who are the characters in the story? [Writes up the word "characters".]
Child:	Ch-
Child:	The goats; and the troll.
Teacher:	Anybody else?
Children:	[after a pause] No. Just the goats and the troll.
Teacher:	[Writes the word "problem".] Do these characters have a problem? Let's take the goats. Do the goats have a problem?
Child:	They are hungry, and they want to go over the bridge and eat grass.
Child:	And they are scared too, because the troll under the bridge will kill them.
Child:	Yeah. Smash em.
Teacher:	[Writes "solution" on the board.] So what's the solution for these goats? Let's act it out.

The children grew familiar with the terms *setting, character, problem,* and *solution,* which is simplified story grammar, by discussing stories they already knew, stories they wrote themselves, stories they read on their own. Figure 9–27 shows the homework of a second grader who was asked to analyze a Raggedy Ann story.

During writing workshop time, both the teacher and the children began using these simple story grammar terms in conferring with each other. Here are some random excerpts from conferences in that class:

Child:	Can a robot be a character?
Child:	Sure, if he's a thinking robot . . .
Teacher:	I have this wonderful setting for my story, but I can't seem to get beyond it. I'm having a hard time thinking of characters . . .

FIGURE 9–27
Sarah
Grade 2

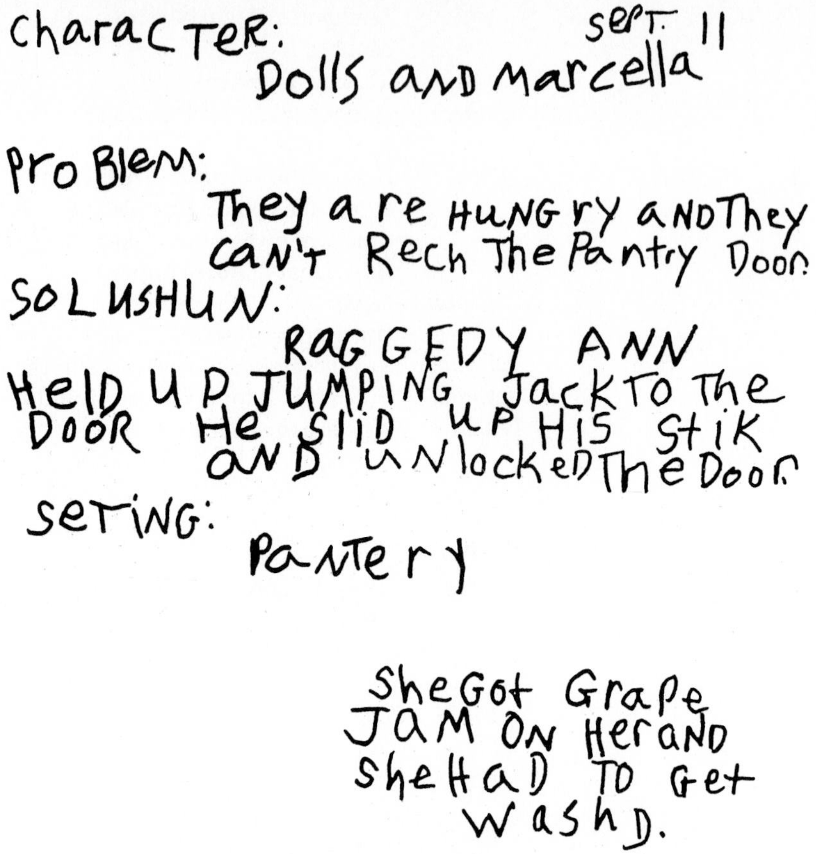

characTeR: sePT. 11
        Dolls aND marcella

ProBlem:
        They a re HuNG ry aNDThey
        caN't Rech The Pantry Door.
SoLusHuN:
              RaGGEDY ANN
HelD uP JuMPING JackTo The
Door He SliD uP HiS StiK
      aND uNlockeDThe Door.
        seTiNG:
              PaNTery

        sHeGot GraPe
        JaM ON HeraND
        sHeHaD To Get
              wasHD.

Child [to another child]:   Teri's nice. She's a good character. But what's her
                             problem? You say she's sad because she's adopted.
                             But then when she finds a ball she gets happy. So
                             maybe she wasn't sad because she was adopted.
                             Maybe it was just an excuse.

The children seem to use story grammar concepts mainly in two ways: to discuss their own and each others' stories more fully, and as a criterion of completeness. That this criterion was internalized seems to be reflected in the children's writing, as seen in a journal entry written during writing workshop time (see Figure 9–28). Sarah was able, on her own, to successfully incorporate the elements of story grammar.

Elizabeth provides the reader with all four elements of story: a vivid setting, a character whose mind and even skin the reader enters, a problem the reader is compelled to share, a solution that makes the reader feel relief.

FIGURE 9–28
Sarah
Grade 2

The fosile

WHeN I was owt ecsPloriNG I fowND This little ThinG. It looKeD To Me like a fosile. But still I wasiNt cwit sher. So I asct my MOM dND Gess what she saiD. She saiD it was aND I was so Happy I coDe of DieD.

FIRST STATION

It's hot in the desert; Tom works hard in slavery. The sun is out and shines on the sand. Tom is barefoot. One day he decides to escape.

He made sure no one was looking and started to run. He ran and ran and didn't stop until he came to a pile of leaves and a couple of sticks. He made a roof and lived four days under that roof.

He was eating a fish and he heard a horse neigh. Could it be true, someone was coming to get him? He ran behind a bush. The horse stopped. Tom peeked through the bushes. The man said: "I see you. Come on out of there. Hop in." It was a friendly voice. Well, it really made Tom feel good. So he climbed in and the man said: "Where to?"

"Anywhere in the North." said Tom.

Elizabeth, Age 8

Teaching with story grammar is a tricky business. For some children the use of structure terms, even such simple ones as *problem* and *solution* can discourage creativity. This happens when a child is allowed to feel that the teacher thinks structures are more important than what the child wants to say. Structural terms are only useful to help the child clarify features she has already become aware of and is trying to control. With very new writers, in particular, it may be better not to mention structural terms at all. The teacher's job as writing coach is to discern the structure inherent in the story the child is writing and talking about, and to ask questions that help the child make it clear to the reader.

Outer Actions and Inner States: Souriau's Dramatic Roles

Although it is certainly not true of the above stories, some stories children write, when viewed through the grid of story grammar, show curious gaps right where they should specify some *psychological* action: an internal response, a goal, a reaction. Compared to stories adults tell, children's stories seem to be heavy on the action, light on the reflection.

Here is a great story by a second grader, which serves to illustrate our point.

The Knight

Once there was a knight named Stanley. He had a suit of steel. He had to fight a dragon, but before he got to the dragon's castle there was a dangerous woods and a dangerous river that he had to cross. He would begin the next morning because it was night time. The next morning he got on his horse and rode away. Soon he came to the woods and there he saw a monster. The monster, whose name was Hckee. Hckee had a green body with 1000 eyes and 1000 legs and 1000 arms with two horns. Hckee ran at Stanley with a sword. Quickly Stanley jumped to the side. Hckee ran right into a tree and Hckee just turned right into a pile of mud. Stanley hopped on his horse and rode away. Soon he came to the river, and Stanley looked at the river. There was no danger. But just then he saw danger: the waves were fire. Stanley hopped on his horse and jumped across the river and landed hard. Stanley rode for a little more. Then Stanley got off his horse and went to sleep. In the morning Stanley got on his horse and rode away. Soon he came to the dragon's castle. Stanley got off his horse. Stanley went across the drawbridge; the drawbridge closed behind Stanley. Stanley was trapped. Stanley took his sword and cut off the dragon's head.

The End

Orion, Age 7

The usual claim is that psychological action, being internal, is not obvious to children, so they leave discussions of characters' inner states out of their stories.[3] Or, perhaps they are aware of inner states, but they are not used to talking about them. Or it may be that the stories they hear and the television shows they watch are heavy on action and light on discussions of inner states—

so they simply might not associate talk about inner states with stories. We believe that children can get better at discussing the psychological dimensions of stories—goals, motives, and inner reactions—and that they should: Certainly it is preferable for children to be able to consider how events make people feel or to take motives into account in deciding whether or not some-one deserves blame.

The work of a French drama critic has provided us with a device for discussing motives in a way that makes sense to young children. Etienne Souriau was interested in discovering the code that enabled the audience to make sense of the action in dramatic scenes on the stage.[11] He was working in the same spirit as the story grammar researchers, in that he thought that there must be a set of conventions that the audience shared with the playwright (or the readers with the author) that made possible their experience of meaning from the work.

Souriau's conventions applied to the *roles* that are played by characters in a scene (these roles work fine in a simple story). He claimed that we can make sense of what's going on if we think of the characters as sharing no more than six dramatic roles. To make it easier to note them symbolically, he assigned each role a sign from the Zodiac.

The first of these roles Souriau called the *lion force,* and represented it this way: ♌ . This is the person who will direct the scene, the main character or hero.

The second is the *sun* ☉ , or desired object: Who or what does the lion force want?

The third is *Mars* ♂ , the rival: Who is trying to stop the lion force from getting what he wants?

The fourth is the helper and is represented by the *moon*: ☽ . There can be any number of helpers, and they can help the lion force, or the rival, or anyone.

The fifth is the *earth* ♁ , or receiver of bounty: For whom does the lion force want the desired object? (Often this is the lion force him- or herself.)

The sixth is *Libra* ♎ , a sort of arbiter or judge: Who or what decides if the lion force gets the desired object?

All of this may sound a bit exotic, but what Souriau provides is a simple framework for looking at the complex interweavings of characters and motives. This is how Souriau's model was used during writing instruction time in one class. The first four character roles were written on the board, and the teacher explained the symbols to the class.

♌ Who is the main character?

☉ What does the lion force want?

♂ Who is trying to stop the lion force from getting what he wants?

☽ Does anybody have a helper?

Teacher: Do you all remember the story of "Jack and the Beanstalk"?

Children: (yesses, nods, yawns)

Teacher: Who do you suppose is the lion force in "Jack and the Beanstalk"?

Children: Jack!

Child: The Beanstalk (laughs).

Child: No, Jack.

Teacher: Does the Beanstalk want anything?

Child: The Beanstalk just grows.

Teacher: I think to be the lion force in a story you have to want something.

Child: In the beginning of the story Jack's mother could be the lion force. She wants Jack to go out and get some food.

Child: But Jack is the hero; I mean, that's who the story is about.

Teacher: Does Jack have a helper?

Child: The old man with the beans.

Child: Yeah.

Child: Well, also the giant's wife helped him.

Child: How about the Beanstalk?

Teacher: Who would the rival be?

Children: The giant!

Child: And *his* helper is the harp. The harp called out to wake up the giant so Jack couldn't steal it.

Teacher: What do you think we should put for the object? What did Jack really want?

Child: Gold.

Child: The hen.

Child: But he didn't know there was going to be any hen up there.

Child: Adventure.

Child: To get away from his mother.

Child: Money. Because remember he was starving. And he took money back to his mother.

Child: In a way the giant was Jack's helper because nothing much would have happened to Jack if the giant hadn't been there.

As a tool for analysis, for getting the children actively interested in and discussing the story, Souriau was already proving his salt.

Clarifying roles is an interpretive process: The discussions give a nice feeling of moving toward of consensus, and yet it is also a divergent process. It is clear that in this class everyone didn't have to agree, that there were often several legitimate interpretations. Children were encouraged to give reasons for their interpretations, but not pushed. Discussions of stories conducted in Souriau's terms often seem more fun and lively than analyses of their simple structure. We think this is because the teacher always knows what the setting of a story is, or who the characters are, whereas in discussions of roles the children have ideas that differ from the teacher's that are valid and interesting and that give the teacher insights into how they see things. To start early with children on this sort of discussion can reassure them that it is quite acceptable and right to make their own interpretation of a story.

After the children seemed confident of the different roles, the teacher tried a game to see how these roles might help in writing stories. She produced two sets of cards. On one set she had written "people" labels: TRUCK DRIVER, TEENAGER, SKINNY GIRL, OLD MAN, MAGICIAN. At the children's request she included some animals, too—BROWN DOG and MOUSE. The class would draw from these all the characters for a story, except the sun (desired objects, as Souriau calls them). For "suns" she made a different set of cards: ADVENTURE, WEALTH, HEALTH, FAME, TO COMFORT, TO DISCOVER. These cards were all marked on the back with a $\odot$.

Here's how the game was played. After telling the children that the group would make up a story together, the teacher asked a child to draw a card for the lion force. He drew TRUCK DRIVER. Another child was asked to draw a card to answer the question, "What does this truck driver want right now?" He drew FAME.

Teacher:	How do you suppose this truck driver wants to become famous?
Child:	He wants to be a rock 'n roll star. He practices singing while he's driving.
Child:	He wants to be in the movies because he thinks he's real handsome.
Teacher:	I wonder if anybody might try to stop him from getting famous. Matthew, want to draw a rival? (Matthew drew a MOUSE) A mouse? How could a mouse stop a truck driver from getting famous?
Child:	He could run out in front of the truck, and then the truck would swerve off the road and run into a tree and that would be the end of the truck driver.
Child:	He could, well, if the guy was recording his song, the mouse could chew a wire or something . . .
Child:	Well, the mouse could just tell him, you're no good, you good-for-nothing truck driver, so forget it.

The discussion got very loud, the children were spilling over with ideas, everyone wanted to talk at once. The teacher then asked the children to take paper and pencil and write a story on their own, using the cards drawn. The three stories that follow were written by the children we quoted in the discussion, two first graders and a second grader (see Figures 9–29, 9–30, and 9–31). Note the variety in character motivation.

FIGURE 9–29
Johanna
Age 6

There once a truk driver
and he loved to
make up sosgs and he
stopt his truk too sing
the sogs to peple
and they loved the sogs
and they clapt and he
sead i must be on me
wae and he klimd in
the truk and went
and he stopt ugen
in the necs tonw and
he wod sing the same
sogs and they clapt
and he got in his
truk and he went to
bed and he wook up
the necs moning at
sun up and he had
brekfis and sag sum
moor sogs and he set
fo and old pepl came
from the nesc town to
here him and aftr the
frset sogs a man came
out fo the crod and
sead you cen sig on
the t.v. he sead ok.

FIGURE 9–30
Jared
Age 7

Once There lived a trucker
he wantid to be a rock star
his Dad was a rock star and he
wantid to be one to. one day
he was driveing along rea coding
a song and a mos startid to choow
on the mike wirer. the truch
driver didit no that The mouse
— was doowing it. then wen he
was dun he trid to lisin to it
he siad wats the mader — with
you! ≥ he siad in madnis. Then
he broke the mike
he was very mad. I will never
bie a ◀● cheep thing lik this
ugen! he went home and went
to bed. The neskt moning he went
to a moovy Thater he siad That
is — what I what to be and so
he did and That is the End

FIGURE 9–31
Juan
Age 6

Juan
a truck edivre wotid to be
famise. but a mosewes afdr him.
and owen Day the mose Sende
gowe awaye your mom and dad
nevr levd you eneews.
yes they did.

As children in a classroom develop throughout the year, both as people and as writers, it is hard to tell what progress can be attributed to a particular teaching practice, to general development, or to some outside event in the child's life. In the class where the Souriau game was played, several first graders who had never before written long or coherent stories were able to do so. Perhaps the game element encouraged them to rehearse their ideas out loud before writing; perhaps the cards served as reminders, as notes enabling them to hold their story in mind for long enough to write it down.

Some of the children spontaneously made "Souriau" into a party game, drawing the cards, and then splitting off into groups to make up stories and work them into skits to present to the whole class. These skits showed a strong awareness of character motivation, which did not always show up in the written versions produced after the skits. However, since the teacher had heard the children discussing motives at length while preparing the skits, she was able to remind them of these motives in the course of conferring about their stories. Many became interested in the challenge of showing character motivation to the reader.

Over the centuries, people who have become good story writers have picked up a sense of the structure and dynamics of stories not from Mandler and Johnson or from Etienne Souriau, but from reading and hearing stories. Daily storytime, books in the classroom and books sent home, time and encouragement to read and write stories will surely do more for the young writers coming along today than any direct instruction. However, the classroom observations above indicate that instruction strategies that encourage discussion and analysis of stories can help young writers enter and learn from the mainstream of literary tradition.

Poetry

It would be sad to conclude this chapter on writing in the poetic voice without some discussion of the writing of poetry. The Oxford English Dictionary defines poetry as: "The expression of beautiful or elevated thought in appropriate language, such language containing a rhythmical element." Often poetry is also understood to mean expressing a lot of sensory and emotional content in a few words.

Because of their wish to express what they truly feel, and because handwriting difficulties force them to economize on words, very young writers often create works of poetry. Joey's Christmas piece, for instance, could probably best be appreciated as poetry rather than as a truncated story.

THE COWS ARE
MOOING THE SHEEP
ARE BAAING
THE BRIGHTEST STAR
IS SHINING SO BRIGHT

WAKES JESUS UP AND
MARY AND JOSEPH

Joey, Grade 1

Influenced by haiku the class had been learning by heart, Chris wrote the following a few weeks into first grade:

HELLO THERE SLOW SMALL SNAIL

Around the same time another first grader (with some spelling help from her sister) wrote:

PEACHES ARE GOOD

She elaborated when asked if she could think of five good things about peaches (see Figure 9–32), and the result was published in the class paper as Rebecca's Peach Poem.

Sometimes it helps students to ask them whether they consider their piece of writing a poem or part of a story. It helps the author to look at his writing objectively, and it helps him realize that there is a difference between the two. It also makes it easier for the teacher to frame conference questions if she knows what the child intends.

FIGURE 9–32
Rebecca
Grade 1

During writing workshop, one child was groping around for a topic and someone suggested dinosaurs. His neighbor Sarah wrote:

DINOSAURS,
OLD DEAD BONES
SAD END.

                                                    Sarah, Age 6

A year later she wrote:

The River
When calm and still it is
peaceful and nice and you
can just sit and watch it,
but when it is rough and
the wind is blowing
all the birds stop singing
and all you can hear is
the splashing of the waves,
but as the wind dies down
the birds start to sing again
and it's peaceful again.
          tweet
          eeeee

Although Sarah did not lose her poetic voice as she became a more fluent writer, many children seem to. Some teachers use form poetry successfully to help children find again the telegraphic intensity of expression they may have had when they were very young, or simply to focus in on the experience they want to convey. Haiku, cinquain, diamante—each form urges the child to condense her thought, to observe her subject. One teacher we know teaches children the haiku form as she encourages them to keep a nature journal. A drama teacher has her students write cinquains about the characters they will portray:

Cassius
Sly, sneaky
hungry for power
persuading, interesting, plotting, killing
Evil

                                                    Elizabeth, Age 8

After reading "Jack and the Wonderbeans" aloud, a teacher got the children as a group to write a cinquain about a particular character, drawing their attention to the story writer's evocation of the character and to the words that triggered it.

Giant
Hands like hams
He comes tromping in
Sniffing and snuffing and snorting
Mean-eye.

Later, in workshop, a child writing a story about two sisters who couldn't get along began her story with these two cinquain portraits:

Jenny
mean, loud
Think she knows everything
Kicking, bragging, talking back
a horse.

Marie
sweet, kind
a real nice girl
smiling, ready to help
a friend.

Erin, Age 8

After a discussion of strip mining and its consequences, the class wrote the following diamante poem:

Mountain barnyard
Squawking, smelly
I'm coming, chickens
Hoeing, growing/standing, staring
Nothing to say
Dead, empty
Slagheap

Group poem

And during workshop, one of the same students wrote this on her own:

Generations
Children
Lively, smart
They are great
Screaming, receiving/praising, knowledging
They are O.K.
Charming, elderly
Parents

Elizabeth, Age 8

Writing group or individual diamante poems about a character as he appears at the beginning and the end of a story can help draw the children's attention to character evolution.

Hansel and Gretal
Extra mouths
Lost, scared
Pushed out of home
Captured, crying/planning, winning
welcomed back home
strong, smart
Children.

Group poem

Many children find it easier to be creative within some constraints, and judging from the popularity of poetry forms with rules governing meter, rhyme, syllables, and so on, that feeling has been shared by many writers throughout history.

Reading good free-form poetry in class, as well as form poetry, and calling the children's attention to examples of free-form poetry in their own work can help dispel the notion that poetry has to fit a particular form. Take what Joey wrote one day in April:

I RAN AWAY WITH THE
RADIO AND SOME COOKIES
IT WAS A HALF MOON
THAT NIGHT, ON THE
RADIO THE SONG WAS
BEAT IT, JUST BEAT IT.

If an adult had written this we might say "What a wonderful beginning to a story," and wonder where it went from there. But we know Joey is not yet up to writing long stories, and we can also recognize that he has said a tremendous amount in these few lines. Taken as a poem, Joey's piece is complete, containing the evocation of a scene (the half-dark night), a sensory connection (cookies clutched in one hand, radio in the other, straining to see, with the music beating away), and a kind of ambivalence of mood (connection between I ran away and Beat It!). Does he want to say how he felt, or would he rather leave it to the reader to guess?

Joey's piece makes a good poem partly because it is still so close to the expressive mode, though a reader who doesn't know Joey can certainly appreciate it. This is the sort of piece that can serve as a bridge for children between the purely expressive and the poetic modes. He probably wrote straight from the heart, without much thought of his readers, yet he chose his words so well that they can communicate to a wide audience. He could get a sense of this by reading it to a number of different people and asking them what they imagine when they hear it. Once he is able to appreciate how much he has communicated in these few words, he can see that a poem is a poem not only because it is short, sits a certain way on the page, or possibly fits a rhythmic structure, but because it also makes the reader see and feel something intensely.

Sometimes teachers and parents are reluctant to recognize these brief poems as complete, particularly if they are written in the first ten minutes of workshop. Because the style is telegraphic and expressive, the teacher sometimes pushes a child toward longer sentences or more new words, feeling it necessary for his development. The child may have an instinctive sense of what is complete for him, but lack the polite vocabulary to tell the teacher to back off: "This is not expository prose, this is poetry."

Children will need practice with other modes of writing—full description, argumentation, and expository prose, that is what the next chapter is about. Writing in these other modes can feel more difficult to young children than writing poetry (though for most adults it is the other way around): They have to hold the pencil longer, they have to worry about punctuation, they have to remove themselves from center stage. But while they acquire other, seemingly more demanding writing skills, their awareness of poetry and skill at writing it can grow, too. We find that for many children writing poetry, or summarizing a draft into a poem, provides a welcome and relaxing change of pace, a sort of homecoming from the rigors of other writing modes.

CONCLUSION

Looking at children between the ages of four and eight, we have seen their progress in learning about the human art of story making. During those same years they are gaining the dexterity to hold a pencil, the strength to write a line and then a page, the confidence to share what they've written or made up, the social skill of anticipating what an audience or reader might want to hear.

A child from a talkative but not a reading family may come to school with a sharp sense of how to interest an audience, but neither the dexterity nor the motivation for putting words on paper. A child who has had many stories read to her but not much other social interaction may bring to school an ingrained feeling for story structure and a great capacity for make-believe, but no confidence in her abilities. What can a teacher go on, as she tries to get these children to share their skills and learn to write in the poetic mode?

Story making can be practiced by children in many ways other than writing. When they are hearing, telling, remembering, or inventing stories, dreams, movies, or happenings at home children are learning to compose. When they play house they are making up a story. Only a small percentage of the stories children invent ever get down on paper, which is not surprising: A complete story requires a lot of words and considerable organization.

But most completed stories do follow certain forms. We have seen children grasping at these forms, putting on paper groups of words, a complex process that Applebee calls chaining and centering. We followed Joey and Sarah in their evolution toward story writing and looked at ways story grammar and Souriau's dramatic roles can be used to reinforce notions of form as children begin to write longer stories.

Much of the writing children do in the poetic mode is not story writing but simply an effort to create with words. This poetry-writing urge needs to be recognized and encouraged as worthy.

REFERENCES

1. Laurens Van der Post. *A Story Like the Wind.* New York: Harcourt Brace Jovanovich, 1979.
2. Arthur Applebee. *The Child's Concept of Story: Ages 2 to 7.* Chicago: University of Chicago Press, 1978.
3. Stephanie McConaughy. "Using Story Structure in the Classroom." *Language Arts* 57 (1980): 157–165.
4. Jean Mandler and Nancy Johnson. "On the Remembrance of Things Parsed: Story Structure and Recall." *Cognitive Psychology* 9 (1977): 111–151.
5. Susan Sowers. "Young Writers' Preferences for Non-Narrative Modes of Composition." Paper presented at the Fourth Annual Boston University Conference of Language Development, Boston, 1979.
6. Wendy Watson. *Lollipop.* New York: Thomas Crowell, 1976.
7. Amos Tutuola. *The Witch-Herbalist of the Remote Town.* Boston: Faber & Faber, 1981.
8. "Taleisen." Translated by Lady Charlotte Guest in *The Mabinogion.* Quoted in Joseph Campbell, *The Hero with a Thousand Faces.* Princeton, N.J.: Princeton University Press, 1972.
9. Robert Scholes. *Structuralism in Literature.* New Haven, Ct: Yale University Press, 1974.
10. Lucy Calkins. *The Art of Teaching Writing.* Portsmouth, N.H.: Heinemann Educational Books, 1986.
11. Etienne Souriau. *Les Deux Cent Mille Situations Dramatiques.* Paris: Flammarion, 1950.

10/ Approaching the Transactional Mode

Alex's mother gave the authors a message she found under his pillow (see Figure 10–1). It's to the Tooth Fairy ("T. fary"). He lost one tooth and now a second has come out. He is asking the Tooth Fairy please to find the first tooth, but also to recognize that "this one has silver in it."

Writing can be used for different purposes. Sometimes we use it to express whatever thoughts and feelings happen to be crossing our minds. Sometimes we use it to tell a story. And sometimes we use it to get something done, as Alex has in his note to the Tooth Fairy. Writing used in this last sense is called *transactional* writing, or writing in the *transactional mode,* because it serves as a piece of business between the writer and the person or persons he is writing for.

In this chapter we shall examine the attempts of some first-, second-, and third-grade children to write in the transactional mode. There are two distinct types of transactional writing that we will observe. Sometimes transactional writing consists of sharing information or explaining something. When these

FIGURE 10–1
Alex
Grade 2

Dear T. fary   I had a tooth come out and I lost it. so they say you are magic so you can get it Plese

this one has silver in it.

thank you

lot of teeth.   alec P.

functions are combined, the result is *expository writing*. In this chapter we will look at two sets of papers that contain expository writing. The second type of transactional writing consists of an attempt to persuade someone to do something or to believe something. This sort of transactional writing is called *argumentative writing,* and we will explore it as well.

Expository and argumentative writing have at least two things in common: The writer stays in the background, and the topic of the writing is in clear focus. It is assumed that the thing that is being described, explained, or argued is more important than what person is doing the writing. When, for example, we read a newspaper story about a train wreck, we do not expect to read a personal account about the reporter's trip to the scene, what the wreckage reminded her of, and so on. When we read a set of instructions for assembling a bicycle, we do not expect to hear the writer's views on bicycle riding, or what happened when he tried to assemble one himself. In both cases we expect the topic to come across to us directly, and we do not expect the writer to enter the picture.

Transactional writing has a definite pattern of organization. This is not to say that all transactional writing has the same pattern, or even that all writing of a certain type of transactional writing does either. Every piece of transactional writing, though, normally has *some* pattern, some structure around which the information is organized. An expository piece that explains something may be ordered around cause and effect or a sequential unfolding of events or steps. It may present a main point and subsidiary details. The possible patterns of organization in transactional prose are more various than the structures of stories we discussed in the previous chapter. For that reason they may seem less distinct to us. But they still exist and they are still important. Readers and writers both count on some sort of organizational pattern to guide them in comprehending and presenting written information.

When children begin to write for transactional purposes, these two features just mentioned—keeping the writer in the background and giving the work a definite structure—are not fully present as a rule. Because children's early writing starts out in the expressive mode, their first efforts to write transactionally will not fully live up to the characteristics of that mode. Their writing is apt to be somewhat expressive and somewhat transactional. This in-between writing, it will be recalled from our previous discussion, is sometimes called *transitional,* with reference to the transition from the expressive to the transactional mode.

Almost all of the papers we will examine in this chapter are transitional. In order to understand them, we have to consider the elements of transactional writing—be they expository or argumentative—that have emerged in them, at the same time noting the aspects of the expressive mode that linger on.

ASSIGNMENTS FOR EXPOSITORY WRITING

We have come to think of the movement from expressive writing to transactional writing as being developmental; that is, of two children the more mature will write in the transactional mode, while the less mature writes in the expressive mode. But judgments of more mature or less mature writing are very tricky. It is not enough to observe what mode the child writes in; we must also note what his purpose for writing was. Expressive writing is acceptable and desirable in many circumstances, such as writing letters or making journal entries. It is only inappropriate when circumstances call for some other purpose for writing, such as reporting an event for a newspaper, or explaining a procedure to an unknown audience.

Those of us who teach the same group of children all year can usually find ways to make sure each child practices various forms of transactional writing. Because we know each child's interests, we can make individualized suggestions for their topic lists, such as cooking instructions or a letter to their senator. Help can be given with these modes, as needed, during conference times in a process-writing classroom.

Other teachers give direct group assignments and notice that, occasionally at least, children seem to benefit from writing to one assignment and comparing notes. For our immediate purpose, which is to study the kinds of successes and problems young writers have with transactional writing, it is interesting to look at batches of papers written in response to the same assignment.

When we give children writing assignments during instruction time, we can often influence the purpose for which they write. Thus, we can give them valuable practice in exercising the different modes of writing and also gain an opportunity to see to what extent they are able to use the different modes. But we must be careful in making judgments, even when children are writing for an assignment because children may not interpret an assignment the same way we teachers do.

An assignment usually specifies three things:

1. A *topic*—what the writing is to be about;
2. A *purpose* or *function*—what the writer should do about the topic (e.g., explain it, give directions, describe it, tell a story about it, or argue for it);
3. An *audience*—to whom the writer should assume the work is addressed.

We should examine our assignments carefully to see how clearly they specify topic, purpose, and audience before we evaluate the writing that results from them. Sometimes children do not adequately honor one or another element of an assignment because the assignment was not sufficiently explicit. Other times they do not honor some of the elements of an assignment because they are developmentally unable to. It is important to know the difference.

As an example, let us consider an assignment that was given to groups of first and second graders.

The "Expert": An Expository Assignment

"How many of you feel you're an expert in something?" asked the teacher. All of the children raise their hands. "Let's talk about who's an expert in what." A class discussion follows. "I have a roll of adding paper tape in my lap. Johnny, you said you know all about sharks. Do you know this much?" The teacher pulls tape to about six inches in length.

"No, I know more than that," said Johnny.

The teacher, pulling tape, asks, "Do you know this much?"

Johnny says, "More."

The teacher continues pulling the tape until Johnny says "stop" and gives him the paper.

Later the teacher says, "Now all of you have your own paper. Today each of us is going to write about something that's very familiar, something we feel we know a lot about. Everyone has chosen his own topic, so every person's paper will be different from his neighbor's. As you write, remember you're the expert and we, your audience, probably know very little about your subject. Keep this in mind as you write, and try to explain exactly what you mean—exactly what you know. If you need more paper you can just tape some extra onto what you've taken. If you've asked for too much, you can just tear the extra off. Feel free to draw if you'd like."

The assignment makes the *topic* very clear: Each student is to write about something in which she or he is an "expert." The *purpose* of the writing is a bit ambiguous: Are the children to tell us *about* something, or are they to tell us *how to do* something? That is, should a child describe the excitement of participating in a particular sport, or should he tell us how to play the game? The writer will have to decide. As for the *audience,* who it is made up of has been made clear: It is the teacher and other students in the class.

As you read the papers in Figures 10–2 to 10–9, ask yourself these questions:

1. Which of the writers stuck to the topic?
2. How did each writer interpret the purpose?
3. Which of the writers consistently addressed whichever purpose was chosen?
4. Which of the writers seemed to keep in mind the same audience all the way through?

The children stuck fairly well to the topic of this assignment. All of the children wrote about something they considered themselves an expert about. Nevertheless, they interpreted the "something" in different ways: Brian wrote about a sport; Rachel, Marc, and Bryan wrote about hobbies. These are alike in that they are activities in which the children participate—activities that might lend themselves to papers that explain how to *do* the activity. Susan, Mara, Ian, and Paul wrote about things they *know* about. These approaches lend themselves to papers that provide facts about the topic. Thus there were

FIGURE 10–2
Rachel
Grade 2

Pins   I have lots of Pins
Hrere they are Health team
all-star, Kingswood camp, A. A, Novice,
Colorado Hi!, Bronies, For E.R.A.,
Caring for the future of your families,
Willoway, You gotta have art Snoopy,
Volunteers make A Difference and
ribons, Zionism, Doggie, One with Stones.
Old fasio gifl. I like my Pins.

potential differences in the way the children approached their topic: One group could have described a procedure, and the other group could have presented facts. Nevertheless, all of the children presented facts.

How well did the children achieve the *purpose* of explaining? What sort of purpose did the children take the assignment to be requesting? All of the students addressed what would be considered an expository purpose; there were no stories, and no purely expressive pieces handed in. Within the expository purpose, as we already noted, none of the children elected to give directions for a procedure, although we might have expected some to from the assignment.

How consistently did the children stick to their purposes? This varied, with strong shades of expressive writing entering into most of the papers.

Brian (Figure 10–5), for example, has interpreted the assignment in a personal way, and we see he has written an inventory of all the positions he can play and things he can do. In total, his paper explains his broad hockey expertise, and indirectly the reader learns a little about the game.

But Brian, the writer, is in center stage in this piece, giving an account of his own experiences and feelings. "Hockey is very very very fun for me." Brian's piece is organized around all of the things he knows how to do. Harking back to Susan Sowers' term (see Chapter 8), we would call this organization a *knowledge-based inventory*—more of a list than a structure. This is a feature of expressive writing. Rachel (Figure 10–2) chose to write a paper about collecting pins. She, like Brian, has also written an inventory, in this case an inventory of the pins she has collected.

Art

Art is fun. You can learn a lot of things from it. And most of all you have to have a lot of pacontes. And I like to make things in Art and one day in art we made paper masa. In school the art teacher is Mrs. Gill. She is very nice. I like it because I am very creative and That is why I like to do Art. And I'm a very, very, very good Artist. And I love making things with clay, and I like makeing things with paper. And I like making things made from paper masa, but, most of all I like making faces of people, cartons, Comics,

Building Modles. It's like a jig saw puzzle at first and now it is so simple I could finish it in a half an hour matring what kind it is I could finish a snap together modle in 10 minits and I could finish a hard glue together in a half an hour and let its dry and put it on my shelf and show it to my freinds I have in motle I glue together and and 7 snap togethers in and oher I get time I paint them I have 18 cars 1 helcoptor and 5 air plane and the ones tat are titeley together I play with and have Fun and with my brother with my air planes and I always win. I never lose.

Hockey. I know how to play forword and defents and goley. I know how to shoot the pyk. I know how to play write wing and left wing. I know how to play

left defents and write defents. Hocky
is Very very very
fyn. I
yshyly play defense.

FIGURE 10-6
Susan
Grade 1

Mice

One thing about mice is that a cat will get Rid
of mice, mice Love cheese most of all. they live in
holes in the wall. People don't like mice so they
put traps in the house. If it dosent work get
a cat. Mice are in some Books in the library.
Mice are good. Mice and cats don't get alon
to well.

FIGURE 10-7
Paul
Grade 2

Space

The sun was made by gases and dust forming a big cloud. one
day the cloud started to burn and the dust and gasses get
tighter turned in to a ball of fire. This is watt the sun is
today. in about 5,000,0000,000, years it will run out of gas to
burn. then it will burn up earth and mars then it will get
white and very smal. A teaspoon of it would way about a ton.
then it would turn in to a hole. The sun is a medeim
size star. there is no air in space so jets can't fly, but rokets can.
When people make rokets they can't make it go so far. the have only
gone to the moon.

From Marc's paper (Figure 10–3), we learn something about art. But just as in Brian's paper, we also learn a great deal about Marc, the writer. The "very, very, very good artist," who feels "very creative" and "who loves making things with clay" and "likes making faces of people, cartoons, and comics" is full of pleasurable feelings he wants to share. He also has the beginnings of conventional expository organization emerging in his paper. He has given us a main idea—"art is fun"—and provided supporting statements for it—"You learn a lot of things . . ." and "you have to have a lot of practice." He lists several important things, and then tells us the most important: "I love . . . ; I like . . . ; but most of all, I like . . . " But his focus is still personal, still expressive.

Bryan (Figure 10–4) is as wrapped up with building models as Marc is with art.

From the papers we have examined so far it might appear that what all these children need to do in order to write better papers is focus a little less on *themselves*. But this is certainly not the case. In exposition, it is not enough for children to keep themselves out of the writing. Limiting the topic is also a consideration.

Mice

1. One thing about mice is that a cat will get rid of mice.
2. Mice love cheese most of all.
3. They live in holes in the wall.
4. People don't like mice so they put traps in the house.
5. If it doesn't work get a cat.
6. Mice are in some books in the library.
7. Mice are good.
8. Mice and cats don't get along too well.

Susan, Grade 1

Susan's composition is less expressive than Bryan's, Brian's, or Marc's. She seems to have taken a step forward by attempting to focus on her topic and limiting her personal intrusion into the paper. Yet we sense she's not nearly so comfortable with her theme as the previous writers were with theirs. Susan seems to be searching for things to say. Her jump from catching mice to "mice are in some books in the library" and "Mice are good" is a disconcerting leap for her readers.

Her paper might have a more natural focus if she were writing about some personal interest, as did the writers whom we've discussed thus far. Although she seems to have moved beyond the focus on her own likes and dislikes, she has yet to replace it with any other strong center. Of course, Susan is only a first grader! Her piece is an inventory. Eventually, for her writing to have a concentrated punch to it, she must learn to limit her topic to one aspect of the facts and integrate the points she makes about her topic into some kind of organization.

FIGURE 10–8
Ian
Grade 1

Siuprman. Siuprman Kam See thrir anenthig Be Cas he has a X rai vitin and he is the Stnogest in the wirild and he Kan fili and he is fatr than a ScPetcy dulat and he is Abul to Lep tul buldeg in a Segeldod and

FIGURE 10–9
Mara
Grade 1

thy Baby mack in thar Pans andcriyall the timethey Sleip in acrip and thr up all niht and slep in the day they crey if they don have fiod whan they Want it they srem in my eras but ther is sum tigfunny Bucus When my mom picshim uP he stops andsum time when my mom pits him down he sceme he only nos tow Wrds he stac uP tilmidniht But Sum times hes Jes fin.

Baby

1. they make in their pants and
2. cry all the time
3. they sleep in a crib
4. and they're up all night and sleep in the day
5. they cry if they don't have food
6. when they want it they scream in my ears
7. but there is some thing funny
8. because when my mom picks him up
9. he stops and some time when my mom
10. puts him down he screams
11. he only knows two words
12. he stays up til midnight
13. But some times he's just fine

Mara, Grade 1

Mara is writing from personal experience, while trying to keep herself in the background. Mara knows a lot about babies because her mother has recently had one. She manages to begin her paper with a detached "expert" voice. Presenting information as one who knows, she writes, "They make in their pants and cry all the time." But Mara's voice changes in the second half of her paper (line 7); now it's more personal and expressive, " . . . when my mom picks him up he stops." Suddenly, "he" substitutes for "they," the specific for the general. Now we leave the detached realm of factual description and enter Mara's world. Mara's composition is a good transitional piece between the expressive and transactional modes. It shows development along the right lines.

Sometimes a child's topic is so removed from personal experience that it's not very difficult for him to sustain an objective point of view. Ian's description of Superman (Figure 10–8) is objective, but this doesn't mean that he is a more sophisticated writer than Mara or the other children. He's learned about Superman indirectly, so he doesn't have the problem of stepping back. Moreover, he has heard the familiar catalogue of Superman's powers again and again. Nevertheless, one can't help but be awed by his extraordinary invented spelling effort. He has forged through his words the way Superman slashes through steel!

Paul's paper (Figure 10–7), "Space," is the last piece we'll discuss. It needs a few adjustments, but Paul's is a fine piece of exposition. He restricts his subject to the sun's evolution and change. He carries his idea through from the time it was "made by ashes and dust" until the time when it will "turn into a hole."

A few children in second grade will write expository papers like Paul's, but not many. Paul's paper satisfies an adult reader's expectation of what expository writing should look like. But teachers should be aware that children must move gradually away from writing that puts themselves first, toward writing that succeeds in giving an organized accounting of a subject and satisfies most of the reader's need to know.

What effect does the audience have on children's writing? These children wrote their pieces in school, for their peers. It seems that this audience invoked personal expression because the writer was justified in assuming that the audience was as interested in herself as in her topic.

When children are writing in school, the writer-audience relationship is known; the child's audience is Miss Jones and the class. Consequently, teachers should assume that expository papers written in school will often be more expressive than transactional. They will often take the form of elementary personal essays, where the child, not the subject, is in center stage. Let us look at another expository assignment that was given to another group of second graders.

Another Expository Assignment: How to Ride a Bicycle
This time the assignment more clearly specified the purpose the teacher was after. Here is the assignment:

Teacher: I'll bet you all know how to ride a bicycle. (Most of the students said they did. Many started to describe the procedure to her.)

Teacher: Well, some people over in Victoria [that is a city where two of the authors worked] want us to write down how to ride a bicycle for them.

Child: Teacher?

Teacher: Yes?

Child: Don't they know how to ride bicycles in Victoria?

As you read the papers the children wrote (Figures 10–10 to 10–13), decide

1. Which children stuck to the topic?
2. Which children honored the purpose of giving directions?
3. Which children kept their audience consistently in mind?

We can see that virtually all of the children stuck to the topic. They all focused on bicycles and how they are ridden.

As for the discourse mode, they stayed within the expository form on this assignment far better than in the previous one. In all of them the writer kept in the background; the focus was on the task of riding a bicycle, not on the person who could do it. There were no personal statements: We did not see "I like to ride my bicycle," or "Riding a bicycle is fun," or even "I'm very, very, very good at riding a bicycle."

FIGURE 10–10
Andy (left)
Grade 2

                                    bicycle
first you must take your
left leg and put it on the
pedal. and then you take

FIGURE 10–11
Russell (right)
Grade 2

your right leg. and put on
the pedal, and push the pedal
with your right leg. and hold
on to the bars. and when
you want to turn you take
your bars and either push
the right or left, and never
ride, without holding onto your
bars.

first thing you do is
to pettle. than you

balance yourself so you

won't fall off your bike
than you steer so
you won't run into
something. and thats
all you have to know.

FIGURE 10–12
John
Grade 2

          Deskib abuot a bike
You got to geep your bales
and pedol and keep the wheel
stat and turn going around
a turn.

FIGURE 10–13
Lois
Grade 2

All you have to do is petel the
bike and the wheels will turn
around and around. And when you want
to stop pull backward on the
petels.

Why did the writers keep themselves in the background of their compositions this time? We suspect it was largely because of the audience. First, they were aware that the papers were being written for strangers—for people they would never see. They may have known that the readers would have been more interested in bike riding than in the writers themselves. Or they may have been shy about sharing a lot of personal material with people they didn't know and couldn't see. However, it could also have been because the topic clearly called for them to explain how to ride a bicycle, not to talk about bicycle riding. The wording of the assignment, that is, made it clearly inappropriate for a child to list all of his experiences and feelings related to bicycles.

Note how well organized most of these papers are. The children kept closely to a sequential, step-by-step pattern for presenting their ideas. By David's question, we may gather that the children understood that their task was to tell their readers how to ride a bicycle. They succeeded very well in thinking through what steps would be helpful to share, and in what order.

The contrast between these papers and the previous assignment is striking. Most of the children responding to the expert assignment put themselves prominently into their papers, but these children did not. Moreover, several of the children writing for the expert assignment chose to write about processes (building model airplanes, playing hockey, doing art, and collecting pins), but none of them explained how to perform those processes. In contrast, all of the children responding to the bicycle assignment explained how to ride a bicycle.

It is not always necessary or desirable to give children explicit assignments for the writing they do. But when the teacher does want to make assignments with the intention of having the children practice writing in a particular discourse mode, the assignment must be worded very carefully. The teacher should discuss the assignment with the children to determine what they understand the assignment to mean. As we have seen, the difference between children's responses to two assignments that purport to generate the same kind of writing may be great indeed. It would be unfortunate if a teacher were to give an assignment of the expert variety and conclude from the children's responses that they *couldn't* write expository prose.

Something like a class newsletter comes in handy in creating new and definite audiences for the children's writing, which, as we have seen, helps children write in the transactional mode. The following instructions were written by a first grader for the class newsletter just after the children had learned to make cornhusk dolls (see Figure 10–14). Complete with drawings, it took Marissa five days of workshop time, or approximately four hours of concentrated effort, to produce this piece, of which she was justifiably proud. Her self-imposed task required her not only to remember every step of a long procedure, but to put herself in the reader's place and judge whether or not the reader would be able to follow the process with only her instructions as guide.

FIGURE 10–14
Marissa
Grade 2

How To Make a Cornhusk Doll by Marissa McHale Blank

School is fun. Today we made cornhusk dolls. I made the one you see.

First you take a piece of cream-colored cornhusk and take two cotton balls and put the cotton balls inside the cornhusk, and bunch the cornhusk and tie a piece of thin cornhusk. Wrap it around the neck of the head you just made. The head should look like this:

Make one long arm by rolling a piece of cornhusk up in a scroll and tying it at both ends, and then you have made arms.

Then take a piece of blue or red cornhusk; take a piece that looks like this

and make a diamond hole in the same one and put it on the head of the body.

Then take five pieces of blue or red cornhusk that look like this, tie them around (the middle of the body) and bend them around.

AN ASSIGNMENT FOR ARGUMENTATIVE WRITING

In general, argumentative writing includes works that attempt to persuade a reader of a certain point of view. In children's writing, however, argumentative writing more often takes the form of an attempt to persuade someone else to do something, such as, give the writer something, allow him to do something, do him a favor, or the like.

Argumentative, or persuasive, writing is an appropriate form for children to practice because in this form the topic and the audience are inherently made clear. The topic is *what we want;* the audience is the person or persons *from whom we want it.* The mode of argumentative writing may pose difficulties, however, that have little to do with writing. Persuasion requires that a person know how to structure an argument according to his social standing vis-a-vis his audience. For example, we can say some things to our close friends by way of persuasion for which we would be sent to our room if we addressed them to our mother, or thrown in jail if we addressed them to the president of the United States. The following is an argumentative assignment that was given to a second-grade class:

> Think of something that you would like to do, but for one reason or another cannot do. Write a letter to persuade the person who is preventing you from doing what you'd like, to change his or her mind.

This assignment was followed by class discussion, and then the children wrote. Several of their papers are reprinted here, but before we look at them, let us decide what to look for.

This assignment points to a definite topic, but it leaves the writer latitude to determine exactly what the topic will be. The assignment leaves it to the writer to decide who his audience is, but it does make it clear that he must decide.

The discourse mode is suggested also. The purpose, at least, is clear: The writer is to persuade someone to let him do something. But it is up to the writer to decide how the persuading is to be done and how to organize his points. It is also for the writer to note that he may wish to structure his arguments differently, to use more or less politeness, depending on his audience. Consider now Figures 10–15 to 10–21. How did the children treat each of the elements of topic, purpose, and audience?

First of all, how many of these children thought of a topic and stuck to it?

FIGURE 10–15
Corey
Grade 2

Corey F.

Dear Mrs. Vargas   why   won't   you
let   us   talk   in   the   cafateoria?   We
have   a   right   to!   after   all   you   talk
in   the   longe.   any   way.

FIGURE 10–16
Johnny
Grade 2

dear mom and dad,

I want to ride my bike on the dirt road. Let me play with frogs. I want to run splash in the mud.

love,

Johnny

FIGURE 10–17
Jeanette
Grade 2

Dear Debbie,
One day Debbie. Pow! Write in the ciser. O.K. Why is it allways we have to play baby. We never ride bikes.

FIGURE 10–18
Annie
Grade 2

Dear Dad,
Why can't I get a hourse? I would keep my room clean. I'd tak care ofit. I'd be extra good I never would fight. pleas! pleas! I would let my sisters ride it.

Sincerly,
Annie

FIGURE 10–19
John
Grade 2

I want to drive a car
Dean Mom and Dad. Would you
let me drive your car no-o-o-o! Ok
I want to no-o. I'll go drive the car
tonight. There asleep I'll go get the car.

The End

FIGURE 10–20
Andy
Grade 2

Dear, Mom and dad. How come I cant ride
into town on my bike. I'm careful enough
around the block. If a car rides on the right
and I'm on the right then I'll stop.
And if a cars on the left and I'm on the
the left I'll stop. And I'll ride on the
side of the road

All of them, really. Johnny chose to write an inventory of all the things he wanted to be allowed to do, rather than pick one and arrange an argument for it. All of the others stated their request and then sought to drive it home somehow. Johnny may have found it easier to make an inventory of requests rather than to structure an argument for one request.

How many of them kept their audience constantly in mind? All but two; John and Alexis did not consistently address their compositions to their parents, the supposed audience. But in John's case that is surely because his request to be allowed to drive the family car was fanciful anyway (see Figure 10–19). His work turned into a story toward the end. The device of dialogue showed up as a method of structuring his composition. This is a manifestation of expressive writing. John's writing did not come off as a persuasive piece. Perhaps if the topic had been derived from a need that was real to him rather than imagined, his paper would have shown a more definite structure.

FIGURE 10–21
Alexis
Grade 2

Dear, Mom
Please let me stay
up to mid - night.
Becouse spring is here8
I want to hear the
frogs sing. please make
up your mind. or I could
wash the dishes. or I'll
cut the yard. and I'll
water the plant's
okay   you can only
stay up to mid-night
for only eight weeks

ALEXIS

Alexis's paper (Figure 10–21) resorted to a bit of dialogue at the end. After making his pitch about being allowed to stay up until midnight, he had his mom say, "Okay, you can only stay up to midnight for only eight weeks." This paper, too, might have stayed more faithfully in the persuasive mode had the child really intended for his parents to read the letter and make a determination on the basis of it.

The children stayed within the argumentative mode of discourse, with the two exceptions we have just mentioned. Their papers generally began with the request and then listed support for it. The arguments they put forward took various forms. Annie's paper (Figure 10–18), for example, was a tit-for-tat argument. She would keep her room clean, be really good, wouldn't fight, and even let her sister ride it, if only her parents would get her a horse. Alexis (Figure 10–21) uses this line of argument too, promising to wash the dishes, cut the yard, and water the plants. Alexis also uses the tack of explaining his request: because spring is here! and he wants to hear the frogs sing.

Corey (Figure 10–15) uses a fair-is-fair approach. If the lunchroom manager gets to talk in the lounge (her rest area away from work), then by rights the children should be allowed to talk in the lunchroom (their rest area away from work).

Jeanette (Figure 10–17) uses the get-tough approach: "One day, Debbie, Pow! Right in the kisser!"

Andy (Figure 10–20) uses perhaps the most sophisticated approach of all. In his piece about bicycle riding on the street he anticipated his parents' objections. He put himself in their place and realized that their objection to his riding his bike on the street was a concern for his safety. Then he set out to convince them that he knew how to be safe. This is a sophisticated approach, and it is also pitched at an effective level of politeness for parents.

Johnny (Figure 10–16) provides no support for his requests, but rather adds other requests to the list and makes an inventory.

The children in this group were able to rise to the challenge of writing an argumentative or persuasive piece fairly well. A couple of them could have used some encouragement when the assignment was given in order to approach it in more realistic terms. This would be easier if the assignment had arisen from a real need, and the letters could actually have been mailed. For the group as a whole, the children raised a remarkable variety of persuasive tactics, from tit for tat to fair is fair to threats to anticipating and allaying objections. The teacher could capitalize on this diversity by sharing the papers and discussing the various approaches. He could ask: "How could we make an argument like Alexis used, to ask permission to talk in the lunchroom?" "How could we make an argument like Annie used to talk Debbie into riding bikes?"

Another issue to which the teacher could call attention is the difference in the way arguments would be couched for different audiences. Jeanette could be asked how she would have worded her argument if she had been addressing her mother. Alexis could be asked how he might have worded his argument differently if he were addressing it to his big brother or to the babysitter. These questions get at an important but often overlooked aspect of language learning. That is, we use different language forms and degrees of formality and directness with different audiences.

The idea of writing persuasive letters and the skills to do so carry over from this type of assignment into writing workshop. Figures 10–22 and 10–23 were written on the children's own initiative.

ENCOURAGING WRITING IN A VARIETY OF MODES

What are some ways to encourage writing in a variety of modes without directive form-centered assignments?

We are convinced that children learn best by being shown the process of writing, and choosing their own topics on which to write. We are also aware that a major problem for many young writers is finding things to write about that seem worthy of all the thought and effort. School life and the information learned in school are a huge part of a young child's life. We want children to realize that not only their home life but everything they study, every story they read, playground, make believe, and school politics are all grist for the writer's

FIGURE 10–22
Elizabeth
Grade 3

Tuesday 11/1/83

Dear Mr. Reagan,
please take apart

missiles to prevent
War, and make som-
thing non-explosof out
of them.
          Recpectfully
     Elizabeth Russo

FIGURE 10–23
Rebecca
Grade 1

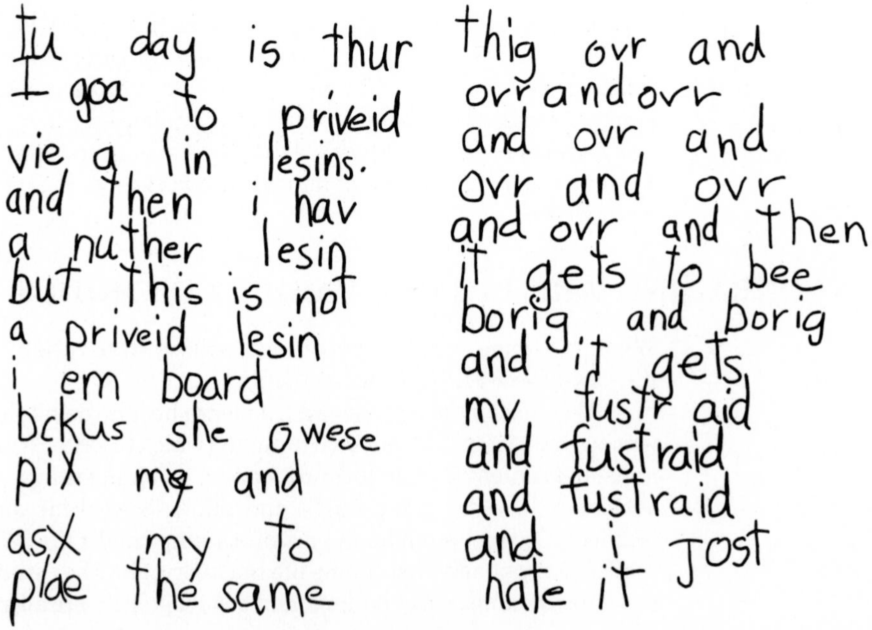

Iu day is thur
I goa to priveid
vie a lin lesins.
and then i hav
a nuther lesin
but this is not
a priveid lesin
i em board
bckus she owese
pix me and
asx my to
plae the same
thig ovr and
ovr and ovr
and ovr and
ovr and ovr
and ovr and then
it gets to bee
borig and borig
and it gets
my fustr aid
and fustraid
and fustraid
and i Jost
hate it Jost

mill. Some teachers promote variety in children's modes of writing by giving occasional assignments like "how to ride a bicycle" or the argumentative assignment previously discussed, usually during a writing instruction time. Others simply model different subjects and modes of writing during workshop time. Others assign writing as part of other areas of study, and let the children continue their efforts during writing workshop time if they so desire. On the following pages are some writings from second, third, and fourth graders who took their inspiration from a social studies investigation of the Roanoke colony and the nine children who were part of it.

David's Diary:
>*April 20th, 1587*
>
>I got aboard the ELIZABETH, with John White as captain. The room for sleeping is three feet, up and down; my bed is a block of wood. It is nicer on the poop deck.
>
>*April 21st*
>
>For meals there is bread, wine, fish. I had fish and meal for lunch. I read stories from the Bible and write in my diary.
>
>*July 20th*
>
>Land in sight. Smoke mysteriously rises from the woods. We will probably land today, we are sailing very fast. White says we will make huts from bark and sticks tied together at the top and bark laid on them to make a bark tepee to live in and tomorrow we'll start on the houses. All we have left to eat is ship biscuits. Sometimes we catch a few fish. I am seasick and homesick.

David, age nine, is able to slip into the shoes of one of the colonist children with no trouble. Orion, on the other hand, who is only seven, finds it easier to write from a detached point of view, in an expository voice, and yet it is clear as his story progresses that he sees himself as one of the crabbers.

>Four hundred years ago a ship came over to Roanoke to drop nine children and a hundred and seventeen women. That day they made huts out of mud and sticks and a few nails that they took over. That night the children coughed upstairs because there was too much smoke. The smoke came from the chimney. The chimney was leaking.
>
>The next morning five boys went to catch crabs with sticks. One boy jumped into the water with his stick and pushed a crab out of the water. The other boys put their sticks down and took rocks and shot them at the crab. The crab died and that's how they killed the crabs. The boy that was in the water got pinched by a crab that was behind him. The boy screamed. All the men and women came to see what was going on. A big Indian and a little Indian were peeking out from behind a rock. The little

Indian ran away like a penguin and the big Indian ran after the little
Indian. The big Indian said STOP in their language, the little Indian
stopped. . . .

Orion's expository writing has turned into an action story, with the
reader drawn right into the middle of it.

Elizabeth, eight years old, maintains one voice throughout; so do Micah,
Orion, and Andrew.

> *January the 17th, 1587*
> Dear Grampa and Granma,
>   I eat mostly deer; it is cold in the winter. I hope we see you
> soon. The people who were here before us which our people call
> savages stole the deer meat so we had to go without anything except
> for water for two days. Micah and I have to go almost every night to
> the neighbor's hut to borrow some fire. We only have one more rag
> for the tinderbox. Granma please send me some of Grampa's rags.
> We send you two wolf skins and five fox skins when a ship comes.
> Our next door neighbor's house burned down. It caught on to ours
> so we had to build another one. Micah and I found ten nails. One
> Indian girl named Pomawak is my friend. I go meet her every day in
> the woods in a clearing. Three days we pick berries together. We
> taught each other our languages with our hands, so we can talk to
> each other a little bit.
>   Love,
>   Your granddaughter Elizabeth

Dear Granny,
     I made a goose trap and my friend and I caught five geese. Every
thing is going fine except for the weather.
     Your grandchild Micah (Age 7)

Dear Grampa,
     I am freezing to death but I don't die. Orion (Age 7)

Dear Grampa,
     Things are getting worse. First I thought the savages were bad, but
now I have to go over to chief Okracoke for medicine and food. My
mother is getting scurvy but she's lucky her teeth aren't falling out. We
are lucky to have the savages. They give us crab, duck, geese and mush,
but now they don't have that much so we are starving. The Indians say
that in forty-one more days the weather will be warmer. If it wasn't for the
Indians we would be dead.
     Your Grandchild Andrew (Age 9)

Some of the children decided to write from an Indian child's point of view:

> Today white people came to this land. They are really white. They look so different from our people. They even dress differently. They have something that covers their legs and also something that covers their chest and back. It doesn't look like they know how to build a house. I was hiding up in a tree with Pakla, my sister. We saw a big canoe. I ran to my village to tell my father, the chief, that a big canoe was coming. He warned me to stay away from them.
>
> With special permission Pakla and I went down to the village that the white people have built. Pakla saw a little girl sitting outside a hut crying. Pakla showed me. I said let's go down and see what the little girl was crying for. We ran down the hill into the village the white people had built. We got to the little baby and kneeled down to see the baby better. All of a sudden a man came out of the hut and was waving his arms and shouting at us. He was shouting something Pakla and I could not understand. But we were smart enough to know we weren't welcome right then. We ran as fast as we could to father, and told him everything.
>
> Elizabeth, 8, with Sarah, 7, and Erin, 8

> On the fourth day Pamawak and I spied ten white people coming up the hill and we ran to tell our father the chief. The chief came down and about halfway we bumped into them making signs that meant corn for a bag of dry biscuits, so our father traded the corn for the biscuits and we had them for supper. They were not very good but they were different.
>
> Sarah, 7, with Elizabeth and Erin

Once again we are struck by what a boon to good writing a strong curriculum is! We often hear it said that to learn to write, children need to be shown the process of writing, that they need to be encouraged to write about things they care about for a real audience. Such statements are true but incomplete: they overlook the importance of subject matter.

The truth is, if they are to have things to write about, particularly in an expository way, children need to be immersed in interesting content. But *immersed:* It is not enough to trot children through disconnected bits of freeze-dried content; they need to engage their imaginations deeply in interesting curriculum, and they need to take the time to explore ideas actively and fully.

Writing is a necessary part of a sound curriculum, and when it is, the power of genuine interest in subject matter, the resonance of rich reading, and the excitement of having their ideas deeply engaged and their ideas taken seriously will go a long way toward enabling children to craft well-structured and vivid prose.

CONCLUSION

Young children write slowly. To write successfully in the transactional mode requires a writer to maintain in her mind her topic, purpose, and audience during repeated trips to the pencil sharpener and conversations with neighbors. It is not surprising that early attempts to write in this voice are highly personal, or that they tend to feature inventories of ideas rather than integrated arguments. It is good practice to steer children toward transactional writing, to remind them of occasions that call for this mode.

But, at least in the early years, we should not be too disappointed if children write mainly in the expressive mode, as long as what they are writing holds their interest. The goal in these formative years is fluency, with variety in writing tasks important to the extent that it helps keep the students' interest sparked.

Nonetheless, children need to be immersed in rich content if they are to write fluently in the transactional mode. Descriptive and expository writing require that children know and care about things to describe and explain. Argumentative writing requires that children have things they care to argue about.

11/ *Writing: The Child, the Teacher, and the Class*

In the previous ten chapters we have been concerned with the question, "What are the *forms of writing*—the configurations that make letters, the patterns that make spellings, the organizations that make composition types—and how do children learn them?" There remains an equally important question: "What is the *activity of writing*, or, if you will, *the process of composing*, and how do children learn to do it?"

WRITING AS A SOCIAL ACTIVITY

As we begin to talk about teaching writing, we must broaden our focus to take in, simultaneously, the individual child and the whole class, including the teacher. Writing is a quintessentially social activity. You cannot teach a child to write without teaching him to interact with others through print. Some of the most important interaction, important because of its value for modeling helpful interaction, is between the child and the teacher. But if there is anything we have learned about writing in the last twenty years, it is that you cannot restrict growing writers to the audience they find in the teacher, any more than you can teach a group of children to square dance if you are the only allowable partner.

What Sort of Learning Is Learning to Write?

Some friends of ours, both college professors, were recently on a long car trip with their two sons, one aged seven and the other just two. They were playing Twenty Questions:

"Are you thinking of something *made by people*?"

"No."

"Are you thinking of something *mineral*?"

"No." And so on.

After the game had gone on for some time the little one couldn't stand being left out any longer, so he suddenly chimed in with perfect intonation:

"inky umping—*doggies*?"

"inky umping—*Mommy*?"

He kept it up until the game dissolved in laughter.

William Corsaro was studying the strategies four-year-old children use to work their way into the group activity of their peers. His young subjects didn't ask "May I play?" because there was a good chance someone would say "No!" They didn't wait to be invited because they couldn't count on being told anything, or told what to do. They simply moved right in and began doing whatever it is the others were doing, and before long, they were part of the group.[1]

A number of researchers have begun to look at school learning as if it were a *game* that children wanted to take part in. Instead of only describing the cognitive learning of individuals, they have begun to describe a significant part of children's learning as *learning to do school*[2]—learning to play one's own role in the ongoing activity of the classroom. Cognitive learning, in turn, is the eventual result of participation over time in school tasks. If we want children to learn to write in school, then we might start by establishing ongoing routines in the classroom that invite and require writing (and reading). We should establish what Nancy Atwell has called a *literate community*.[3]

By now, thanks to the vigorous research and observation that have been focused on the writing process over the last decade, we have a fairly clear idea what activities people must carry out in order to become and to be writers. We will summarize these activities—what we call the *process of composing*—in this chapter. Then we will lay out in much finer detail the procedures that have helped us set up literate communities in our own and others' classrooms.

A DESCRIPTION OF THE WRITING PROCESS

Milan Kundera came of age in Czechoslovakia under a government whose policy of censorship would not allow him to publish his books. He was put in jail more than once; some of his friends are still there. As a group they dreamed of the West, where even schoolchildren could write and publish what they wanted to. They longed for the almost unimaginable power to write what one truly wished to say and share one's most important thoughts with an attentive public.

Kundera's is the strongest demonstration we know of the point that writing begins with a will to say something to someone else. Marvelously, we have found that, although many of our own adult voices have been muted by our school experiences or displaced by the canned excitement of the electronic media, children still want to write. In the following pages we will share what one professional writer and writing teacher describes as the process he and many other writers go through in order to write—the stages, step by step. But you should always keep in mind that before any set of strategies will work, the will to say something to someone else must be present, and encouraged. A classroom that focuses on these strategies without the communicative intention they are to serve will not keep faith with its children.

The Stages of Writing

Donald Murray has written a description of the writing process professional writers appear to use.[4] His description seems just as viable for school writing. In Murray's model, writing is a *process of continuous thinking, experimenting, and reviewing.* The activity of writing a paper develops in three stages: rehearsing, drafting, and revising.

Rehearsing, the stage in which writers discover what they have to say is the rehearsing stage. Teachers can encourage rehearsing by means of brainstorming sessions, in which children think and write down as many details as they can about a person, a place, or an event that is meaningful to them. Sometimes teachers promote free writing during the rehearsal stage. Free writing is timed writing in which the writer puts down absolutely anything that occurs to her, without stopping and without making any corrections, for a specified period of time, usually five or ten minutes.[3] Both methods are intended to bring out into the open a wide range of particular ideas and details, which a writer can subsequently employ in his deliberate writing. There are other activities used during the rehearsal stage that we will describe later.

The second stage in the process of writing is *drafting.* The term "drafting" is chosen because this sort of writing is a tentative activity. When we speak of a first draft or a second draft, we imply that a piece of work is undergoing change, that other drafts may follow. It is during the drafting stage that the writer experiences clearly what she has to say. Drafting enables the writer to put her thoughts outside of herself and to consider them as if they belonged to someone else. The writer may thus have a dialogue with herself through the drafting process. She can appraise the work with some detachment in this stage, considering it as something that can stand on its own before a reader.[4]

Revising is the final stage, although we should remember that revision can lead to further rehearsal and further drafts. The writer examines her piece and clarifies for herself what the writing should say. When necessary, the writer prunes words or adds them, all in an effort to make the meaning that is in the piece speak more clearly. Sometimes revising is a matter of patching up phrases or sentences in order to make them smoother or clearer. Sometimes, however, the writer discovers whole new possibilities that should be developed in the work. In the latter event, revision can mean changes to larger parts of a work, and sometimes to the whole work. In Murray's words, "the writing stands apart from the writer, and the writer interacts with it, first to find out what it has to say, and then to help the writing say it more clearly and gracefully."[4]

Betty Flowers[5] suggests a way to make the different mental forces that are at work in writing comprehensible to children. She presents students with four role models, the *madman,* the *architect,* the *carpenter,* and the *judge.* Ideally, a writer takes on each of these roles, one at a time, as he works through his drafts. We have found it very helpful to children who have begun to acquire some fluency in writing. We remind you, however, before examining Flowers's work, that writing is not usually a linear process. The roles Flowers outlines are just that, roles. While contemplating her role models we should remember, for example, that revision can lead to further rehearsal and new drafts.

The *madman* is, of course, doing what Murray calls rehearsing. He is "full of ideas, writes crazily and perhaps rather sloppily, gets carried away by enthusiasm or anger, and if really let loose, could turn out ten pages in an hour."[5]

The second worker, who might be called in the next day, is the *architect.* She comes in, reads over what the madman has written, and looks for parts that are worth keeping and developing. "Her job is to select large chunks of material and to arrange them into a pattern that might form an argument. The thinking here is large, organizational, paragraph level thinking."[5] Also the architect might ask, are there any basic supports missing for what we want to say?

Once the architect has gotten together the basic structure of the piece — and this might involve cutting and taping and adding to the madman's work — we are ready for the carpenter.

The *carpenter* nails the ideas together in a logical sequence, making sure each sentence is clearly written, contributes to the paragraph, and leads logically and gracefully to the next sentence. When the carpenter finishes, the piece of writing should be smooth and watertight.

Only at this point are we ready to call in the last of the workers, the *judge.* The judge reads over the whole piece as a newcomer, reflects on what he hears, and compares it with what the author wanted to say. Is the idea or argument convincing? Is the tone right? Does the whole seem polished and ready?

Madman, architect, carpenter, judge is an easy sequence for most children to remember, and it promotes the same process that we see in Murray's sequence of *rehearsal, drafting, revision,* and *possible redrafting.* An added advantage of Flowers's method for young writers is that it gives a sense of individual purpose to each draft or each rereading, and keeps the judge at bay until suitably late in the process.

Before we leave Murray's stages and Flowers' roles, we should remind the reader that both of these approaches to the writing process are ideals, approximations that are not always honored in practice. Some writers find that thinking about what they are going to write before they write it fills them with dread: writer's block. Others write so slowly and thoughtfully that they rarely need to revise what they say. More to the point of this book, first-grade writers invest so much energy in the crafting of even a line of print that revising may seem like cruel punishment for them. Now, having said all that, after years of working with both these models, the authors still believe that devoting some attention to generating ideas and planning writing, drafting with an experimental attitude, and being prepared to rewrite their works to satisfy an audience are worthy goals for all children.

ATMOSPHERE, ASSIGNMENT, AND RESPONSE: THE TEACHER'S ROLE IN THE WRITING PROCESS

It is now time to discuss the teacher's role in all this. In light of our previous discussion on the writing process, what are the classroom characteristics and activities that are most helpful to children in their growth toward literacy? We will explore the issues of atmosphere, assignments, and responses in an effort to forge an answer.

An Atmosphere for Writing

Every classroom has both a physical and an intellectual atmosphere. Some basic features of the physical atmosphere are crucial to children's well-being, for example, lighting and ventilation. Provided these necessities are met, however, the intellectual atmosphere is far more important. A healthy intellectual atmosphere is one with a curriculum rich in substance, where writing is received with enthusiasm and respect, where praise is judiciously bestowed, where children are helped to discover their next goal, and where a purposeful audience exists for each student's writing. In a healthy intellectual atmosphere, young authors feel they can take risks and make mistakes without fear of censure. Ideally, children come to know that trying new forms and experimenting are an important part of the writing process. Most nonessential physical constraints can be overcome in the classroom. Extraordinary writing centers, dazzling with prepared booklets, notebooks, borrowed typewriters, paints, crayons, and paste, are fine—but not essential. All too often they are more show than we care to believe. Intellectual constraints—those that take discovery out of the writing classroom and replace it with formulas for sentence patterns, rules for punctuation, and demands for correct spelling—are more difficult for children to overcome. Concerns for mechanics have their place, but teachers who are sensitive to their children's writing development make sure that a preoccupation with correctness does not take the place of the intellectual "romper room" that effective composition demands.

Choosing Topics for Writing

Just as the atmosphere in a classroom affects children during every stage of the composing process so do the topics we encourage children to choose. A person's choice of topic can either set the writing stage or destroy it. Generally, when we write about things that matter to us and that we know about, we welcome the rehearsing and drafting stages for the chance to better express how we feel and say what we know. At such times, we are glad to revise because we have the opportunity to try and get closer to our thoughts, closer to what we really mean. On the other hand, if we are forced to write about issues that inspire no images or ones that strike no emotion, revision is pointless: We have nothing in mind that we're trying to capture.

Appropriate Responses to Children's Writing

An important part of the composing process is receiving some response to one's writing. Writing is, after all, an attempt to trigger some kind of mental experience in a reader. Writers, like target shooters, improve their aim as they see where their efforts go, which depends in large part on the nature of the response. In this chapter we will be concerned with who makes the response, when it is most useful, and in what forms it should be made. Responses to what has been written and the discussions that ensue provide the classroom dynamics for children's writing development. Unfortunately, in many classrooms response is limited to bright stickers and stamped smiling faces. If we see our task as encouraging writing development, this type of response must yield to a more sensitive and knowledgeable commentary from the teacher.

What follows is a discussion of two writing programs that have proven successful for us, for the teachers with whom we work, or for teachers whose programs we have read about in national journals. The first program centers upon the kindergarten year. The latter program is intended for first, second, and third graders. Both these programs are sensitive to the composing process Murray describes and to the important areas of the writing teacher's responsibility: atmosphere, assignment, and response.

THE KINDERGARTEN YEAR

In Chapter 8 we defined composition as the act of putting together the details of a message in a form that is understandable to an audience. We went on to point out that children can compose before they can write. In fact, they do it all the time in kindergarten. Watch any five year old compose as she pretends to be pouring coffee for a friend in her classroom's playhouse corner. And isn't it composition at its best when a kindergarten child rescues her buddy from a "fire" that's blazing and consuming the class jungle gym? Composition doesn't always come in letters upon pages. Composition is thinking and creating. Composition is moving ideas from hidden spaces within our minds to detectable spaces in our outside world.

Marilyn Snyder, a kindergarten teacher from Walled Lake, Michigan, knows that writing has its beginnings in oral composition. From opening day, her children begin writing through their talk. Marilyn schedules "writing" early in the day. She always calls this activity writing, as opposed to sharing, drawing, or coloring, because she wants her children to understand that composition entails pulling together one's thoughts for others to interpret and enjoy. The children come close to her and sit in a group. They talk of things they want to write about or topics that she has asked them to consider: melting snow, hatching chicks, growing seeds.

After the children talk, they go back to their tables to "write." They draw and chatter while she moves about the room helping individual children. She finds herself commenting on drawings, asking questions, giving suggestions, taking dictation, and occasionally helping children sound out words.

Time is set aside later in the day for sharing. The children are pulled together in a group and called one by one to the author's chair.[6] Once seated, each youngster holds up his drawing and begins to speak. The rest of the class listens and is encouraged to ask questions. Marilyn asks questions, too.

In this way, Ms. Snyder is addressing three needs of a beginning writing group:

- the need to establish an approximation of a literate community, in a room where almost none of the children can read or write in the conventional sense!
- the need to draw out children's language, and lead them to compose orally, and
- the need to find a connection between written representation and spoken language.

Setting Up a Literate Community

We need not dwell on this point here because later in this chapter we will consider in detail procedures for setting up classroom environments that encourage interaction among students by means of and concerning the medium of writing. Note for now how Marilyn has set up routines for discussing, writing, and sharing, which will be durable frameworks to support children's growth. Those children who can only draw, can draw. Those who are ready to experiment with letters can do so. In fact, this activity format can organize the writing time through all of the elementary school years. Imagine the good fortune of the teacher who gets Ms. Snyder's children next year. These children will already know how to plan and write and share.

Drawing Out Oral Language

When the children ask questions of the child who is sharing his or her paper in Ms. Snyder's classroom, they are participating in a most important part of the composing process. By answering questions, children are forced to sustain their topics, to tell more, and yet more. With encouragement and regular opportunities for asking and answering questions, children will eventually be able to ask their own as they write.

James Britton[7] says that sustained narrative speech is likely to be a lead-in to writing. James Moffett suggests why:

> The first step towards writing is made when a speaker takes over a conversation and sustains some subject alone. He has started to create a solo discourse that while intended to communicate to others is less collaborative, less prompted, and less corrected by feedback than dialogue. He bears more of the responsibility for effective communication. . . . The cues for his next line are not what his interlocutor said, but what he himself just said.[8]

Connecting Writing and Speech

As we suggested in the early chapters of this book, young children need to develop an understanding of how writing represents ideas. Dyson[9] found that children in kindergarten used letters and pictures interchangeably. One child, for example, drew a picture of a boy and wrote the letters J–I–M, then said, "These both say 'Jim.'" At this early stage, however, both pictures and letters seemed to serve as tokens, as reminders of a longer discourse. In Chapter 9 we described how Tyler wrote the letters OSOPNOTM, then told a story about a unicorn. Asked to read her writing a second time, Tyler produced essentially the same story, but with different words.

During the kindergarten year, we expect children to move from a point where they talk about print in the same loose way that they might talk about a picture, to the realization that print represents language in an exact way. Then we expect children to acquire the alphabetic principle, the realization that print represents language by its sounds, and represents sounds at the level of phonemes. They will also have to learn the identity of the letters of the alphabet and learn several concepts about print, including the conventions by which print is arranged on the page. They will have to acquire the *concept of word,* the ability to divide language mentally into units of words, and to find a match between the bound configurations on the page and the words they hear the teacher pronounce when she reads aloud.

Teachers must take care to see that children develop these concepts that orient them to print. Normally, the children's own active discovery processes, along with guidance from the teacher, is sufficient to enable children to acquire these concepts. However, it must be stressed that if children think about print in a way that is highly variant from the way it actually works, their early writing experiences will be more confusing than productive.[2]

Judith Hilliker, a kindergarten teacher from Durham, New Hampshire, has developed means of working children through this transition from picture to picture-plus-print to print. She begins with lots of shared book experiences: reading aloud to children from enlarged versions of books, pointing to the words, and calling attention to the ways the letters signal the sounds of the words she reads. At the same time, she encourages children to make their own print productions with paper and pencil.[10] As soon as her children begin to recognize that letters represent sounds, she invites them to use that knowledge at the writing table.

Hilliker points out that at first the text might be just one letter, but "when a child who knows that 'P says puh' prints a capital P next to a four-legged oval with a squiggle, he's communicating more fully that his picture shows a pig." Hilliker goes on to say that pretty soon he'll be asking her how to make a "guh." Then he'll want some medial consonants, and later long vowels. Writing helps the prereader understand how reading works because by this point the text has enough clues for him to read it. The young writer who prints "BOT" can probably read it as boat, even without the picture. "And when he does," says

Hilliker, "his concept of reading suddenly tumbles out of the realm of mystery."[10]

Many kindergarten teachers prefer asking children to choose their own topics, rather than choosing topics for them. In these classrooms the children draw and write as best they can while the teacher circulates around the room. Teachers help, the way Judith Hilliker does, by supplying letters and giving encouragement. When a child completes a piece Hilliker dates it, transcribes the invented spelling (inconspicuously), then places it in her ready-to-read box for her class's next story time. After a child's piece has been read to the class, she stores it in a writing folder. She watches for the child's progress and assesses his development in three areas: "letter formation, phonics skills, and understanding of the mechanics of print."[10]

THE PRIMARY YEARS

In the remainder of this chapter we will discuss a general system for implementing a writing program for first through third grades—a system, like the kindergarten program, that is sensitive to the writing process Murray describes[4] and to classroom characteristics that support writing growth. The discussion will be divided into eight sections:

1. an overview of a process-writing classroom;
2. an outline of what to do the first day;
3. a typical day;
4. suggestions for setting up a writing classroom, in general, and writing folders, in particular;
5. the dynamics of moving a promising draft along;
6. conferencing techniques;
7. publishing possibilities; and
8. suggestions for evaluation.

We have found this system to work well for us over the years, but we assume that our techniques will be modified by anyone who chooses to use them. We have not found it easy, by any means, to set up and sustain process-writing classrooms, but the rewards continue to make the effort worthwhile. We reflect with pleasure on the honest industry we have seen each day in children who are writers, the sound of pencils scratching furiously across page after page of text, the earnest voices of children talking to one another about their evolving drafts, the pride we see in children's faces as they share their finished products, and the heightened, almost collegial curiosity our young authors show over the adult authors who write the stories they read and love.

An Overview of a Process-Writing Classroom
In process-writing classrooms we attempt to create an atmosphere where even a professional writer would feel at home. Here children choose their own topics

and write for people that matter: themselves, their classmates, their friends in the school community (pieces are shared between classrooms), their teachers, their parents and siblings, as well as the literary community at large (work is submitted for publication).

You will see boxes that hold writing folders; trays for works in progress; jars of pencils, crayons, and colored markers; shelves of published books; an author's chair; and bulletin boards, which sometimes celebrate a published author, but just as often celebrate a member of the class. Large round tables are placed well apart for group conferences, and small places are created (spaces under tables, for example) where pairs of children can collaborate in peace.

Though a part of each writing period is quiet, perhaps fifteen minutes, a good portion—twenty minutes, or so—is not. Like professional writers, children are encouraged to talk to others about their drafts. They talk to their teachers and their classmates. They ask for an ear, first to attend to meaning and later to attend to grammar and style. They ask for an eye, first to attend to spelling and later to attend to mechanics.

Writing is a cooperative effort between teachers and children in these classrooms. It is joyful, noncompetitive, and nourishing, while at the same time highly demanding: Children write at length, they revise, and they edit, but in an atmosphere of acceptance and *respect.* This milieu has been set up and maintained with several purposes in mind, but perhaps the major purpose has been to prevent loathing of the whole process later on, as Peter nearly did (see Figure 11–1).

What to Do on the First Day

According to Donald Graves,[11] the tone is set in process-writing classrooms by what the teacher DOES, not by what the teacher SAYS. We agree. First you will have to show children how you go about making your own topic choices, an overhead projector is helpful here. We try and choose topics that are simple

FIGURE 11–1
Peter
Grade 1

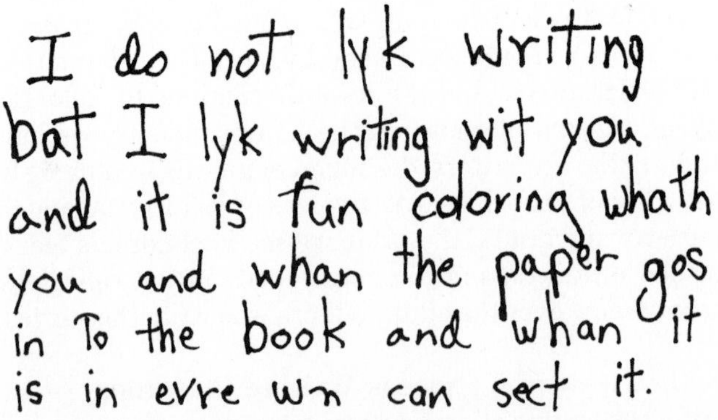
I do not lyk writing
bat I lyk writing wit you
and it is fun coloring whath
you and whan the paper gos
in To the book and whan it
is in evre wn can sect it.

(I do not like writing, but I like writing with you. And it is fun coloring with you and when the paper goes into the book. And when it is in, everyone can see it.)

and close to home, like watching a caterpillar spin a coccoon or building with Legos. Generate at least three or four topics and then tell the children why you have chosen your topic from the three or four you have listed on the overhead. We tend to choose topics that conjure up lots of memories or ones that would make us feel good in the writing.

Then, take time to let your children generate their own topics, encouraging them to talk about their list with a friend. Ask each child to circle just one topic for today. (Prior to beginning writing in your room, you might want to review the teaching suggestions from Chapter 7 in order to get over the spelling hump.) First graders often draw pictures of possible topics, rather than listing their topics using invented spelling.

Next, still using the overheard, we write (or draw) our favorite topic in the middle of a transparency, circle it, and then begin letting words that come into our mind flow onto the sheet. When we do this, we are showing children how to prepare a *cluster sheet,* one prewriting strategy we use frequently. We write slowly, but deliberately. With first graders, we might only draw little figures around our topic. Figure 11–2 is one of our cluster sheets about a best childhood girl friend, Marilyn. (The numbers represent the order in which the words were written.)

You will notice when looking at the numbers in the diagram that all the words related to a subtopic (i.e., "alley picking," "playhouse," "looked like," etc.) were not written before another subtopic came to mind. This is how prewriting works: One idea leads to another, then back again.

Believe it or not, even first graders can do this. However, in Matt's example (Figure 11–3) you will notice that the smaller circles are not connected in a logical way. For this reason, first graders often just draw a picture for their prewriting experience.

FIGURE 11–2
Sample cluster sheet

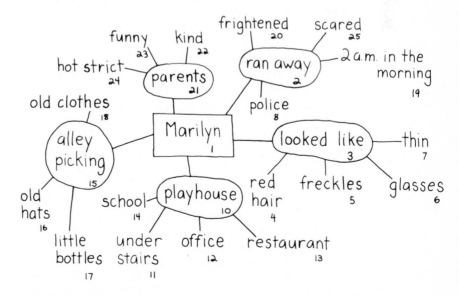

FIGURE 11–3
No Name
Grade 1

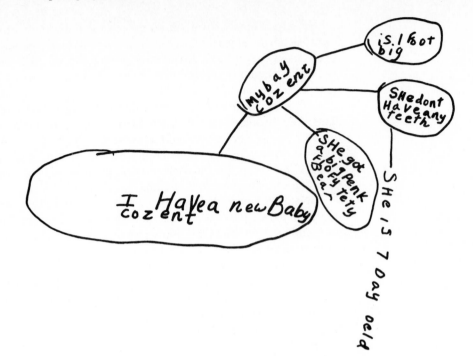

Once you have finished this activity, let the children chat with a partner for a few minutes with their cluster sheets in hand. Then pass out some draft paper (we use either tossed-out computer paper or primer paper, the kind with a lot of wide lines) and begin writing. We encourage those who want to add to their drawing, or cluster sheet, to do so. Again, we write/draw on the overhead using a new transparency while the children write/draw at their desks. Everyone is quiet now and we insist on not being disturbed.

After about five minutes into our own writing we leave the overhead and begin walking around the room to help any children in trouble. Usually a simple question centering on some aspect of their cluster sheet or picture is enough to get a youngster moving along.

After about fifteen or twenty minutes, bring the children, with their drafts, to a corner of the room where you have set up two chairs, a child's chair and a large one (we use ours). Have a few children in mind, and one by one ask them to share what they have written or drawn. Be sure to guide your first reader to the *larger* chair, while you take the smaller one. This puts the child, literally, on top of her world, even if only for a few minutes. After you have told the author how you felt hearing the draft and you have mentioned something specific you liked, encourage the other children to tell the author how *they* felt when they heard the piece, and what they liked or remembered. Then allow a few children to ask the author questions.

Continue this routine for at least a week until each child has written on several topics. Once a number of drafts have been completed (any number more than one; but, perhaps just one for your reluctant writers), a single draft can be chosen for publication. Let us put off publication for just a bit, though, and describe a typical writing day later in the year, a day that will come sooner than you think.

Beyond Day One: A Typical Day

Our writing periods are usually forty-five minutes long (see Figure 11–4): fifteen minutes for writing, twenty minutes for having conferences, and ten minutes for sharing. The order—writing, having conferences, and sharing—frequently changes.

As with the very first day, it is usually best to begin each writing period with everyone writing, including the teacher. We, as well as our children, need a chance to get in touch with our own writing processes. What's more, children need to see us write.

After about five minutes of writing, we suggest that you walk around your room, talking briefly with a few of your students, the ones you believe may need you the most. It helps if you have taken the time the night before to review your children's writing folders. *Hunt for youngsters having problems.* Watch for either very little writing or for drafts that look extremely scribbled-up or holey. Consider such marks or a lack of writing as clues to children in trouble, and choose these children for your early rounds. Sometimes writers in trouble just

FIGURE 11–4
Writing period

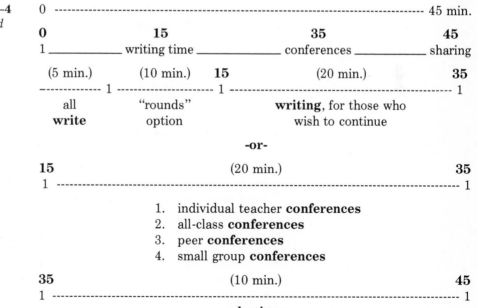

1. individual teacher **conferences**
2. all-class **conferences**
3. peer **conferences**
4. small group **conferences**

Note: We go into greater detail about types of conferences later.

need a few minutes of your undivided attention. Giving this needed attention early in the day helps: You will have let these youngsters know that you care and you *may,* incidentally, prevent unwanted interruptions later on.

After you have circulated among your students, call four to six children to the conference table. Since it helps children to know when you are going to conference with them—they have a chance to think about what they're going to say—consider assigning them to certain days. That is, specific children may be assigned to Mondays, others to Tuesdays, and so on. Alternatively, you may choose to have a conference box in your room. When a child has a draft that she needs to share with you, as opposed to sharing it with a peer, the youngster may put her draft in the general conference box. We signify "general" because later, when children are publishing, we have several conference boxes, marked for specific purposes.

While some children are holding conferences with you, the other children should continue writing. (It might seem impossible to keep twenty or thirty children busy while you're holding conferences, but it's not. By the end of this chapter you will understand just how busy your children will be. Trust us for right now.) As the year progresses, the class members not in conference with you may do other things as well. For example, children may

- continuing writing/illustrating,
- hold peer conferences,
- illustrate a piece for someone else,
- read to another child from the author's chair,
- be part of a group conference, and
- publish.

Conference time usually lasts about twenty minutes, although at first you may be frustrated and want more time. The thing you can do that will make the biggest difference is to *read your children's drafts the night before.* Beginning a conference unprepared will naturally result in a less efficient meeting.

Quite often it's helpful to hold all-class conferences rather than individual conferences. During these conferences, work with the entire class, or a group of children, on one skill, such as the use of commas in a series. Take a child's rough draft that needs some work (with the child's permission, of course) and transfer it to an overhead. We frequently make a ditto as well, so each child can follow along easily. Then work together to locate some of the rough spots and correct them together.

Although adding commas is an example of an editing skill covered in all-classroom conferences, all-class conferences can be used to demonstrate revision as well. We especially like dealing with problems of audience sensitivity this way. For example, children often use pronouns without specifying who their "he" or "she" is supposed to be; or they refer to a previously unmentioned character, assuming you, the reader, know exactly who the character is. These types of audience sensitivity problems are easy for children to detect, *when they're not reading their own writing,* which is why we like working on this troublesome issue. Other easy problems to work on together are

- prying apart drafts that have more than one topics,
- hunting for dead wood (unnecessary words),
- expanding *telling* lines (e.g., "it was funny") into *showing* lines or paragraphs (i.e., lines that describe the events that were funny), and
- choosing the best words, using varied sentence patterns.

Don't worry too much if your first attempts at all-classroom conferences fall short of perfection; you will find the experience of holding all-classroom conferences to be your best teacher.

The last few minutes of every writing day should be spent sharing. Since you want this to be a time when children hear well-written work, choose volunteers carefully; it's probably best to choose pieces you've read recently.

Setting Up the Classroom

The Classroom.   We have never needed very much: a lot of paper; colored markers and pencils; a folder/binder for each child, complete with pockets and clips for holding papers, to house work in progress; a manila folder for everyone, to house already published or unwanted drafts; some colorful baskets, which we number to accommodate the steps that drafts go through on their way toward publication; an author's chair that the children use whenever they read their work, which we decorate;[3] some bulletin board space to celebrate our authors or to depict the writing process; at least one round table for group conferences, whether teacher-led or child-led; a bookshelf to house our ever-growing classroom library; and a typewriter or computer to print out our final drafts.

Most classrooms have these materials, or things similar, available to them as part of the school budget. An author's chair can be found at a garage sale and bookshelves can be makeshift, if need be. The point is, you shouldn't need too much. Two luxuries we allow ourselves, however, are pads of stick-on note paper and a rubber stamp that says DRAFT. The sticky pads allow us to record all sorts of information for authors, or let authors take their own notes, while freeing the author to place the sheet wherever he needs it on his draft. The DRAFT stamp encourages young authors to write freely, without worrying about mechanical, grammatical, or spelling errors. Drafts are just that, drafts and the DRAFT stamp proves it!

The Writing Folder.   Works in progress have to be housed in a folder/binder, and we use ones with pockets and center clips. When open, they look like Figure 11–5. The left hand pocket holds topics and cluster sheets, and the

FIGURE 11–5
Writing folder

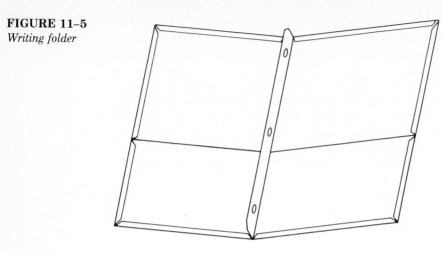

right hand side holds drafts in progress. We save the center for our ever-growing writing manual.

Topic Sheet.   We've tried all types, but we find ones similar to the one in Figure 11–6 work the best. Children fill in their names on day one and then, as topics occur to them, they write them down right on their topic sheets. When they choose a topic to write on, they fill in the square under the number. Here is one second-grader's topic sheet (see Figure 11–7).

First-grade teachers might prefer fewer spaces for topics, like the one in Figure 11–8. You will notice that this topic sheet has several triangles beneath each number, whereas the previous topic sheet has only one square. The teacher who designed this topic sheet told us many children like writing on the same topic several times, hence she added more triangles.

Another option for first-grade teachers is to simply fold a piece of manila paper in half and have the children draw just two possibilities.

Cluster Sheets.   One way to engage children in prewriting is through the use of cluster sheets. Some children don't want to use them, preferring to draw, while many children find them helpful. Like a picture, a cluster sheet serves as a memory bank for young authors. You'll find that first graders often add onto them even after a draft has been started. Figure 11–9 is one type of cluster sheet.

The Manual.   A writer's manual for first, second, and third graders isn't going to be very detailed. Nevertheless, there are guidelines and resource materials that we find helpful to have on hand. We don't pass the manual sheets out all at once (and a few teachers we work with don't use them at all). What follows are some suggestions of what to include in a writer's manual.

FIGURE 11–6
Topic sheet (left)

FIGURE 11–7
No Name (right)
Grade 2

TOPICS
Your Name_____

1.   7.
☐   ☐
----

2.   8.
☐   ☐
----

3.   9.
☐   ☐
----

4.   10.
☐   ☐
----

5.   11.
☐   ☐
----

6.   12.
☐   ☐

TOPICS
Your Name_____

1.   7.
☐ bike rideing ☐ Kivin
----

2.   8.
☐ seling   ☐   socer
----

3.   9.
☐ goldfish ☐ fishing
----

4.   10.
☐ skoll   ☐
----

5.   11.
☐ pano   ☐ t. chess
----

6.   12.
☐   ☐

FIGURE 11–8
*First-grade
topic sheet*

Topics   Name_____
_____

1.
△△△△

- -

2.
△△△△

- -

3.
△△△△

- -

4.
△△△△

Name_____

FIGURE 11–9
Cluster sheet

FIGURE 11–10
*Sample manual
sheet*

Things I Can Do During Writing Time

☞1. I can add to my topic list. ✚✚

☞2. I can brainstorm a new topic.♀♀

☞3. I can begin a new draft. ✎

☞4. I can improve or add on to a
draft I have started. ✎✎✎

☞5. I can draw some pictures for one
of my drafts.🖌🖌🖌

☞6. I can underline misspelled words.
(This is proofreading.)

☞7. I can look for words that should
be capitalized.
(This is also proofreading.)

☞8. I can read my drafts to myself
and decide which one I want to
publish.

Figure 11–10, entitled "Things I Can Do During Writing Time," allows children to review their options before they begin writing. As the year progresses, children color in the little hands by the options that have been discussed and are in use at the time. Teachers vary on how they use this sheet—some allowing children to use all the possibilities at once, others going more slowly—but it has been our experience that most teachers use the sheet in one form or another.

The sheet in Figure 11–11, entitled "What I Can Do During Conference Time," is also a popular one because, like its predecessor, it lets the children know what they are allowed to do. Unlike the silent nature of the writing-time activities, most of the conference-time activities involve interaction. You will note that writing is still an option during conference time, that period when conferences are permitted and talking is encouraged. Children especially love option number three: writing with a friend. They either pull their desks together or crawl under a nearby table with their drafts.

In addition to the writing-time and conference-time sheets, we include a sheet outlining simple conference guidelines in the manual (see Figure 11–12). Although the children can meander from our formula when they need to, the guidelines provide a starting point for peer interaction.

As with everything else, we model peer conferences several times before we expect the children to confer with each other. Some of us have our children use a listener's guide (see Figure 11–13) during a peer conference to keep them on task.

FIGURE 11–11
Sample manual sheet

Things I Can Do During Conference Time

☞1. I can do anything from my <u>Writing Time</u> list.

☞2. I can hold a conference with a friend. ☺ or ☺☺

☞3. I can write at a friend's desk or at a place we find comfortable. ✏☺✏☺✏

☞4. I can draw some pictures for one of my friend's drafts. 🖌🖌🖌

☞5. I can hold a conference with my teacher. 👤 or 👤

FIGURE 11–12

Conference Guidelines for
2nd, 3rd, & 4th Graders

1. Listen to your partner's draft.

2. Tell your partner what you liked about the draft or what you thought was interesting.

3. Listen to your partner's draft again.

4. If you have a question about your partner's topic, this is a good time to ask it. (If you have time, write your question down and give it to your partner. This will help your partner remember what you asked.)

FIGURE 11–13 Listener's Guide to a Peer or Group Conference

YOUR NAME_____   Date_____

CONFERENCE WITH:_____

THEIR STORY TITLE/TOPIC_____

What I liked or thought was interesting:

_____
_____
_____
_____
_____

What I would like to know more about:

_____
_____
_____
_____
_____

Suggestions for improvement:

_____
_____
_____
_____
_____

****

To bring closure to the writing period, we use a writing log, which is also part of the manual. Figure 11–14 is one example.

Children write in these eagerly, so teachers go through the folders periodically and read them. Fundamentally, however, the logs are meant for the children, to chronicle their own writing behavior. A typical example reads, "I had a hard time getting started today, but I wrote a lot finally. Jason helped me!"

FIGURE 11–14

Writing Log   Name_____

Date	What I did today	How today went Great OK Slow Moving

The Dynamics of Moving a Promising Draft Along

Publishing children's work is an important part of process-writing classrooms, but because children write so much, we find we cannot publish everything. This state of affairs is probably healthy. After all, professional writers don't publish every draft they produce: *everything* isn't good enough. For professionals, what does get into print is always a matter of choice, and so it should be for children.

Right from the beginning of the year the children are told that some of their work will be published, but some will not. Every time they have completed a certain number of drafts on separate topics, perhaps two or three, maybe even four, they are to choose one and send it on a publishing journey. We explain that professional writers must do this too, often sending their work back and forth through the mail five or six times. Children have no problem understanding this, and they eagerly await our explanation and instructions to guide their foray into publishing. This is what we tell them.

When you have selected your best draft, we would like you to make a sandwich with it. This might sound kind of funny, but listen carefully. Your *draft* will be like the peanut butter or the tuna fish you would use if you were making a sandwich: it will be your filling. Your top piece of bread will be a journey sheet (see Figure 11–15) and your bottom piece of bread will be a proofreading sheet (see Figure 11–16). Use the stapler and staple your sandwich together, at the top. Then, follow the instructions on your journey sheet and send your draft on its way. (Some experts with whom we have corresponded, find the term "sandwich" condescending. It has never hit us this way, but you may prefer a different term, perhaps publishing packet.)

Though we will talk about this journey sheet (Figure 11–15) as if it were the only one, in truth they are as varied as the teachers themselves. This one was designed by Betty Morris, a second-grade teacher in Birmingham, Michigan, with Ruth Nathan, one of this book's coauthors.

Stepping through Betty and Ruth's journey sheet, you'll notice the first thing a child must do after choosing a draft is to write the date on the journey sheet (Step 1). Then, the youngster must read his draft to a friend (Step 2). Since writing time is a quiet time, conference time is the natural sharing slot. (During writing time, this child would have to work on another draft.)

After conferring with a friend, our youngster will work on revising his piece if he needs to (Step 3). We find that children ask their peers questions all the time, and many youngsters opt to add on after their conference sessions. Here are several questions a classmate asked Amy, the second-grade author of the draft on witches (see Figure 11–17).

1. How do you know all of this?
2. What do they do when the bats perch on their noses?
3. Can you describe the stubs?
4. How come they have the power of 300 strong men?

FIGURE 11–15

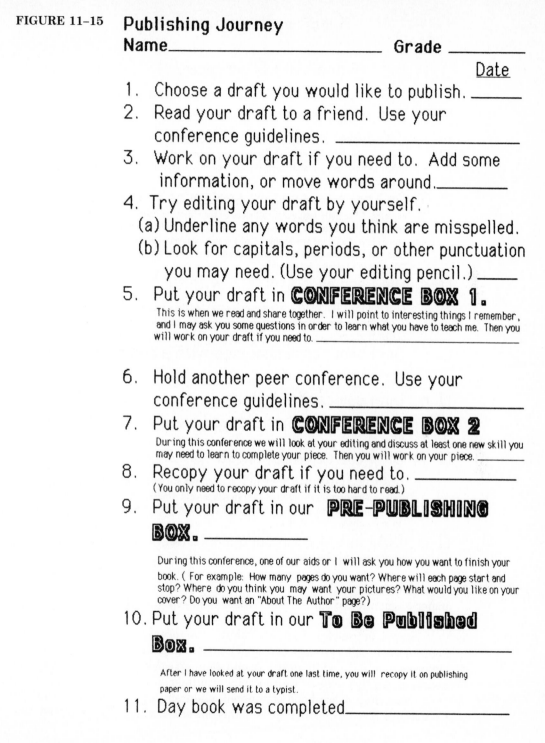

Publishing Journey

Name_____ Grade _____

<u>Date</u>

1. Choose a draft you would like to publish. _____
2. Read your draft to a friend. Use your conference guidelines. _____
3. Work on your draft if you need to. Add some information, or move words around._____
4. Try editing your draft by yourself.
   (a) Underline any words you think are misspelled.
   (b) Look for capitals, periods, or other punctuation you may need. (Use your editing pencil.) ____
5. Put your draft in **CONFERENCE BOX 1.**
   This is when we read and share together. I will point to interesting things I remember, and I may ask you some questions in order to learn what you have to teach me. Then you will work on your draft if you need to. _____
6. Hold another peer conference. Use your conference guidelines. _____
7. Put your draft in **CONFERENCE BOX 2**
   During this conference we will look at your editing and discuss at least one new skill you may need to learn to complete your piece. Then you will work on your piece. _____
8. Recopy your draft if you need to. _____
   (You only need to recopy your draft if it is too hard to read.)
9. Put your draft in our **PRE-PUBLISHING BOX.** _____

   During this conference, one of our aids or I will ask you how you want to finish your book. (For example: How many pages do you want? Where will each page start and stop? Where do you think you may want your pictures? What would you like on your cover? Do you want an "About The Author" page?)
10. Put your draft in our **To Be Published Box.** _____

    After I have looked at your draft one last time, you will recopy it on publishing paper or we will send it to a typist.
11. Day book was completed_____

FIGURE 11–16
*Proofreading
checklist*

Proofreading Checklist

☐ 1. Did I spell all words correctly?
(Underline/circle words you are unsure of. Try looking some of them up.)

☐ 2. Did I write each sentence as a
complete thought? (Here is an incomplete thought, " On the street."
Here is a complete thought, " The little puppy stood all alone on the street.") Note:
Sometimes writers use an incomplete sentence on purpose to create a certain effect.
Here is an example, "Not me!"

☐ 3. Do I have any run-on sentences? (Here is a run-on
sentence: " The little puppy stood all alone on the street and he couldn't find his
mother and he was so, so frightened that he thought he would die and so he looked
around to find a friend and he didn't find one so he walked on and on.)
Note: Sometimes authors deliberately write run-on sentences. See Shel
Silverstein's Lafcadio for examples.

☐ 4. Did I end each sentence with the correct
punctuation? (Here is a sentence that has the wrong punctuation at the
end, "Could the puppy find his mother." This sentence needs a question mark, not a
period.)

☐ 5. Did I begin each sentence with a capital
letter?

☐ 6. Did I use capital letters
correctly in other places? (Names, days of the week, months,
titles, etc.)

☐ 7. Did I use commas, apostrophes, and other
punctuation correctly? (Commas are used between words in
lists, before a conjunction introducing an independent clause, after salutations, etc.
Apostrophes are used with possessive forms [Jimmy's shoes, the boys' lockers] and
in contractions [can't, it's].)

☐ 8. Did I indent each paragraph? (New ideas require new
paragraphs, dialogue also.)

Amy kept track of these questions, which were written on the sticky
paper we mentioned earlier, and worked some, but not all, of the answers into
her draft.

Step 4, editing the draft, is a helpful step for two reasons: Teachers like
knowing their children respect them enough to give them readable work, and
children benefit from attempting to edit alone. We ask our students to use red
pencils when they edit so we can celebrate their discoveries with them.

Once Step 4 has been completed, children put their "sandwiches" in
Conference Box 1 (Step 5). Papers in this box are now ready for us to read. We

FIGURE 11–17
Amy
Grade 2

All witches are very ugly. They have long gren Bumpy noises, and some Bats might purtch on it. Witch noiseslook like there made of Paper mashy. They have wiges with sowigly measy hair on them. They are all Bald and wair maecks, Becaus they have stuøs. They have Black cat's with Gleewing green eyes. They alse have monsters what they keep in cages chaned to walls. They feed them Banana peals and They also eat long sticks of Butter. Witches sleep on semcnt flowers. They alwes wear capes, hats and Dark Black clower There head's a shaped like Onions, and shell like skunks, And There head's are as fragle as mash pataitos. Same witches are geod But Mast are Bad. Witches have the pawe of Soo strong men from the circes. They are very strong and have the magic of 79 Migishons. They can tur into the tallest Giant to the smalest fly. Witches eat flys and slime. And there favret Dish is Spider wibe pie, with honey on top. The good witches are very, very good, and very, very, nice. But witches eat childrer with a Bit of Salt and a Bit of Pepaer. They have a specl masheen. It's a Bike with the Back wheel in a p@t with Baling hot water. And knives stalded in to yeu, way Down, deep. You peadel And the Back whel and it mixkes you the Salt, pepar a your Blod. And that Tastes Better Than Spider wibe pie with honey on top.

read four or five of them after school, in preparation for the formal teacher-child conferences we will hold the next day, or on the next writing day. (We refer to these as formal conferences because during our daily rounds we often talk with children informally about their drafts.)

The first conference we hold with a child centers on meaning. We frequently tell them how their draft makes us feel and point to interesting parts of the draft. Sometimes we ask the child to identify the part(s) that works best for her. If a piece isn't too long, we may ask the youngster to read the whole draft out loud. Just hearing a child read her piece gives us information about what we should do next. For the sake of clarity, rather than going into conferencing techniques now, we will defer this discussion to our conferencing section and move on to Step 6 of the journey sheet. One last comment before we do. At the end of Conference 1 we ask the children to look over the Proofreading Checklist (Figure 11–16) and mark the editing skills they think they can use by themselves. This way, before putting their drafts in Conference Box 2, they have had an opportunity to try their hand at editing *once again*. Several first and second graders check off numbers four and six; many have already completed number one. Again, the children are asked to use red pencils, so that we can see which improvements they were able to make without our help.

Step 6 calls for another peer conference. The more interaction young authors have with audience, the better. This is because children are egocentric: They aren't quite aware of what their audience knows and doesn't know, nor of what their audience needs to understand in order to comprehend the message. (Our early drafts are egocentric to some extent, as well.) Consequently, the journey sheet provides many opportunities for interaction.

Our second formal conference with a child is an editing conference. During this second editing conference (Step 7), we look at how well they have corrected what they said they could manage. If they haven't done a very good job, we help them with one of the skills they identified as being "known"; if they have found all of their errors, we celebrate this and then move on, teaching them one, and only one, *new* skill.

Once a child has edited as much as he can, we frequently do the rest alone, although sometimes we do this with the youngster nearby. We use a different color pencil when editing to tune us in to the skills we need to teach. Then, if the draft is readable, the piece moves on to the Pre-publishing Box; if not, it has to be recopied (Step 8). We try and avoid Step 8 at all costs, especially with less mature children. During the Pre-publishing conference (Step 9), we do little things like decide on page breaks. If we are fortunate enough to have an aid or a volunteer parent on hand, he or she holds this conference with the child. Sometimes children from older grades help us as well.

When the draft is ready for publication, it moves on to Step 10 where it is placed in our publishing folder or box. It either gets sent to a typist—often a parent in the room—or the draft is recopied onto special publishing paper by the child or teacher. The letter you see in Figure 11–18 is one a writing consultant sent to teachers who were initiating a process approach in their classrooms.

Several schools we work in have a central clearing house for drafts that are to be published. Teams of parents collect these drafts periodically and type them, using school computers. Papers are sent to the office with a slip similar to the one in Figure 11–19, and drafts come back all typed and ready to be illustrated.

When a child's book is completed, which means it has been printed and illustrated, the date is written on the last line of the journey sheet, Step 11. This is a big day for a youngster because he knows that soon he will be sitting in the author's chair sharing his work with the class. And the class will clap when he's done and tell him about their favorite parts. Some will say, "I love your illustrations," some will comment on the parts of the story (poem, essay,

FIGURE 11–18
Letter to teachers about publishing

Dear Teachers,

We are extremely fortunate to have five parents available to type for us. Here's how the system will work.

1. Attach a "Publishing Request" form to each draft you'd like typed. (The forms are located over your mailbox in the office.)

2. Fill out the form exactly as you wish it typed. Circle the type size you want.

3. Put the draft (with publishing request attached) into the metal box over your mailbox.

4. Your typed draft will be delivered to you.

Remember: 1. All drafts must be edited-completely

2. page breaks must be clearly visible
(Sample: _____]p1t _____]p2b)

3. State, by each page number, where you want the words typed
t = top   m = middle   b = bottom
c = centered over entire page

FIGURE 11–19
Publishing request

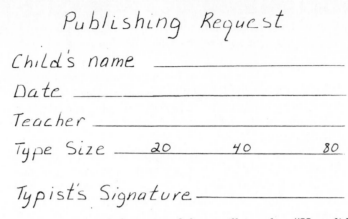

etc.) they enjoyed the most. Others will wonder, "How did you think of all that?" while still others will wish they had written the book themselves, and they will say so.

As we have said earlier, the particular journey sheet we have led you through is just one example. Once teachers are aware of the journey concept, they create their own. A first-grade teacher designed the one in Figure 11–20; a second-grade teacher, Kevin Keller of Walled Lake, Michigan, used some original graphics for his (see Figure 11–21).

Conferencing Techniques
Conferences can be arranged between the teacher and children, between two children, or among small groups of children. We'll take a look at each type in turn.

Teacher-Child Conferences.   Teacher child conferences can be of two types: *individual*—one teacher, one child—or *teacher-group*—one teacher, a few children. Individual conferences can be *informal,* conducted during your writing-time rounds, as we've mentioned earlier; or they can be *formal,* meaning prearranged. Drafts going through publication journeys are formal encounters, one-to-one interactions with authors during conference time.

During informal encounters we find ourselves helping children trouble-shoot, usually by listening to problems, asking relevant questions, or making open-ended suggestions. For example, Randy, a second grader, might tell us he doesn't know how to end his piece. We might respond by suggesting he write two endings and then pick the one that sounds the best. In this case, we'd encourage a peer conference as well. If Sandy, a first grader, tells us she doesn't know how to get started, we might ask to see her drawing or cluster sheet, and then start asking questions. Informal conferences are short, the purpose being to help a child move on quickly.

Formal individual teacher-child conferences are different: They've been arranged and frequently center on a draft pulled from one of the conference

FIGURE 11–20
*First-grade
journey sheet*

First Grade Journey Sheet

Your name _____

Date _____

1. Read your draft to yourself. ☐

2. Read your draft to a friend. ☐

   Whom did you read it to?_____

   [Let your friend tell you what was great. Let
   your friend ask you questions.]

3. Put on your editing hat.
   Edit your draft for
   ☐ spelling [Underline words that need help.]
   ☐ capitals [$\underline{f}$ means make it a capital.
   $\not{f}$ means make it lower case.]

4. **Put your draft in our
   Publishing Box.** ☐

FIGURE 11–21
*Alternative
second-grade
journey sheet*

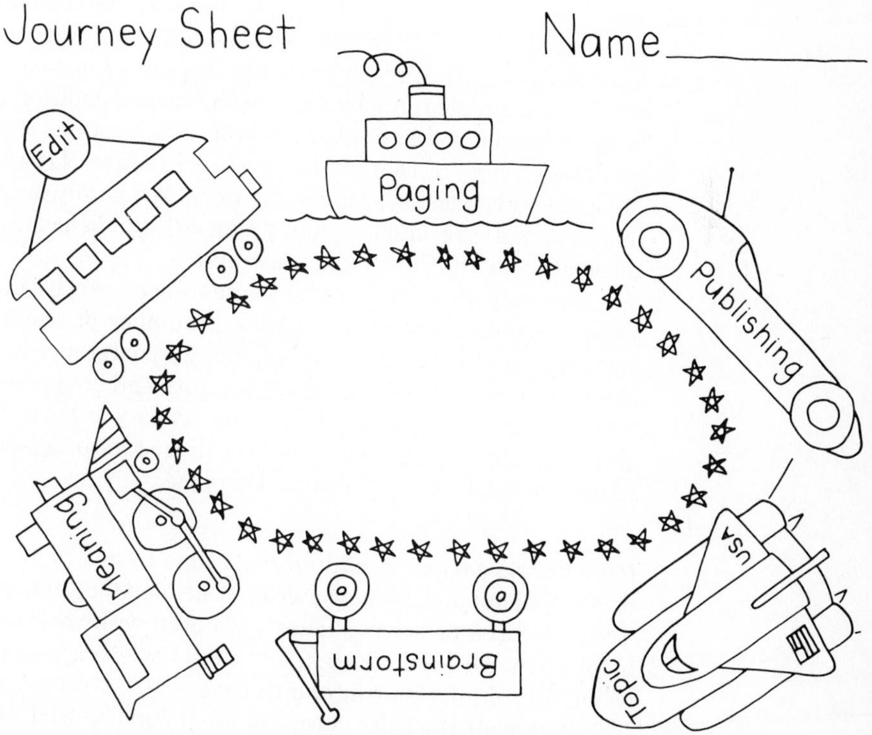

Journey Sheet   Name_____

Edit   Paging   Publishing

Meaning   Brainstorm   Topic   USA

boxes or folders. During early, planned conferences over drafts pulled from Conference Box 1, which center upon meaning rather than upon mechanical or grammatical issues, we often begin by telling the youngster how we felt about her piece reading it, and by pointing to what we enjoyed the most. Then, we may attempt to help a youngster make her piece better, often by inviting the child to put down her pencil and talk about her topic. During the early years we generally ask for elaboration: "Would you tell me more about your bike? Where do you like to go on it? What does it look like? Whom do you like to go riding with?"

The last suggestion may sound blasphemous to some writing scholars, but we feel there is a place for teachers to ask questions in elementary process-writing classrooms. It is not always possible to follow the child's lead because some children simply don't know enough about composing to be of much help to themselves. As the year progresses this changes, of course. The more children hear good literature and respond to their peers' writing during conference time, the more they become attuned to recognizing shortcomings in their own texts, and the less you will have to say during conferences.

In order to help you help your children grow as writers, we have included Donald Murray's "Qualities of Good Writing" (see Figure 11–22), a list one of his students shared with us at a workshop we attended. This list will help you to identify what you most certainly know intuitively about good writing, but for which you may not have found good labels. We refer to this list all the time as we sort out what we might say to a child during our teacher-child conferences.

Following Murray's list you will find one of our own (see Figure 11–23), which has examples of questions we have asked children to help them grow as writers. Nested within our list you will find questions that relate to Murray's qualities. A note of caution, however, is in order: Try not to overdo it when "helping" a youngster improve his work. We hardly ever address more than one issue at a time, and frequently a piece is published that is short on most of these aspects, but long on at least one.

We said that teacher-child conferences can be individual or teacher-group. Sometimes it helps to have a number of children around you and available for talking when you're holding a conference with a child. The other children listen and make good suggestions, and hold group conferences often. Small groups are also nice to arrange when you have a particular skill that several children need help on. (Review the section on all-classroom conferences in the section labeled, "Beyond Day One.")

Peer Conferences.   Children need time to talk to one another about their drafts, and not just about work that is headed for publication. They get stuck. They get tired of writing. They get bored with their own ideas. They need inspiration. All good reasons, we think, for letting them talk to one another, which they do during conference time.

There are rules, for sure, and procedures as well. (1) We like children to

FIGURE 11–22

The Qualities of Good Writing
Donald Murray

1. **MEANING**

   There must be content in an effective piece of writing. It must all add up to something. This is the most important element in good writing, but although it must be listed first it is often discovered last through the process of writing.

2. **AUTHORITY**

   Good writing is filled with specific, accurate, honest information. The reader is persuaded through authoritative information that the writer knows the subject.

3. **VOICE**

   Good writing is marked by an individual voice. The writer's voice may be the most significant element in distinguishing memorable writing from good writing.``

4. **DEVELOPMENT**

   The writer satisfies the reader's hunger for information. The beginning writer almost always overestimates the reader's hunger for language and underestimates the reader's hunger for information.

5. **DESIGN**

   A good piece of writing is elegant in the mathematical sense. It has form, structure, order, focus, coherence. It gives the reader a sense of completeness.

6. **CLARITY**

   Good writing is marked by a simplicity which is appropriate to the subject. The writer has searched for and found the right word, the effective verb, the clarifying phrase. The writer has removed the writer so that the reader sees through the writer's style to the subject, which is clarified and simplified.

   It is my belief that these qualities are the same for poetry and fiction as well as non-fiction.

sign up for peer conferences, so we can think about the pairs and make sure we approve. (2) We insist on not being disturbed during conference time because we're busy too. (3) If children are in a peer conference, we ask them to log it in their writing logs (see the section entitled, "The Manual"); we may ask them to tell us what they accomplished later on. (4) We frequently ask them to write down one comment they made to their conference partner and one question they asked as well. We confess that we abhor asking them to do this (we don't use these sheets with first graders, obviously), but classroom control is an issue and little tactics like this help. Once the children appreciate how interesting process writing is, tricks like this become unnecessary.

FIGURE 11–23   **CONFERENCE QUESTIONS TEACHERS MAY CONSIDER**

Introductory Questions
-Tell me about your piece of writing.
-Why did you choose this subject to write about?
-What surprises you most about this draft?
-What kinds of changes have you made from your last draft?
-What questions did your conference partner have of you?
-What problems did you have or are you having?
-What questions did your conference partner have of you?
-Where is this piece of writing taking you?
-What questions do you have of me?

Questions That Deal With Meaning
-Do you have more than one story here?
-Underline the part that tells what this draft is about.
-What is the most important thing you are trying to say here?
-Explain how your title fits your draft.

Questions That Deal With Authority
-Can you tell me more about this?
-This part isn't clear to me. Can you tell me what you mean?
-Can you describe this for me?

Questions That Deal With Voice
-How does this draft sound when you read it out loud?
-Circle the part that is most exciting.
-Show me a place where I can tell **you** have written this piece.

Questions That Deal With Development
-Can you tell me more about it?
-Do you have enough information?
-Can you tell me where you are going in your draft?
-How did you get to this place in your draft?

Questions That Deal With Design
-Are you happy with your beginning and ending?
-How does the beginning of your piece grab your reader's
 attention?
-How have you tied your ending to your beginning?

Questions That Deal With Clarity
-Can you be more specific here? (e.g. How did you go into the
 house?)
-What are your action words? Can you add others?
-Can you think of a different way to say this?
-Is this the best word here?

Questions (when a draft is not finished) That Help a Writer Move On
-What do you intend to do now?
-What do you think you can do to make this draft better?
-What works so well you'd like to try and develop it further?

Questions That Help Children See Their Growth As Writers
-What did you learn from this piece of writing?
-How does this piece compare to others you have written?Why?
-Can you think of something new you tried in this draft that
 you have never tried before?
-How are you a better writer now than you were at the begin-
 ning of the year?

During the first few months of the school year, we're not sure how much gets done during peer conferences. Children simply haven't had enough time with us: We haven't modeled question-asking much or shared and discussed quality literature. As the year progresses, however, the children get better, both in terms of their behavior and in terms of the quality of their peer conferences.

All-Classroom Conferences and Small Group Conferences. A lot of one-to-one teaching goes on in process classrooms, but it can't all be this way! Sometimes it's advantageous (and life-saving) to teach a concept to everyone or to a small group. All-classroom conferences can be oriented toward meaning or editing concerns; the procedure is the same for both. Identify a problem in a draft. Ask the youngster if you can reproduce it on an overhead transparency. Make a ditto of the draft, if you can, and pass out red pencils with the copies. If you'd prefer not using a child's draft, make up one highlighting the issue and use this instead.

We discuss the problem with the class first. For example, in the piece about fish (see Figure 11–24), the problem we were to address was sentence order. We mixed up a paragraph from the basal reader first, then asked the children what was wrong. Later, we talked about how writers might get themselves into this fix. We noted that writing is difficult and demands

FIGURE 11–24
Fish draft

My fish have little mouths but they eat like pigs but thats ok. **1**

I feed them every morning just a pinch. **2**

I started out with five fish 3 femails and 2 mails. **3**

Now I have 8 fish. **4**

And I like them a lot to. **5**

It's hard to hold the food in two fingers but I can do it. **6**

They are gupies. **7**

We did not name them yet. **8**

The cup we put the food in is about two inches long. **9**

I have pebbels that are colored and plants to in it. **10**

attention, and that sometimes it is worthwhile just to get the whole draft out first, worrying about other things later: Drafts are just that, drafts.

Our next step is to put the draft we have prepared on the overhead and pass out the copies. Each child tries to make the piece better by himself, then pairs meet and work together. While working with the fish example, one child suggested we cut the transparancy apart, by sentences. The children then took turns coming to the overhead rearranging the sentences and explaining their improvements. Talking about forming paragraphs was a natural outflow of this exercise, as was pronoun comprehension (the "it" in line 10?). Correcting the spelling was also fun, but this came last (what a switch!).

Sometimes children can hold small-group conferences, which are like extended peer conferences. When a number of children would like to conference together, all sharing their drafts and getting feedback from one another, we let them do so. We ask them to follow their conference guidelines and not to leave the group until everyone has had a chance to read. To insure this, we keep oaktag cards labeled Group A, B, C, etc. and numbered sequentially. We pass one card out to each child (e.g., A1, A2, A3, A4), and the children keep them in their folders until everyone is finished. If conference time is over before everyone has had a turn, the children keep the cards and meet with their group during the next conference period, when they finish hearing everyone's draft.

Publishing Possibilities

The list is endless. Of course, books are a favorite and we like to keep them simple. Since parent-teacher organizations are eager to know how best to spend their hard earned money, we suggest binding machines (available in all office supply stores and costing about $300). Once a book is typed, illustrated, and a cover is made, the binding process takes less than a minute.

Classroom literary journals are another option, and they can be sophisticated or kept simple. Simple ones entail children copying their drafts onto dittos, and teachers, or aides, running them off. Children can do the collating and stapling, and love to do so. Since literary journals can be sold, advertising proves to be yet another writing outlet. As we've said, journals can be sophisticated as well. Berkshire Middle School in Birmingham, Michigan, wanted a fancy one, so they had a professional printer do theirs. Such journals get paid for through pledge campaigns, bake sales, or incentive grants offered frequently nowadays.

Classroom newspapers are also a natural outlet for children's writing. Children often write about trips and visitors, so why not use these drafts in your paper? A literary corner might become a permanent column, along with traditional news and editorial slots. Feature articles certainly could come from your children's writing.

National magazines such as *Stone Soup, Highlights,* and *Cricket* encourage children to write and to send in their work. A list of magazines that publish children's works can be found in the Appendix, at the back of the book.

There are many ways to publish student writing in the classroom. In the Appendix you will find a list of forty-three innovative suggestions for student publishing.

Evaluation

It is hard writing about evaluation without getting philosophical. After reading a text written by Marjorie, a seven year old, you can see that giving this piece a grade would not be easy.

> I have to
> atmit that I
> wot get a sicker (sticker)
> on my unit. Because it
> was hard.
> And I don't
> whnat tu be a
> scardy cat.
> so I will tell
> ya that I am not
> a scardy cat.

Marjorie, Grade 1

What will our grade reflect? Our ability as teachers? Marjorie's prior knowledge? Her product in light of other products written by children her age? The piece's meaning? Grammatical and mechanical correctness? Spelling correctness? Marjorie's effort? How much she has grown since her last effort?

From our point of view, we want to provide children with the type of evaluation and feedback that will produce skillful writers. For us, this means we must evaluate and give feedback throughout the writing process. Carol Steele, a writing consultant from Grand Rapids, Michigan, says, "Evaluation needs to happen at the point in the process when the input will be most helpful."[12] So when children stare at their empty topic sheets, we *help* them think of interesting aspects of their lives; we *read* first drafts and *point out* what has been said well; we *ask* for clarification when we feel lost as readers; we *look* for closure in pieces that lack endings; we *evaluate* and then *teach* the skills that need to be learned. The list could go on.

By providing checklists and sets of questions we teach self-evaluation too. As Steele says, "self-evaluation helps train students to turn their powers of observation and analysis toward their work."[12] Through all-classroom conferences, small group conferences, teacher-child conferences, and peer conferences, children become increasingly adept at analyzing their writing. While we might consider evaluating their growing awareness of their writing needs or weaknesses, one quickly sees that the amount of teacher-child interaction is a crucial element in the equation. So we are back to square one, at least in terms of giving Marjorie's piece a grade.

If we have to give grades for writing, evaluating Marjorie on her new performance in class seems a bit more realistic than assessing the quality of her drafts. But before evaluating Marjorie, even upon her performance instead of her products, we had better evaluate ourselves. Here is a list of teachers' behaviors that we routinely use to evaluate our *own* performance. It is our belief that if we do well in all of these areas, Marjorie will do well also.

Teacher's Behavior

1. Insists upon writing during writing time in order to grow as a writer him/herself.
2. Shares his/her own evolving drafts with the class.
3. Keeps track of children's progress in a systematic way.
4. Has a structure or system in the classroom to support the writing period.
5. Provides opportunities for children to publish in a variety of forms.
6. Sees to it that children share their work with other children.
7. Seeks out support materials to help children write.
8. Has a literature component in his/her writing program.
9. Shares professional material with other teachers.
10. When holding teacher-child conferences, is sensitive to the child's intention as well as his/her development level.
11. Periodically shows students how they are growing as writers.

Student's Behavior

1. _____ writes during designated time
   always   sometimes   rarely

2. _____ uses constructive strategies for getting drafts started
   always   sometimes   rarely

3. _____ takes the Conference Period seriously
   a) Is willing to help classmates by listening to their drafts
   b) Realizes other children may have meaningful suggestions
   always   sometimes   rarely

4. _____ is growing in his or her understanding of the difference between revising (e.g., adding on) and editing
   quite a bit   some   very little

5. _____ uses the support systems in the classroom (e.g., manual guidelines, spelling sheets, dictionaries, etc.)
   frequently   occasionally   infrequently

6. _____ is learning to view revision as part of a healthy writing process
   yes   no

7. _____ is an active participant during Share Time
   almost always   on occasion   almost never

We don't mean to be glib by avoiding product evaluation, but at this point in time we simply don't know how, nor do we see any purpose in doing so. By sharing our interpretation of Marjorie's writing behavior with her, however, we feel we may help her products indirectly. If she isn't using support systems, we can show her how; if she seems to be playing around during conference time, we can let her know *we* know, and that this matters; if she doesn't write during writing time we might encourage her via our checklist, to become more serious; if she never talks during Share Time, again, the checklist might help. Some children benefit by knowing their behavior is being chronicled, and difficult as it is to admit this, we do believe it to be true. Therefore, we encourage periodic process evaluation. Like everything else we have written in this section, however, our checklist is by no means the end all. It is a prototype meant to be altered.

CONCLUSION

What we have described in this chapter is a support system for the process of writing, which can be used with some variations throughout elementary school. For the sake of clarity, we have focused on the procedures that the teacher needs to initiate to set up a process-writing classroom—topic choice, expanding a topic, peer conferences, revisions, teacher conferences, editing, etc.—at the risk of making the school day seem rather mechanical. Although it may take some time for both children and teacher to get used to these procedures, in our experience they do provide children with a sense of security and control, thus encouraging creative and productive work. Knowing the procedural ropes doesn't suppress the excitement children get from their writing; it channels it and keeps it alive.

What we have only touched on in these recent chapters is the essential complement to this program, the sources of inspiration with which teachers and parents surround young writers: conversations, explorations, substantive information. The process-writing classroom works best within a cultural context as rich and exciting as teachers and community members can make it. This means continually bringing the world into the classroom and the childen into the world. The many ways of doing this, fascinating as they are, must be the subject of other books.

REFERENCES

1. William Corsaro, " 'We're friends, right?': Children's Use of Access Rituals in a Nursery School." *Language in Society, 8* (1979): 315–336.
2. Ann Haas Dyson. "Learning to Write/Learning to Do School: Emergent Writers' Interpretations of School Literacy Tasks." *Research in the Teaching of English, 18* (1984): 233–264.
3. Nancie Atwell, "Writing and Reading from the Inside Out." *Language Arts, 61* (1984): 240–252.

4. Donald Murray, "How Writing Finds Its Own Meaning," in *Eight Approaches to Teaching Composition,* Timothy R. Donovan and Ben W. McClelland (*ed.*). Urbana, Ill.: NCTE, 1980.

5. Betty Flowers, "Madman, Architect, Carpenter, Judge: Roles and the Writing Process." *Language Arts, 58* (1981): 834–836.

6. Donald Graves and Jane Hansen. "The Author's Chair." *Language Arts, 60* (1983): 176–183.

7. James Britton. *Language and Learning.* Harmondsworth, England: Penguin Books, 1970.

8. James Moffett. *Teaching the Universe of Discourse.* Boston: Houghton Mifflin, 1968.

9. Ann Haas Dyson. "Research Currents: Young Children as Composers." *Language Arts, 60* (1982): 884–891.

10. Judith Hilliker. "Kindergartners Can Write." *Learning, 15* (1986): 74–75.

11. Donald Graves. *Writing: Teachers and Children at Work.* Portsmouth, N.H.: Heinemann Educational Books, 1983.

12. Carol Steele. "Evaluation of Writing." *Michigan Council of Teachers of English Newsletter., 38* (1986): 11–12.

Epilogue:

Playing with Literature and Language: Amy's Story

> Ma Goodness she's coming a-skippitty skoppetty
>   skippitty skoppetty
>   skippitty skoppetty
>
> Ma Goodness she's coming a-skippitty skoppetty
>   All doon the hill.
>
>   Pop Corn he's a-coming a-hippitty hoppetty
>   hippitty hoppetty
>   hippitty hoppetty
>
>   Pop Corn he's a-coming a-hippitty hoppetty
>   All doon the hill.[1]

Children are language lovers and eight-year-old Amy is no exception. When she was five, Edna Preston's magical words, "skippitty-skoppetty" mesmerized her at every sitting. So did Winnie the Pooh's famous hum:

> Tra-la-la, tra-la-la, tra -la -la,
> Rum-tum-tiddle-um-tum.
> Tiddle-iddle, tiddle-iddle, tiddle-iddle,
> Rum-tum-tum-tiddle-um.[2]

And then there was John Ciardi's humorous poem, "Sit Up When You Sit Down," and Charlotte Zolotow's comforting words about William's need for a doll:

"He needs it," she said
"to hug
and to cradle
and to take to the park
so that
when he's a father
like you,
he'll know how to
take care of his baby
and feed him
and love him
and bring him
the things he wants,
like a doll
so that he can
practice being
a father."[3]

These were some of Amy's favorites.

At first, literature's effect on children is very subtle—just moments in time, shared and treasured by parents and children alike. But soon, it seems, rhymes are imprinted on their lips.

"Little pig, little pig, let me come in."
"Not by the hair of my chinny-chin-chin."
"Then I'll huff and I'll puff and I'll
    blow your house in."[4]

Chanted over and over by little people, and Amy too, magical words like "Little pig, little pig" stick powerfully in their memories.

A, B, C, tumble-down D,
the cat's in the kitchen
and can't catch me.[5]

. . . yet another rhyme remembered.

Slowly, as children grow older, the effects of literature become more profound. By the age of six, Amy began creating her own poems, chants, and stories. Quite often they sounded familiar:

Peanut butter, peanut butter
Smooth as silk,
You really taste good,
with a glass of milk.

It didn't take much for Amy's parents and teachers to realize that something was becoming internalized within her: a sense of sound, a sense of rhythm, a sense of language, perhaps a sense of form. Fortunately, some of Amy's language play was recorded by her mother using a dictated language-experience format. Just a few days after the peanut butter rhyme, Amy coaxed her mother to record this paragraph:

Last night it started snowing.
When I woke up this morning the
ground was covered with snow and
ice. I feel happy that it is finally winter.

Is it just coincidence that Amy heard Charlotte Zolotow's story, *Hold My Hand,* a few days earlier?

<table>
<tr><td>. . . The wind stops.</td><td>I look at you
and suddenly the air</td></tr>
<tr><td>Everything is still</td><td>is full of snow.</td></tr>
<tr><td>There is only the cold</td><td>the snow flakes cling</td></tr>
<tr><td>cold cold cold.</td><td>like bits of ice</td></tr>
<tr><td>Oh hold my hand.</td><td>to our mittens.[6]</td></tr>
</table>

Later, that same month, Amy wanted this popular song recorded:

I told the witch-doctor I was in love with you,
  bum, bum, bum, bum.
I told the witch-doctor I was in love with you,
  bum, bum, bum, bum.
And then the witch-doctor, he told me what to do.
He said, "OO, EE, OO, AH, AH, TING, TANG, WALLA
  WALLA, BING-BANG
    OO, EE, OO, AH, AH, TING-TANG, WALLA-WALLA,
BANG-BANG!"[7]

Amy had etched into her memory another string of cherished sounds, another string of words she wanted to capture for herself.

First grade brought many changes. By January Amy was writing alone— no more dictation, no more middlemen! At first her stories came on little bits of paper. Her mother remembers Amy tiptoeing downstairs in her pink pajamas, clutching her first hand-written "story" (Figure 1). Slowly she crept into the living room, slipped this note onto her mother's desk, and barely audibly, she whispered, "Here's a *real* story."

As the year progressed, Amy's little descriptions turned into full blown accounts. Try and follow her development (see Figures 2 to 7). What seems to be changing?

When Amy was eight and in second grade, her teacher shared many tall tales with the class, mostly Paul Bunyon episodes. Amy tried writing her own (Figure 8).

FIGURE 1
Amy
6 yrs. 9 mos.

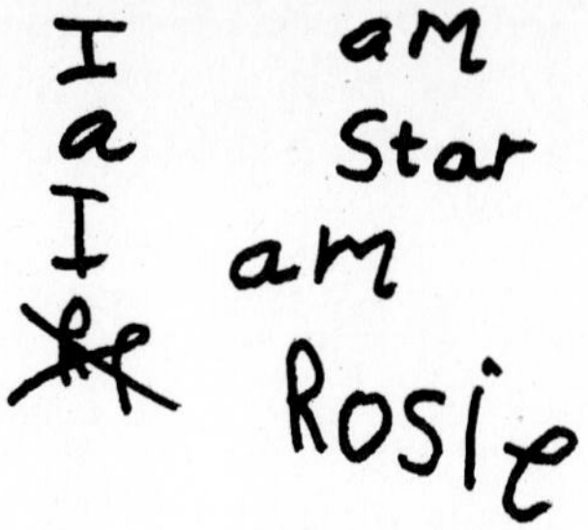

I   am
a   Star
I   am
❋   Rosie

FIGURE 2
Amy
6 yrs. 10 mos.

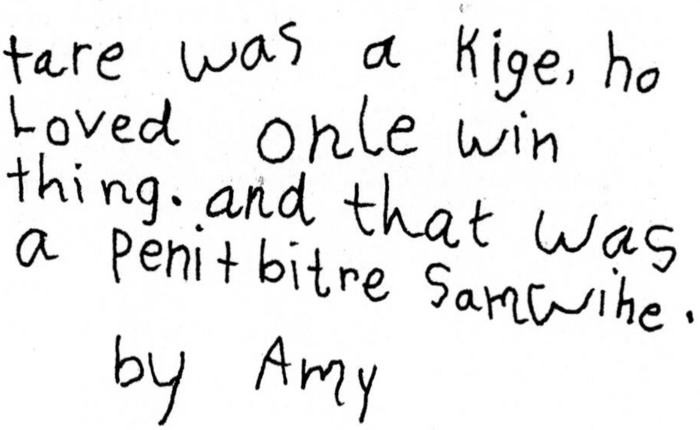

tare was a Kige, ho
Loved onle win
thing. and that was
a peni+bitre samcwihe.

by Amy

FIGURE 3
Amy
6 yrs. 10 mos.

a Mouse was in
a house. the Mouse
Was So happe.
he had a Little
chare. and a Little
tabil.

by AMy

FIGURE 4
Amy (left)
6 yrs. 11 mos.

FIGURE 5
Amy (right)
7 yrs. 0 mos.

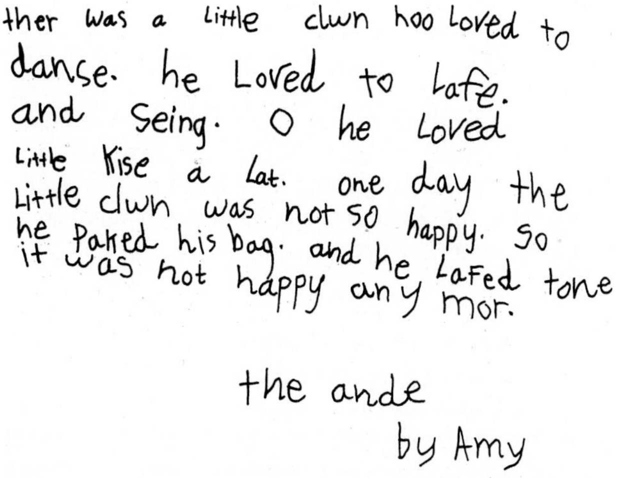

The Mose
That wes
a Mose
hoe lived
in a hose
The hose
lived in
The forist
The forist
Lived in
The wild

Thar was
a little gril
how onle liRed
One Thing and
Thet was a flowr

FIGURE 6
Amy
7 yrs. 1 mo.

ther was a little clwn hoo loved to
danse. he Loved to Lafe.
and Seing. O he Loved
Little Kise a Lat. one day the
Little clwn was not so happy. So
he Paked his bag. and he LaFed tone
it was not happy any mor.

the ande
by Amy

FIGURE 7
Amy
7 yrs. 6 mos.

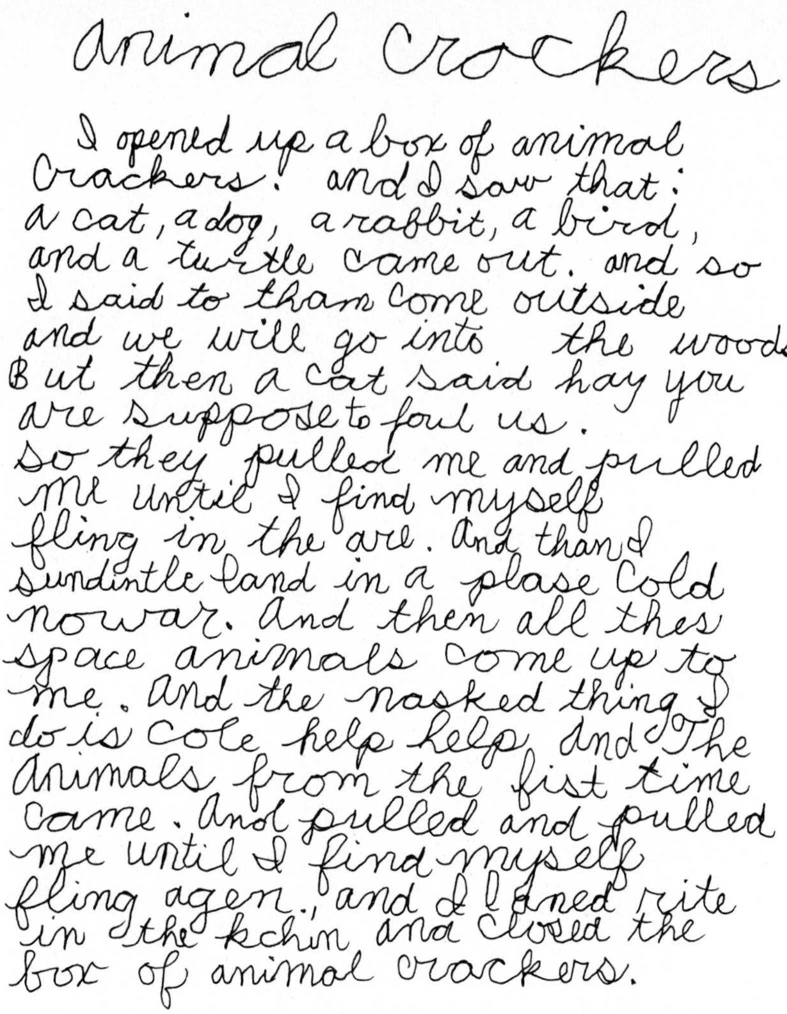

animal crackers

I opened up a box of animal
Crackers! and I saw that:
a cat, a dog, a rabbit, a bird,
and a turtle came out. and so
I said to tham come outside
and we will go into the woods.
But then a cat said hay you
are suppose to foul us.
So they pulled me and pulled
me until I find myself
fling in the are. And than I
sundintle land in a plase cold
nowar. And then all thes
space animals come up to
me. And the nasked thing I
do is cole help help. And The
Animals from the fist time
came. And pulled and pulled
me until I find myself
fling agen. and I laned rite
in the kchin and closed the
box of animal crackers.

Now Amy is thirteen and in eighth grade. A few nights ago, as her mother was working on this book's revision, Amy reread the epilogue—her story, really. She started talking about herself as a writer, as a little kid, as a child who loved dressing up. She sat down, deciding to share some of her feelings with you. Here is what she wrote:

Reflection

Dressing up was always fun, but dressing up as *I'm Really Rosie* was the best. As I reread *The Beginnings of Writing,* I remembered putting on a huge floppy hat, a black and white polka dot dress, my mother's high-healed shoes, and wobbling around the house whenever I wanted to be

FIGURE 8
Amy
7 yrs. 11 mos.

The Dancer That Could Srach her Leg

Once a dancer went to her stoodeo, and she leeped ocross the the room. One of the other things she could do was was strach her leg. (Her name was mary) One day she strached her leg to the liberdy bell and mary rang it. The people thout there was going to be war with no warning. Mary was so scard for the people soon found out about this.

And that is how Mary almost mad war.

Rosie. I see now that my love for Rosie, and Rosie's glamour, came through in my first real story, "I Am Rosie, I Am a Star."

My stories are longer now, at 13 years, 9 months (as my mother, Ruth Nathan, would say), but I love looking over my old stories. I realize I loved fantasy, like in my story "Animal Crackers." In around 5th grade I really got into fairies. Unfortunately I don't know where all those stories have gone.

In closing I'd like to share a poem I've written just recently; it's about my cat, Sammy. We have breakfast together, as you will soon see. I hope you like "Breakfast for Two?".

Amy Nathan
January, 1987

Breakfast for Two?

Trudging down the stairs,
7:10 AM.
And the cat whips by my ankles.
I don't talk in the morning. Never
Make me talk in the morning.
Pull the cereal out,
Grab the milk,
Get a spoon and a bowl.
And the cat skids and stops in his tracks as I pour my milk.
All set, I raise
The first spoonful
To my mouth.
And the cat jumps up on the table and stretches out beside my
Bowl, the perfect actor: The Prince.
I start to crunch.
And the cat slowly, hesitantly lifts his paw and slowly,
Hesitantly tries putting it in my bowl for his first taste.
I slap away his paw and
Continue eating.
And the cat tries diving his head right down into the bowl.
I push his head away
And then see that
I am done,
Just the sweetened milk
Is left. I fill a spoon
Full with it
And lift it towards
The cat.
And the cat sticks out his tiny pink tongue and laps it up,
Squeezing his eyes shut with pleasure.

Amy Nathan

Amy is not an exceptional youngster. The only thing that may be exceptional is her warm relationship with the adults that surround her and her personal desire to make written language a part of her life. Since Amy's relationship with literature has been nurtured, and since love of language has been modeled by her teachers and parents, it's no wonder that Amy has become a writer.

Let children know you treasure language, and they'll treasure it also. Help them understand, as early as possible, that language is theirs to manipulate, and they'll respond. There's no magical ingredient that gets children to write.

FIGURE 9
Amy
7 yrs. 11 mos.

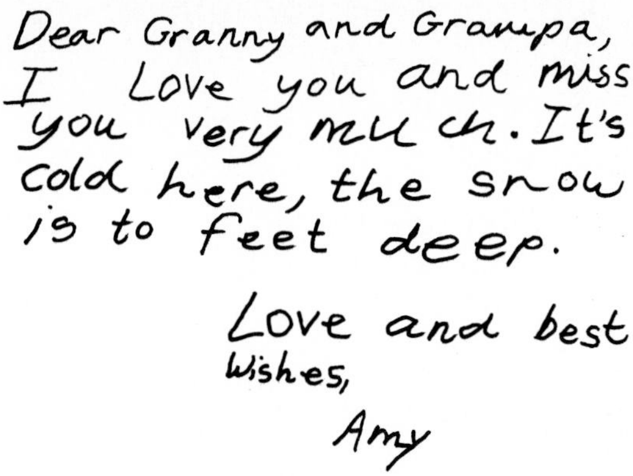

Dear Granny and Grampa,
I Love you and miss you very much. It's cold here, the snow is to feet deep.

Love and best wishes,

Amy

We have shared with you aspects of Amy's growth as a writer. Her development as a language aware youngster can be every child's accomplishment. The ingredients? Lots of literature, an outward and enthusiastic love of language on the part of teachers and parents, a profound respect for what children say and what they want to record, and the understanding that growth as a writer is a slow-moving process. Everything children write will not be spectacular, as Figure 9 shows. Be patient and accepting; give feedback and love; and chuckle when you get "love and best wishes."

REFERENCES

1. Edna Mitchel Preston. *Pop Corn and Ma Goodness.* New York: Viking Press, 1969.
2. A. A. Milne. *Winnie-the-Pooh.* Racine, WI: Whitman Publishing Company, 1926.
3. Charlotte Zolotow. *William's Doll.* New York: Harper & Row, 1972.
4. Joseph Jacols, collector. "The Story of the Three Little Pigs," in Bryna Untermeyer and Louis Untermeyer, *Stories and Poems for the Very Young.* New York: Golden Press, 1973.
5. Sonia DeLaunay. *Alphabet.* New York: Crowell, 1970.
6. Charlotte Zolotow. *Hold My Hand.* New York: Harper & Row, 1972.
7. Sheb Wooly. *"The Witch Doctor Song."* BMI.

Appendix

MAGAZINES THAT PUBLISH CHILDREN'S WORK

Highlights for Children, Inc.
803 Church Street
Honesdale, PA 18431
(poems, stories, art, riddles, jokes,
Ages 3–12)

Humpty Dumpty
P.O. Box 567
1100 Waterway Blvd.
Indianapolis, IN 46206
(artwork only, Ages 4–6)

Childlife
P.O. Box 567
1100 Waterway Blvd.
Indianapolis, IN 46206
(art, stories, articles, book reviews
up to 500 words, jokes, riddles,
Ages 7–9)

Turtle
P.O. Box 567
1100 Waterway Blvd.
Indianapolis, IN 46206
(artwork only, Ages 2–5)

Children's Playmate
P.O. Box 567
1100 Waterway Blvd.
Indianapolis, IN 46206
(poems, art, jokes, riddles,
Ages 5–7)

The National P.T.A.
Reflections Contest
700 North Rush Street
Chicago, IL 60611-257
(poetry, prose, drama, art, music)

Childrens Digest
P.O. Box 567
1100 Waterway Blvd.
Indianapolis, IN 46206
(fiction, nonfiction, poetry—up to
700 words, favorite jokes, riddles,
Ages 8–10)

Prism
1040 Bayview Drive
Suite 223
Fort Lauderdale, FL 33304
(poetry, fiction, nonfiction photo-
graphs, art, Ages 5 and up)

Stone Soup
P.O. Box 83
Santa Cruz, CA 95063
(poetry, fiction, plays, art, photos,
Ages 5–13)

Cricket Magazine
Box 100
La Salle, IL 61301
(poems, drawings, stories according
to Contest Rules, Ages 6–13)

Raintree's Pub-A-Book
330 East Kilbourn Ave.
Milwaukee, WI 53202

Shoe Tree
Prequest Publications
P.O. Box 356
Belvidere, NJ 07823

PUBLISHING POSSIBILITIES FOR CHILDREN

1. Response to writing contests found in children's magazines such as *Cricket* or *Ranger Rick*

2. Classroom poetry corners

3. Classroom newspapers, fairly simple nowadays because of easy-to-use computer programs that set columns and incorporate drawings

4. School newspapers that include original student writing

5. Bulletin boards that highlight an author-of-the-week

6. Bulletin boards that demonstrate the writing process—from first draft, through all revisions, to final product

7. Bulletin boards on selected topics

8. Books—both individual and class

9. Classroom literary journals

10. Grade-level literary journals

11. All-school literary journals

12. Program notes for class or school productions

13. Plays—written and produced by the children

14. Puppet shows—written and produced by the children

15. Research reports destined for a classroom book on a topic under study

16. Books on selected topics that go to waiting rooms in the community

17. Books written by older children for younger children

18. Radio shows on selected topics transmitted through the school's loud-speaker: sports broadcasts, author-of-the-week, etc.

19. Student anthologies of their best writing over the school year

20. Letters to: authors, important public figures, people of interest to the class (e.g., local newspaper editors), thank you notes, letters of inquiry, etc.

21. Student magazines: fashion, cars, computer information, etc.

22. Student tip sheets: tips on computer programs, school rules, dress code, lunchroom behavior, interesting and/or unusual games (e.g., ones that only require chalk, for example)

23. Instruction manuals ("how-to" books)
24. Signs for political campaigns, lemonade stands, school bake sales
25. Advertisements for used toys, old clothes, homeless puppies, etc.
26. Computer programs, with manuals, originated by the children
27. Game rules
28. Cookbooks
29. Cards: holiday, get-well, congratulations, birthday, unbirthday, etc.
30. Song lyrics
31. Author's biography page on the last page or cover flap of a book
32. Notes sent to parents about class trips—before *and* after
33. Classroom sayings, proverbs, jokes, etc.
34. Chain novels—class or school-based
35. End-of-the-year "send-off" letters to school friends
36. Classroom door covers (poems, sayings, chants, rules of conduct, etc.)
37. Author's Chair—sayings, cheers, etc. (to be pasted on)
38. Classroom dictionaries
39. Make-believe products that require written language (e.g., cereal boxes, tooth paste tubes, boxed soup [directions needed], etc.)
40. Year books
41. Documented picture albums from class trips, or about class projects
42. Travel brochures written after a special trip
43. School handbooks

Suggested Further Reading

Bissex, Glenda. *Gyns at Work: A Child Learns to Write and Read.* Cambridge: Harvard University Press, 1980. A detailed, longitudinal study of one child's development in writing and reading. If all research was like this, teachers would be happy to read it.

Calkins, Lucy. *The Art of Teaching Writing.* Portsmouth. NH: Heinemann, 1986. Calkins shows teachers and children in the writing process. The book moves from the kindergarten writer to the early adolescent writer. The multiple aspects of a quality writing program are presented in this well-written book.

Cooper, Charles and Lee Odell. *Evaluating Writing.* Urbana, IL: National Council of Teachers of English, 1977. Six researchers report a variety of measures that can be used to evaluate writing.

Goelman, Hillel, Antionette Oberg, and Frank Smith. *Awakening to Literacy.* London: Heinemann, 1984. This book is for the teacher who is interested in research studies.

Graves, Donald. *Writing: Teachers and Children at Work.* Portsmouth, NH: Heinemann, 1983. Graves calls this a collection of workshops. He helps teachers look at what they do to support young writers, how children grow in the writing process and how to record and report progress.

Hanson, Jane, Thomas Newkirk, and Donald Graves. *Breaking Ground: Teachers Relate Reading and Writing in the Elementary School.* Portsmouth, NH: Heinemann, 1985. Teachers report their experiences with children who are learning to write by reading. Literature connections for classrooms from kindergarten through early adolescence are shared.

Harste, Jerome, Virginia Woodward, and Carolyn Burke. *Language Stories and Literacy Lessons.* Portsmouth, NH: Heinemann, 1984. The authors suggest a theoretical framework for literacy that views children as participants in the "authoring cycle" from their first scribbles. A thought-provoking examination of traditional curriculum that raises questions based on what we now know about children moving into literacy.

Jagger, Angela and M. Trika Smith-Burke. (eds.) *Observing the Language Learner.* Newark, DE: International Reading Association, 1985. A collection of papers from an IRA sponsored conference presents the research and insights of many well-known writers in this field.

Jensen, Julie. (ed.) *Composing and Comprehending.* Urbana, IL: National Conference on Research in English and ERIC Clearinghouse on Reading and Communication Skills. 1984. This set of articles from *Language Arts* includes current theory and research along with the learning and teaching of writing.

Fox, Mem. "The Teacher Disguised as Writer in Hot Pursuit of Literacy." *Language Arts,* 64 (1987): 18–32. Australia's best-selling children's writer shares her view of children and the reading/writing process.

Murray, Donald. *Learning by Teaching.* Upper Montclair, NJ: Boynton Cook Publisher, 1982.

———. *Write to Learn.* NY: Holt, Rinehart & Winston, 1984. Murray continues to develop fresh insights into the craft of writing. He could be considered the teacher for the teacher who writes.

Strunk, William and E.B. White. *The Elements of Style.* 2nd ed. NY: Macmillan, 1972. This slim book on clear writing first appeared in 1959. The brevity makes it an easy starting place for those who want to improve communication with their readers.

Welty, Eudora. *One Writer's Beginnings.* NY: Warner Books, 1984. This brief autobiogrpahy shares her view of the act of writing.

Zinsser, William. *On Writing Well.* 3rd ed. NY Harper & Row, 1985. This book presents general principles for clear writing and the requirements for various forms of nonfiction. This edition also includes tips on writing with a word processor. The new chapters on trusting your material and your attitude toward writing offer recent insights from his own development as a writer.

Index

A

Adults' role in children's language development, 8–9
All-classroom conferences, 243–244
Alphabetic writing, 14–15
Applebee, Arthur, 146–147
Argumentative writing, 138–139
  assignment, 200–205
Assessing children's spelling development, 105–107
Assignment(s):
  argumentative writing, 200–205
  expository writing, 188–200
    expertise-based, 189–197
    how to ride a bicycle, 197–199
Atmosphere for writing, 215
Atwell, Nancy, 212
Audience and compositions, 127–131
Author's chair, 217, 222, 225, 237

B

Brandenberg, Aliki, 136
Britton, James, 128, 129, 130–131, 132, 217

C

Caxton, William, 81
Characters in children's stories, 145
Child(ren) (*see also* Composition(s)):
  early graphics and, 41–52
  ideographic writing and, 12
  language development, adults' role in, 8–9
  and, language rules, 3–6, 9
  making print, encouraging, 47–52
  peer conferences, 240–243
  poetry, 180–185
  progress in spelling, 107–115
  stories (*see also* Writing):
    grammar, 170–174
    otherness in, 144–148
    psychological action of, 174–180
    Souriau's dramatic roles, 175–180
    structure, 147–148
  syllabic writing and, 13–14
  teacher-, conferences, 238–240
  writing:
    appropriate responses to, 216
    name, 44–45
    perception of, 21–25
Chinese writing, 13–14
Classroom:
  conferences, 243–244
  literary journals, 245

Classroom (*Continued*)
  newsletter, 199
  newspapers, 245
  process-writing, 219–225
    setting up, 225–231
Clay, Marie, 26, 33, 39, 45, 47, 48, 110
Cleary, Beverly, 169
Cluster sheet(s), 221–222, 226
Coarticulation, 75
Composition(s) (*see also* Writing):
  kindergarten year, 216–219
  menu of writing forms, 127–131
  moving a promising draft along, 232–238
Conceptual learning, 107–108
Conference(s):
  all-classroom, 243–244
  editing, 236
  guidelines, 230
  listener's guide for, 230
  peer, 240–243
  questions, 242
  small group, 243–244
  teacher-child, 238–240
  techniques for, 238–244
  -time sheets, 229
Consonant(s):
  blends, 60, 73
  digraphs, 60–61, 63–64
  letter-name spelling and, 57–60
  nasal, 64–66
  production of, 61–63

D

Descriptive writing, 138
Dialogue, 131
Digraphs, 60–61, 63–64
Directional principles, 35–38, 41

Drafts, 213, 214, 222–223, 225, 243–244
  publishing journey, 232–238
    examples, 233, 239
Dyson, Ann Haas, 218

E

Early phonemic speller, helping, 109–112
Early phonemic spelling, 101–102
Editing (*see* Revising)
Egocentrism, 124
English spellings (*see* Spelling, English)
Evaluation, 245–247
Exposition, 136
Expository writing:
  assignments for, 188–200
    expertise-based, 189–197
    how to ride a bicycle, 197–199
Expressive mode, 128, 131–134

F

Fabre, Jean Henri, 138
Ferreiro, Emilia, 41–44
Flexibility principle, 27, 31–33
Flowers, Betty, 213–214

G

Generative principle, 27, 28–29
Gibson, Eleanor, 19, 22, 23
Grammar, story, 170–174

Graphic, early, what children do with, 41–52
Graves, Donald, 113, 220
Greek alphabet, 14

K

Kindergarten year, composition in, 216–219
Kundera, Milan, 212

H

Halliday, Michael, 6–8
Hieroglyphics, phonetic use of, 13
Hilliker, Judith, 218–219
Holdaway, Don, 110

L

Language:
  children's development, adults' role in, 8–9
  children's rules, 3–6, 9
  seven different functions, 7–8
Lap Method, 109–110
Lavine, Linda, 22–25, 39
Learning, conceptual, 107–108
Letter-name speller, helping, 112–114
Letter-name spelling, 56–61, 101, 102–103
Letter-name strategy, 56
Letters, to represent sounds, 76–77
Linear principles, 33–38
Literary journals, classroom, 245
Literate community, setting up, 217
Logos and sign concept, 31
Long vowels, invented spellings of, 66–67

I

Ideographic writing, 11–12
Initial consonants, and letter-name spelling, 57–60
Inner states in stories, 174–180
Invented spellings (*see* Spelling, invented)
Inventory, 132
  knowledge-based, 191
  principle, 47

J

Japanese writing, 13
Johnson, Nancy, 147
Johnson, Samuel, 81
Journey sheets, 232–238
  examples, 233, 239

M

M, the letter, 64–66
Magazines, 244–245
Mandler, Jean, 147
Manual, writer's, 226–231
Marking rules in English spelling, 67, 83–86

Modes of writing, 127–131
   encouraging writing in a variety of,
     205–209
   expressive, 128, 131–134
   poetic, 128, 129–131, 140–142
     developing in school, 170–185
   transactional, 128, 131, 136–139
Moffett, James, 109, 217
Monologue, 131–132
Montessori, Maria, 48
Morpheme conservation rules,
   92–96
Morris, Betty, 232
Murray, Donald, 213–214, 219,
   240–241

N

N, the letter, 64–66
Nasal consonants, 64–66
Nathan, Ruth, 232
Newsletter, classroom, 199
Newspapers, classroom, 245

O

Olson, David, 48
Oral language, drawing out, 217
Otherness in children's stories,
   144–148
Outer actions of stories, 174–180

P

Page-arrangement principles, 27,
   33–38

Parents:
   providing models of writing,
     48–49, 108
   role in children's language
     development, 8–9
   role in children's spelling, 112, 113
Peer conferences, 240–243
Perception, theory of, early writing,
   and, 19–21
Phonemes, segmenting words into,
   75
Phonemic speller, early, helping,
   109–112
Phonemic spelling, 74–75
   early, 101–102
   pre-, 100–101
Phonetic use of hieroglyphics, 13
Phonological rules of English
   spelling, 90–92
Piaget, Jean, 124
Poetic mode, 128, 129–131, 140–142
   developing in school, 170–185
   writing in, 144–186
Poetry, 180–185
Post, Laurens van der, 144
Prephonemic speller, helping, 108
Prephonemic spelling, 100–101
Preston, Edna, 249
Primary years, writing program,
   219–247
Principle(s), 26
   directional, 33–38
   flexibility, 27, 31–33
   generative, 27, 28–29
   inventory, 47
   linear, 33–38
   page-arrangement, 27, 33–38
   recurring, 27–28
Print, encouraging children to make,
   47–52
Process-writing classroom, 219–225
   setting up, 225–231

Proofreading checklist, 234, 236
Psychological action of stories, 174–180
Publishing:
  class newsletter, 199
  journey, 232–238
    examples, 233, 239
  moving a promising draft along, 232–238
  possibilities for student writing, 244–245

R

Read, Charles, 67, 68
Rebus, 13
Recurring principle, 27–28
Revising, 213, 214, 224–225, 232–234, 236, 240

S

Scribal rules of English spelling, 85, 86–90
Self, in compositions, 127–131
Setting, in children's stories, 145
Shared book method, 110
Short vowels, invented spellings, 67–68
Sign concept, 27, 29–31, 41–45
Small group conferences, 243–244
Snyder, Marilyn, 216–217
Social activity, writing as, 211–212
Sounds, letters to represent, 76–77
Souriau, Etienne, 175–176
Souriau's dramatic roles, 174–180
Sowers, Susan, 132, 191
Spaces between words, 38–39

Speech, and writing, connecting, 218
Speech sounds, 61–73
Spelling:
  correct, 104–105
  development, assessing, 105–107
  English:
    difficulties of, 55–56
    marking rules in, 83–86
    modern, learnable patterns of, 82–96
    morpheme conservation rules in, 92–96
    phonological rules in, 90–92
    scribal rules in, 85, 86–90
    strange, 80–82
  helping children make progress in, 107–115
  invented, 55–61, 63–68, 71–73
    developmental dimension of, 73–76
    effect of age on, 99
    long vowels, 66–67
    short vowels, 67–68
  letter-name, 56–61, 101, 102–103
  making progress in, 99–115
  phonemic, 74–75
    early, 101–102
  prephonemic, 100–101
  stages of, 100–105
  standard, learning, 79–97
  transitional, 74, 103–104
Steele, Carol, 246
Stories, children's (*see also* Writing):
  centering in, 146–147, 150
  chaining in, 146–147, 150
  grammar, 170–174
  otherness in, 144–148
  psychological action of, 174–180
  Souriau's dramatic roles, 174–180
  structure, 147–148
Student's evaluation, 245–247
Syllabic writing, 13–14

T

Talking, early, 3–11
  similarities to learning to write,
    10–11
Teacher–child conferences, 238–240
Teacher's evaluation, 247
Teacher's role in the writing process,
    215–216
Topic(s):
  in children's stories, 146
  and compositions, 127–131
  sheet, 226
  for writing, 215
Transactional mode, 128, 131,
    136–139
Transitional spellers, helping,
    114–115
Transitional spelling, 74, 103–104
Transitional writing, 134–136, 188
Tutuola, Amos, 165–166

V

Vowels:
  historical changes in, 81, 82
  laxness as feature of, 70–71
  long, invented spellings of, 66–67
  marking, 67, 83–86
  pairing of, 71
  production of, 68–73
  short, invented spellings of, 67–68
  tenseness as feature of, 70–71

W

Watson, Wendy, 165
Wells, Gordon, 8
Word(s):
  concept of, 75–76

segmenting into phonemes, 75
sorts, 114–115
spaces between, 38–39
Writer's manual, 226–231
Writing (*see also* Composition(s)):
  alphabetic, 14–15
  argumentative, assignment,
    200–205
  atmosphere for, 215
  children's appropriate responses
    to, 216
  children's perception of, 21–25
  of child's name, 44–45
  Chinese, 11–12
  early:
    strategies for, 45–52
    theory of perception and, 19–21
  evaluation, 245–247
  expository, assignments for,
    188–200
  folder, 225–226
  forms, menu of, 127–131
  ideographic, 11–12
  Japanese, 13
  learning to, 1–15
    similarities to learning to talk,
      10–11
  log, 231
  materials in early childhood
    classrooms, 50–51
  precursors of, 18–25
  process, description of, 212–214
  process, teacher's role in, 215–216
  process-, classroom, 219–225
    setting up, 225–231
  program, primary years, 219–247
  providing models of, 48–50
  as a social activity, 211–212
  speech and, connecting, 218
  stages of, 213–214
  suggestions, 51–52
  syllabic, 13–14
  systems, organization of, 11–15
  -time sheets, 228–229
  transitional, 134–136, 188